African American Voices

The Life Cycle of Slavery

Second Edition

African American Voices

The Life Cycle of Slavery

Second Edition

Edited by
STEVEN MINTZ

BRANDYWINE PRESS • St. James, New York

Cover Photo: In 1862 T. H. O'Sullivan made this extraordinary photograph of five generations of a slave family. All were born on the plantation of J. J. Smith in Beaufort, South Carolina. *Courtesy: Library of Congress.*

ISBN: 1-881089-46-0

Second Edition 1999

Telephone Orders: 1-800-345-1776

Printed in the United States of America

TABLE OF CONTENTS

PREFACE TO
THE SECOND EDITION

Though the subject evokes deep shame and guilt, it is essential that Americans study the history of slavery and the slave trade. For there is no better way to learn about the development of the modern world economy, the construction of modern conceptions of race, the nature of evil, or the costs of progress.

The history of the United States was profoundly shaped by slavery. African slaves and their descendants furnished the basic labor power that created dynamic New World economies and produced the first mass consumer goods such as sugar, rice, tobacco, and cotton. At its abolition, slavery left a legacy in racism, economic inequality, and the social and economic underdevelopment of large parts of the Third World.

In recent years, slavery has become a divisive political battleground. Americans have even debated whether to issue a national apology for slavery and to pay reparations to the descendants of slaves. To participate intelligently in this debate, it is essential to correct certain myths and misconceptions that many Americans hold about slavery: that it was a marginal and insignificant institution; that it was unprofitable and inefficient; and that freedom was a gift granted to African Americans solely by whites.

The history of slavery is profoundly unsettling. In the pages that follow you will discover that many of the most progressive societies in history were slave societies, including ancient Greece and Rome, the centers of Islamic civilization, Renaissance Italy, and, of course, the United States. You will learn that slavery attended Europe's rise to global power; that slave labor was indispensable to the European settlement and development of the New World; and that some Africans were complicit in the slave trade and exercised considerable control over it. You will also discover that while politicians sought to suppress this fact, slavery was the supreme issue in American politics. Slavery played a pivotal role in the meaning and outcome of the American Revolution; the creation of the Constitution; the growth of competing political parties; and, of course, the escalating sectional conflicts that resulted in civil war. Above all, you will learn that far from being a minor aspect of the past, slavery was a key to the creation of the modern world: to a modern consumer economy, multinational trade, and modern conceptions of race.

This book will tell two very different stories about slavery. One describes the origins, development, and significance of the most extreme form of dehumanization and exploitation in history. But there is another story that is more inspiring. Slavery is also about human resilience and cultural survival under the most exploitative conditions imaginable. And it is about resistance: of how slavery involved a process of constant negotiation and testing of boundaries. Above all, it is the story of how enslaved Africans and their descendants helped shape everything that we think of as American: our language, music, food, religion, and even our ideals of freedom. Today, African Americans constitute about twelve percent of the American population—about one in eight. But the influence that African Americans exert on American culture is far greater—an influence that began during this country's formative period.

FOREWORD

The experience of slavery defies simple generalizations. Readers of Harriet Beecher Stowe, whose treatment of slavery was broad and subtle for its own time, learned to separate slaves into docile and deferential Uncle Toms and militant and rebellious George Harrises, and masters into brutal and sadistic Simon Legrees and gentle, guilt-ridden Augustine St. Clares, but the realities of slavery were far more complex. A larger view of slavery requires us to look at slavery from the inside, from the perspective of the enslaved. In this volume, readers will encounter such famous figures as Frederick Douglass and Nat Turner, as well as lesser-known individuals who will help answer the question: What was it like to be a slave?

This volume begins with an introduction that summarizes what we now know about the history of slavery, the African slave trade, the conditions of slave life, the impact of slavery on the southern economy, and the process of emancipation. The introduction is followed by substantial excerpts from published slave narratives, interviews with former slaves, and letters written by enslaved African Americans. Together, these documents draw a comprehensive portrait of slavery. The selections move from memories of growing up in Africa to the trials of the Middle Passage, the horrors of the auction block, the sustaining forces of family and religion, acts of resistance, and the meaning of the Civil War and emancipation. Together they present a collective life cycle of an enslaved people.

1-14
41-90

INTRODUCTION
A History of Slavery

A woman listed in the census simply as Celia was just fourteen in 1850, when a sixty-year-old Missouri farmer named Robert Newsome purchased her. A widower with two grown daughters, Newsome raped Celia before he had even brought her to his farm. For five years, he kept her as his sexual slave, forcing her to bear two illegitimate children. In 1855, pregnant a third time and ill, she struck back. She knocked her abuser unconscious by hitting him on the head with a club and burned his body in her fireplace. During her murder trial, Celia's attorneys argued that a woman had a right to use deadly force to prevent rape. But the court ruled that in Missouri, as in other slave states, it was not a crime to rape a slave woman. Celia was found guilty and hanged.

A Virginia-born slave named Benjamin Montgomery was seventeen when he was purchased by a Mississippi planter named Joseph Davis in 1850. Davis, Confederate President Jefferson Davis's elder brother, had met the British utopian reformer Robert Owen, and wanted to apply Owen's ideas to his own plantation. He instituted a system of self-government on his plantation, including a court system in which slaves ruled on any cases of misconduct, and gave slaves like Benjamin Montgomery access to his personal library. Montgomery educated himself and became a skilled mechanic. He managed the plantation's steam-powered cotton gin and ran a retail store, eventually earning enough money to purchase his family's freedom. Nevertheless, he and his family decided to remain on the plantation. After the Civil War, Montgomery actually purchased the property from Davis, and ran it until his death in 1877.

The experience of slavery varied widely, depending primarily on a slaveholder's character and whims. Some masters, like Joseph Davis, attempted to treat their slaves in a kindly if paternalistic manner. Yet as Celia's example reveals, the institution of slavery

1

could also bring out the very worst characteristics of human nature, for it allowed masters to treat a human being as a piece of property, to be exploited however they wished.

Slavery in Historical Perspective

During the nineteenth century, slavery was often described as "the peculiar institution." But throughout much of human history, free wage labor, not forced labor, was the truly peculiar institution. Most people worked not out of a desire to better their condition in life but because they were forced to: as slaves, serfs, peons, or indentured servants.

Slavery in the United States was not unique in treating human beings like animals or as property. The institution of slavery could be found in societies as diverse as ancient Assyria, Babylonia, China, Egypt, India, Persia, and Mesopotamia; in classical Greece and Rome; in Africa, the Islamic world, and among the New World Indians. At the time of Christ, there were probably between two and three million slaves in Italy, making up thirty-five to forty percent of the population. England's Domesday book of 1086 indicated that ten percent of the population was enslaved. Among some Indian tribes of the Pacific Northwest, nearly a quarter of the population consisted of slaves. In 1644, just before the Dutch ceded Manhattan to the British, enslaved Africans made up forty percent of the population.

It is notable that the modern word for slaves comes from "Slav." During the Middle Ages, most slaves in Europe and the Islamic world were people from Slavic Eastern Europe. It was only in the fifteenth century that slavery became linked with people from sub-Saharan Africa.

Defining Slavery

How does slavery differ from other forms of exploitation such as serfdom, indentured servitude, or the subordination of women in patriarchal societies? The traditional definition of slavery was legal. Slaves were peoples' property and could be bought, sold, traded, leased, or mortgaged like livestock.

Recent research has revealed great diversity among slavery's forms and functions. In the ancient and non-Western world some slaves served as field laborers. But others served as sex objects in harems; as eunuchs; and as bureaucrats, doctors, and soldiers. In the American South, slavery's primary functions were economic. But in many ancient and non-Western societies, slavery served psychological, religious, sexual, and honorific functions.

To encompass slavery's diversity, scholars today tend to define the institution culturally. Slaves, according to this view, are people totally subject to an owner's whim. They belong only to their owner, who can force them to labor, subject them to sexual exploitation and cruel punishment, and hold over them the power of life and death. In addition, slaves are people who are cut off from their traditional culture and dishonored in a variety of ways (for example, by being branded, tatooed, or required to wear distinctive collars, clothing, or hairstyles). The most common form of dishonor is to disparage slaves' character and their intellectual capacities. Regardless of place, time, or the slaves' ethnicity, all societies have imposed certain common stereotypes on slaves—that they were licentious, childlike, lazy, irresponsible, and incapable of freedom.

Slavery in the Ancient, Medieval, and Early Modern Worlds

Slavery dates to prehistoric times and was modeled on the domestication of animals. From the earliest periods of recorded history, slavery was found in the world's most advanced regions. The first civilizations—along the Tigris and Euphrates rivers in Mesopotamia, the Nile in Egypt, the Indus Valley of India, and China's Yangtze River Valley—all had slavery. The earliest known system of laws, the Hammurabi Code, recognized slavery and stated that slaves could be sold or inherited. But the percentage of slaves in these early civilizations was small, in part because these societies kept relatively few male slaves. In the tales of Homer and in the Old Testament, male war captives were typically killed, while women were enslaved as field laborers or taken as concubines.

Although slavery was a universal institution in the ancient world, only a handful of societies made slavery the dominant labor force. The first true slave society in history emerged in ancient Greece between the sixth and the fourth centuries B.C. In Athens during the classical period, a third to a half of the population consisted of slaves. Ancient Rome would be even more dependent on slavery. It is not an accident that our modern ideas of freedom and democracy emerged in these slave societies. Most early societies lacked a word for freedom. But large-scale slavery in classical Greece and Rome made people more aware of the distinctive nature of freedom and the contrast between slavery and liberty.

Slavery never disappeared from medieval Europe. While slavery declined in northwestern Europe, where it was replaced by serfdom, it persisted in Sicily, southern Italy, Russia, southern France, Spain, and North Africa. Continuing warfare between Christians and Muslims generated large numbers of slaves to work in agriculture. Most of these slaves were "white," coming from areas in Eastern Europe or near the Black Sea.

When Europeans began to colonize the New World at the end of the fifteenth century, they were well aware of the institution of slavery. As early as 1300, Europeans were using black and Russian slaves to raise sugar on Italian plantations. During the 1400s, decades before Columbus's "discovery" of the New World, Europeans exploited African labor for slave plantations on sugar-producing islands off the coast of West Africa. European colonization of the New World led to a dramatic expansion in slavery. During the sixteenth century, Portugal and Spain extended racial slavery into the New World, opening sugar, coffee, and cotton plantations in Brazil and the West Indies and forcing black slaves in Mexico to work in mines. During the seventeenth century, England, France, Denmark, and Holland established slavery in their New World colonies.

The Newness of New World Slavery

Was the slavery that developed in the New World fundamentally different from the kinds of servitude found in classical antiquity or in other societies? In one respect, New World slavery was not unique. Slavery everywhere permitted cruelty and abuse. In Homer's Greece, it was not a crime for a master to beat or kill a slave, and the testimony of unskilled slaves was not allowed in court unless it was obtained through torture. Nor does the Bible prohibit the beating of slaves. In the Roman Republic, a master might kill a slave. Vedius Pollio, a citizen of Rome, reportedly fed the bodies of his slaves to his pet fish. Flavius Gratianus, a fourth century Roman emperor, ruled that any slave who dared accuse his master of a crime should be immediately burned alive. Roman slaves who participated in revolts were crucified on crosses. In ancient India, Saxon England, and ancient China, a master might mistreat or even kill a slave with impunity. Aztec Mexico publicly staged the ritual torture and killing of slaves. Yet in certain fundamental respects New World slavery differed from slavery in classical antiquity and in Africa, eastern and central Asia, or the Middle East.

For one thing, slavery in the classical and the early medieval worlds was not based on racial distinctions. In ancient times, slavery had nothing to do with the color of a person's skin. In ancient Rome, for example, the slave population included Ethiopians, Gauls, Jews, Persians, and Scandinavians. Unlike seventeenth-, eighteenth-, or nineteenth-century Europeans, the people of the ancient world placed no premium on racial purity and attached no stigma upon racial mixture. Ancient societies, however, did tattoo, brand, or mutilate their slaves as a symbol of their debased status.

Racial slavery originated during the Middle Ages, when Christians and Muslims increasingly began to recruit slaves from east, north-central, and west Africa. As late as the fifteenth century, slavery did not automatically mean black slavery. Many slaves—both in southern Europe and in Islamic lands—came from the Crimea, the Balkans, and the steppes of western Asia. But after 1453, when the Ottoman Turks captured Constantinople, the capital of eastern Christendom, and began to monopolize the supply of "white" slaves, Christian slave traders drew increasingly upon captive black Muslims, known as Moors, and upon slaves purchased on the West African coast or transported across the Sahara Desert. By the eighteenth century, Islamic societies also became dependent almost exclusively on sub-Saharan African slaves. For the first time, the most menial, arduous, and degrading forms of labor were associated with black slaves.

Another distinction between modern and ancient slavery was that the ancient world did not necessarily regard slavery as a permanent condition. In many societies, slaves were allowed to marry free spouses and become members of their owners' families. In ancient Babylonia, for instance, freeborn women and male slaves frequently married, and their children were considered to be free. Access to freedom tended to be far easier under ancient slavery than it was under American slavery. In Greece and Rome, manumission of slaves was not uncommon, and former slaves carried little stigma from their previous status.

A key difference between ancient and modern slavery was that slaves did not necessarily hold the lowest status in pre-modern societies. While we today draw a sharp distinction between slavery and wage labor, such a distinction was largely nonexistent in the world of classical antiquity, and slaves could be among the wealthiest or most influential people in a city. The Bible, for example, tells the story of Joseph, sold into slavery by his brothers, who became a trusted governor, counselor, and administrator in Egypt. In classical Greece, many educators, scholars, poets, and physicians were in fact slaves. And in ancient Rome, slaves ranged from laborers in mines to merchants and urban craftsmen. In the ancient Near East, slaves could conduct trade and business on their own. In certain Muslim societies, rulers were customarily recruited among the sons of female slaves.

Finally, it was only in the New World that slavery provided the labor force for a profit-making capitalist system of plantation agriculture producing cotton, sugar, coffee, and cocoa for distant markets. While many slaves in the ancient world toiled in mines and agricultural fields, or on construction and irrigation projects, and suffered extremely high death rates, it appears that slavery then was primarily a household institution. In general, ancient peoples did not breed slaves or subject them to the kind of regimented efficiency found on slave plantations in the West Indies or the American South. It seems that most slaves in Africa, in the Islamic world, and in the New World prior to European colonization worked as farmers or household servants, or served as concubines or eunuchs. They were symbols of prestige, luxury, and power rather than a source of labor. Under modern New World slavery, slaves became the dominant labor force in plantation agriculture.

Justifications of Slavery

Over time, justifications for slavery have changed profoundly. Many ancient societies considered slavery a matter of bad luck or accident. Slaves in many early societies were war captives or victims of piracy or children who had been abandoned by their parents. It was easy to think of enslavement as a fate that could befall anyone.

Writing in the 300s B.C., Aristotle, one of the most influential thinkers in Western culture, advanced the notion of the "natural slave." Slaves, in his view, lacked the higher qualities of the soul necessary for freedom. Slavery was not only good for the master, according to Aristotle, but also good for slaves, who received the guidance and discipline they were incapable of providing themselves. The idea that slaves were naturally suited for slavery would appeal to many future generations of slave owners.

In the Christian world, the most important rationalization for slavery was the so-called "Curse of Ham." According to this doctrine, the Biblical figure Noah had cursed his son Ham with blackness and the condition of perpetual slavery. In fact, this story rested on a misunderstanding of Biblical texts. In the Bible, Noah curses Canaan, the ancestor of the Canaanites, and not Ham. But the

"Curse of Ham" was important in being the first justification of slavery based on ethnicity.

It was not until the late eighteenth century that pseudo-scientific racism provided the basic justification for slavery. Yet even before this era, there can be no doubt that racism inclined many Europeans to see sub-Saharan Africans as fit for little more than slavery. In the fifteenth and sixteenth centuries, many European Christians associated Africans with their Islamic enemies. At the same time, many Europeans devised a clear color symbolism. They associated whiteness with purity, while blackness had sinister and even satanic connotations since black was the color of the Devil.

Slavery in Africa

Slavery existed in Africa before the arrival of Europeans—as did a slave trade that exported a small number of sub-Saharan Africans to North Africa, the Middle East, and the Persian Gulf. It would be a grave mistake, however, to assume that the kinds of slavery found in Africa prior to the Atlantic slave trade were identical to the system of plantation slavery that developed in the New World.

For one thing, hereditary slavery, extending over several generations, was rare. Many African slaves were eventually freed and absorbed into their owner's kin group or society. One reason why hereditary slavery was uncommon was that most slaves were female. Women were preferred because they bore children and were responsible for most productive labor. They were responsible not only for agricultural production, but for spinning and weaving and many other tasks. Another difference between traditional African and New World slavery was that the gap in status between masters and slaves was not as wide in Africa. To be sure, most African slaves were field workers. But many served in royal courts, where they were officials, soldiers, servants, and artisans.

Slavery in traditional African society took a variety of forms. There was some chattel slavery, under which slaves could be bought and sold like livestock. But under a system known as "pawnship," youths (usually girls) served as collateral for their family's debts. If their parents or kin defaulted on these debts, then these young girls were forced to labor to make repayment. In many instances, these young women eventually married into their owner's lineage, and their family's debt was canceled. Under a system known as "clientage," slaves owed a share of their crop or their labor to an owner or a lineage. Yet these slave "clients" owned the bulk of their crop and were even allowed to participate in the society's political activities. These slaves were often treated no differently from other peasant or tenant farmers.

The trans-Atlantic slave trade profoundly changed the nature and scale of slavery in Africa itself—and imposed a heavy economic, political, and psychological cost on the continent. The development of the Atlantic slave trade led to the enslavement of far greater numbers of Africans than ever before. It also resulted in more intense exploitation of slave labor within Africa. Over time, traders sought slaves deep in the interior. One of the slave trade's most profound consequences was demographic. While the trade probably did not reduce the overall population, it did produce a radically skewed sex ratio, since most of the slaves exported to the New World were adult men. During the slave trade era, in most parts of West and Central Africa for every hundred women from fifteen to sixty years of age there were only eighty men. In Angola, there were just forty to fifty men per hundred women. The slave trade left fewer adult men to hunt, fish, rear livestock, and clear fields.

The slave trade had momentous social consequences. It generated violence, spread disease, and resulted in massive imports of European goods, undermining local industries. It also slowed population growth. According to one estimate, in the absence of the slave trade, there would have been 100 million Africans in 1850 instead of 50 million.

Why Africa?

Why was Africa so vulnerable to the slave trade? The answer lies especially in West and Central Africa's political fragmentation. By the era of the slave trade, many of the region's larger political units—such as the empires of Ghana and Mali—had declined. The absence of large, strong, stable political units made it difficult for western and central Africans to resist the slave trade. In western and central Africa, many new commercial states, merchants, and traders, chronically short of capital, thrived by enslaving some people and selling others abroad. Birth rates often exceeded agriculture's capacity to feed the population. Drought, famine, or periods of violent conflict might lead a ruler or a merchant to sell slaves. In addition, many rulers sold slaves in order to acquire the trade goods—textiles, alcohol, and other rare imports—that were necessary to secure the loyalty of their subjects or clients. Over time, however, the quest for slaves led to social disintegration and the spread of warfare in many parts of western and central Africa. Social conflict, in turn, generated fresh supplies of slaves.

In retrospect, it seems clear that the Atlantic slave trade resulted from a highly complex—and contingent—set of variables. The rapid decline in the population of New World Indians created an enormous demand for labor—to clear forests, mine precious metals, and raise cash crops. Trade winds and ocean currents made it easy to sail from the western African coast to Brazil and the Caribbean. The importation of new food crops from the Americas—such as cassava, squash, and peanuts—stimulated a population growth in Africa that helped make the slave trade possible.

Enslavement

Many Americans, influenced by images in the television miniseries "Roots," mistakenly believe that most slaves were captured by Europeans who landed on the African coast and seized people. While Europeans did engage in some slave raiding, most people who were transported to the Americas were enslaved by other Africans. Europeans were incapable, on their own, of kidnapping twenty million Africans. Indeed, the system became so institutionalized that most European slave traders had little direct contact with the actual process of enslavement. Some African societies—like Benin in southern Nigeria—refused to sell slaves. Others, like Dahomey, appear to have specialized in enslavement. Still other societies, like Asante, in present-day Ghana, and the Yoruba in western Nigeria, engaged in wars that produced as many as half of all eighteenth- and early nineteenth-century slaves. In most cases, rulers or merchants were selling not their own subjects, but people they regarded as aliens. Africans thought of themselves not as Africans, but as members of separate nations.

The overwhelming majority of slaves sold to Europeans had not been slaves in Africa. They were free people captured in war or victims of banditry or enslaved as punishment for certain crimes. In Senegambia, the Guinea Coast, and the Slave Coast of West Africa, war was the most important source of slaves. In Angola, kidnapping and condemnation for debt were very important. Many were captured in wars or in surprise raids on villages. Adults were bound and gagged and infants were sometimes thrown into sacks. One of the earliest firsthand accounts of the African slave trade comes from a seaman named Gomes Eannes de Azurara, who witnessed a Portuguese raid on an African village. He said that some captives "drowned themselves in the water; others thought to escape by hiding under their huts; others shoved their children among the sea-weed."

Apologists for the African slave trade long argued that European traders did not enslave anyone: they simply purchased Africans who had already been enslaved and otherwise would have been put to death. Thus, apologists claimed, the slave trade actually saved lives. Such claims are a gross distortion. Some independent slave merchants did in fact stage raids on unprotected African villages and kidnap and enslave Africans. Most professional slave traders, however, set up bases along the west African coast where they purchased slaves from Africans in exchange for firearms and other goods. Before the end of the seventeenth century, England, France, Denmark, Holland, and Portugal had all established slave trading posts on the west African coast in response to massive European demand.

While there had been a slave trade within Africa prior to the arrival of Europeans, the massive European demand for slaves and the introduction of firearms radically transformed West and Central African society. A growing number of Africans were enslaved for petty debts or minor criminal or religious offenses or following unprovoked raids on unprotected villages. An increasing number of religious wars broke out with the goal of capturing slaves. European weapons made it easier to capture slaves.

In the earliest years, most slaves came from coastal areas. Over time, the source moved farther into the African interior. Many Africans at first retained females and sold off males. About two-thirds of the slaves sent to the New World were male. After capture, the captives were bound together at the neck and marched barefoot hundreds of miles to the Atlantic coast. African captives typically suffered death rates of twenty percent or more while being marched overland. Observers reported seeing hundreds of skeletons along the slave caravan routes. At the coast, the captives were held in pens guarded by dogs and armed men. Our best guess is that another fifteen to thirty percent of Africans died during capture, the march from the interior, or the wait for slave ships along the coast.

The captives who survived the forced march to the sea were then examined by European slave traders: "The Countenance and Stature, a good Set of Teeth, Pliancy in the Limbs and Joints, and being free of Venereal Taint, are the things inspected and governs our choice in buying," wrote one slave trader. Those who were bought were branded with hot irons, assigned numbers, and forced aboard ships; the others were simply abandoned. (Representatives of the Catholic Church sometimes branded enslaved Africans with the cross as a sign that they had been baptised.)

The Middle Passage

The trans-Atlantic slave trade was the largest movement of people in history. Between ten and fifteen million Africans were forcibly transported across the Atlantic between 1500 and 1900. But this figure grossly understates the actual number of Africans enslaved, killed, or displaced as a result of the slave trade. At least one million Africans—ten to fifteen percent—died during the infamous "Middle Passage" across the Atlantic. Many others died during the march to the coast or confinement along it. Altogether, for every hundred slaves who reached the New World, another forty had died in Africa or during the Middle Passage.

The Atlantic slave trade, however, was not the only slave trade within Africa. Nearly as many Africans were exported across the Sahara, the Red Sea, and the Indian Ocean from A.D. 650 to 1900 as were shipped across the Atlantic. Islamic traders probably exported ten million slaves into north Africa, Arabia, Yemen, Iraq, Iran, and India. In addition, it now seems clear that during the era of the Atlantic slave trade, many and perhaps most of the enslaved were kept in Africa. It is imaginable that as many as sixty million Africans died or were enslaved as a result of these various slave trades.

The level of slave exports to the New World grew from about 36,000 a year in the early eighteenth century to almost 80,000 a year during the 1780s. By 1750, slave ships usually contained at least 400 slaves, with some carrying more than 700.

Once on shipboard, men and women were separated, men usually toward the vessel's bow and women toward the stern. The men were chained together and forced to lie shoulder to shoulder, while women were usually left unchained. Slaves were crammed into spaces sometimes less than five feet high. One observer said that slaves were packed together "like books upon a shelf . . . so close that the self would not easily contain one more." Conditions within the slave ships were unspeakably awful. Inside the hold, slaves had only half the space provided for indentured servants or convicts. Urine, vomit, mucus, and horrific odors filled the hold.

The Middle Passage usually took more than seven weeks. During the voyage, the enslaved Africans were typically fed only once or twice a day and brought on deck for limited times. The death rate on these slave ships was very high—reaching twenty-five percent in the seventeenth and early eighteenth centuries and remaining around ten percent in the nineteenth century—as a result of malnutrition and such diseases as dysentery, measles, scurvy, and smallpox. This was a much higher death rate than that found among white immigrants, and it appears to have been due largely to dehydration, resulting from inadequate water rations. Diarrhea was widespread, and many Africans arrived in the New World covered with sores or suffering fevers.

On shipboard, many slaves mutinied, attempted suicide, jumped overboard, or refused to eat. The most recent estimate suggests that there was a revolt on one in every ten voyages across the Atlantic. To prevent their captives from starving themselves, slavers sometimes smashed out their teeth and fed them by force. To discourage acts of resistance, some captains actually cut off the arms and legs of a few kidnapped Africans.

Upon arrival in the New World, Africans underwent the final stage in the process of enslavement, a rigorous process known as "seasoning." To prepare them for sale, Africans were rested, washed, better fed, and given medical care. In some cases, lead was placed in their anus to disguise signs of bleeding. Many newly-arrived slaves died of disease or suicide, but a few captives conspired to escape slavery by running away and forming "maroon" colonies in remote parts of South Carolina, Florida, Brazil, Guiana, Jamaica, and Suriname.

The Slave Trade's Significance

Slavery had a critical role in the development of the modern world economy. Slaves provided the labor power necessary to settle and develop the New World. Africans possessed many skills that were valuable in this task. They were experienced in intensive agriculture and in raising livestock and knew how to raise crops like rice that were unfamiliar to Europeans. Slaves also produced the products for the first mass consumer markets: sugar, tobacco, coffee, cocoa, and later cotton. Slavery was an integral part of the earliest multinational systems of credit and trade that arose in the fifteenth and sixteenth centuries. While slavery did not create a major share of the capital that financed Europe's industrial revolution (profits from the slave trade and New World plantations did not add up to five percent of Britain's national income at the beginning of the industrial revolution), the African slave trade stimulated European shipping, manufacturing, and gunmaking. Africa became a major market for iron, textiles, firearms, and rum.

During the earliest phases of capitalist development, planters, master craftsmen, and others could not afford to pay wages. Chronically in debt, New World planters could exploit slave labor without expending scarce currency. Slavery provided the cheapest and most expedient way to meet the demand for labor in mining as well as agriculture. Between the early 1500s and the early 1800s, the slave trade became one of Europe's largest and most profitable industries. Profits were said to run as high as three hundred percent. In the mid-eighteenth century, a third of the British merchant fleet was engaged in transporting fifty thousand Africans a year to the New World. American shipowners, farmers, and fisherman also profited from slavery. Slavery was essential to the growth of commercial capitalism in the colonies. The slave plantations of the West Indies became the largest market for American fish, oats, corn, flour, lumber, peas, beans, hogs, and horses. New Englanders distilled molasses produced by slaves in the French and Dutch West Indies into rum.

The Extent of the Atlantic Slave Trade

Before the nineteenth century, most immigrants to the New World were African. Enslaved Africans arrived in the New World at least as early as 1502. During the peak years of the slave trade, between 1740 and 1810, Africa supplied 60,000 captives a year—outnumbering European migrants by a ratio of three or four to one. According to one recent estimate, about eighty percent of women immigrants and ninety percent of child immigrants came from Africa. By 1820, about 8.4 million Africans had been forcibly imported into the Americas compared to just 2.4 million European immigrants. Even in the area that would become the United States, about half of all immigrants to the thirteen colonies from 1700 to 1775 came from Africa.

By the beginning of the eighteenth century, black slaves could be found in every New World area colonized by Europeans, from Nova Scotia to Buenos Aires. While the concentrations of slave labor were greatest in England's southern colonies, the Caribbean, and Latin America, where slaves were employed to work in mines or on sugar, rice, tobacco, and cotton plantations, slaves were also put to work in northern seaports and on commercial farms. In 1690, one out of every nine families in Boston owned a slave. In New York City in 1703, two out of every five families owned a slave.

The Origins of New World Slavery

It was not inevitable that Europeans in the New World would rely on African slaves to raise crops, clear forests, and mine precious metals. In every New World colony, Europeans experimented with Indian slavery, convict labor, and white indentured servants. For example, as late as the early 1700s, a third of South Carolina's labor force consisted of Indian slaves.

Why, then, did every European power eventually turn to African labor? Was this, as some have argued, the product of deep-seated racial prejudice? Or was it the result of a haphazard and random process that took place gradually with little real sense of the ultimate outcome? Or were other forces at work?

Certainly there is a great deal of evidence showing that sixteenth-century Europeans held deeply racist sentiments well before the establishment of slavery. We know, for example, that the Elizabethan English associated blackness with evil, death, and danger. They portrayed the devil as having black skin and associated beauty with fair skin. Through their religion, the English denigrated people of color, claiming that Negroes were the descendants of Noah's son Ham who was cursed by having black offspring for daring to look upon his drunken and naked father. Long before the English had contact with Africa, racist stereotypes were widespread. One English writer claimed that Negroes were naturally "addicted unto Treason, Treacherie, Murther, Theft and Robberie." It was easy for the English to accept slavery because they regarded Negroes as an alien people. But it also seems clear that racism was as much a consequence of racial slavery as it was a cause or justification.

In colony after colony, Europeans shifted from Indian to African slaves partly for demographic reasons. Epidemic diseases reduced the native population by fifty to ninety percent. Initially, colonists in every English colony relied on neither Indian nor black slavery but on indentured white servants. During the late fifteenth and early sixteenth centuries, England's population grew by over a third—much faster than its economy. To address a sudden explosion of crime and poverty, England's rulers forced the poor to toil in workhouses, and, beginning in 1547, enslaved persistent vagabonds and branded them with the letter "S." In the early 1600s, England viewed New World colonization as a providential solution to their country's problem of overpopulation. Thousands of England's unemployed and underemployed farmers, urban laborers, debtors, and criminals were sent as "indentured servants" to the New World, where they contributed to England's wealth by raising tobacco and produced other goods. Over half of all white immigrants to the English colonies during the seventeenth century were convicts or indentured servants.

Indentured servants agreed to work for a four- or five-year term of service in return for their transportation to the New World as well as food, clothing, and shelter. In certain respects, the status of white servants differed little from that of slaves. Like slaves, servants could be bought, sold, or leased. They could also be punished by whipping. Unlike slaves, however, servants were allowed to own property, and, if they survived their term of service, received their freedom along with a small sum of money known as "freedom dues." During the seventeenth century, indentured servants suffered an appalling death rate. Half of all white servants in the Chesapeake colonies of Virginia and Maryland died within five years of their arrival. Since servants cost half as much as slaves, they were a more economical investment.

Black slavery took root in the American colonies slowly. As early as 1619, a Dutch ship carried the first Africans to Virginia, but it would not be until the 1680s that black slavery became the dominant labor system on plantations. In 1640, there were probably only 150 blacks in Virginia (the colony with the highest black population), and in 1650, three hundred. But by 1680, the number had risen to three thousand and by 1704, to ten thousand.

As the supply of English servants diminished, colonists in the Chesapeake imported increasing numbers of slaves directly from Africa. Many were sent to inland plantations, where planters believed that it would be easier to control the slave population. To meet planters' growing demand for slaves, the English government established the Royal African Company in 1672. After 1698, when Britain ended the Royal African Company's monopoly of the slave trade, the number of enslaved Africans brought into the colonies soared. Between 1700 and 1775, more than 350,000 African slaves entered the American colonies. By the mid-eighteenth century, blacks made up almost seventy percent of the population of South Carolina, forty percent in Virginia, eight percent in Pennsylvania, and four percent in New England.

Slavery in Colonial North America

Slavery was a legal institution in all of the thirteen American colonies. A majority of the founding fathers owned slaves, including the author of the Declaration of Independence (Thomas Jefferson), the Father of the Constitution (James Madison), and the commander of the Continental Army (George Washington).

Slavery during the colonial era was not a static institution. It was dynamic, evolving, varying greatly across time and space. The first generation of Africans in the New World were remarkably cosmopolitan. Few of the first generation came directly from Africa. Instead, they arrived from the West Indies and other areas of European settlement. These "Atlantic Creoles" were often multilingual and had Spanish or Portuguese names. Sometimes they had mixtures of African and non-African ancestry.

Slavery during the early seventeenth century is shown by the case of Anthony Johnson, one of Virginia's first slaves. Arriving in 1621, he was put to work on a plantation along the James River, where he took a wife, Mary, and raised at least four children. During the 1630s, Johnson and his family gained their freedom, probably by purchase. Johnson subsequently acquired an estate of 250 acres, which he farmed with the help of white indentured servants and at least one slave. Just as remarkably, Johnson successfully sued in court for the return of a slave, who he claimed had been stolen by two white neighbors. As Johnson's life suggests, the black experience in seventeenth-century America was extremely complex. Some blacks were permanently unfree; others, however, were treated like white indentured servants. They were allowed to own property and to marry and were freed after a term of service. A few slaves, like Francis Payne who lived in eastern Virginia, were assigned plots of land remote from their master's homes, and were allowed to raise extra tobacco and other crops and purchase their own freedom. In several cases, black slaves who could prove that they had been baptized sued successfully for their freedom. In one eastern Virginia county in 1668, twenty-nine percent of all blacks were free. Racial lines had not assumed the rigidity that they would subsequently acquire. White and black servants worked together, received the same punishments, and plotted escapes together. Blacks fathered about one third of all the illegitimate children born to white servant women. In 1677, at the end of Bacon's Rebellion (a revolt against Virginia's royal government), the last holdouts were twenty white indentured servants and eighty black slaves.

Beginning in the late 1660s, colonists in the Chesapeake colonies of Maryland and Virginia imposed new laws that deprived blacks, free and slave, of many rights and privileges. At the same time, they began to import thousands of slaves directly from Africa. Yet slavery remained dispersed and decentralized. Even the wealthiest Chesapeake planters tended to divide their estates into many separate quarters where small groups of slaves lived and worked. In the South Carolina and Georgia Low Country, slavery was also remarkably fluid during the pioneering period. Black soldiers played an indispensable role in protecting the colonies against the Indians and the Spanish. White planters were heavily dependent on the knowledge and skills of African-born slaves in growing rice, raising cattle, and building irrigation dikes.

The Diversity of Colonial Slavery

During the late seventeenth and eighteenth centuries, three distinctive systems of slavery emerged in the American colonies. In the Chesapeake colonies of Maryland and Virginia, slavery was widely used in raising tobacco and corn and other grains. Most slaves in this region lived on relatively small farms or plantations presided over by resident owners. Beginning in the 1720s, slaves in the Chesapeake region became the first slave population in the New World able to reproduce its numbers. Eager to encourage a rapid population increase, slave owners in the Chesapeake consciously imported many female slaves. While raising tobacco or corn was less debilitating and taxing than growing sugar cane in the West Indies or rice in the South Carolina and Georgia Low Country, slavery in the Chesapeake may have been more difficult psychologically. Even in the eighteenth century, slaveholders in the Chesapeake supervised their slaves much more closely than in the South Carolina or Georgia Low Country or the Caribbean and intervened much more frequently in their lives.

In the South Carolina and Georgia Low Country, slaves raised rice and indigo and were able to reconstitute African social patterns and maintain a separate Gullah dialect. Although slaves were subjected to a harsh labor regime, the task system of labor, permitting a measure of independence, became the norm. Each day, slaves were required to achieve a precise work objective. This allowed them to leave the fields early in the afternoon to tend their own gardens and raise their own livestock. Slaves often passed their property down for generations. The kind of slavery that emerged in the Low Country was similar to some west and central African forms of slavery and was very different from the kinds of slavery found in the Chesapeake. Far more than in the Chesapeake, planters in the Low Country openly acknowledged sexual unions with black women. An elite of free light-skinned people of color emerged that served as intermediaries between whites and blacks.

In the North, slavery was concentrated in productive agriculture on Long Island and in southern Rhode Island and New Jersey. Most slaves were engaged in farming and stock raising for the West Indies or as household servants for the urban elite. A massive influx of Africans in the mid-eighteenth century inspired the creation of many African churches and benevolent societies. Northern slaves developed a vibrant African-American culture. They celebrated a number of popular festivals like Election Day, during which roles between whites and blacks were temporarily reversed.

Toward Slavery

As early as the late 1630s, English colonists began to make a sharper distinction between the status of white servants and that of black slaves. Beginning with Maryland in 1639, colonies made it clear that baptism as a Christian did not make a slave a free person. Discrimination against black servants began to increase. In 1640, when two white indentured servants and a black servant named John Punch fled from Virginia to Maryland, all three received thirty lashes. The whites also had their terms of service extended by four years, but Punch, the black servant, was condemned to lifelong servitude. In 1669, Virginia became the first colony to declare that it was not a crime to kill an unruly slave in the ordinary course of punishment. By the end of the seventeenth century, Virginia and Maryland had forbidden interracial marriages and sexual relations. Laws adopted in several colonies in the early eighteenth century confiscated slaves' property, forbade masters from freeing their slaves, permitted masters to mutilate and dismember disobedient slaves, and declared that slave status was inherited through the mother. The law now defined Africans as chattel property, under the complete legal control of their masters.

Slavery's Evolution

At the time that Thomas Jefferson was born in 1743 most slaves were born in Africa, few were Christian, and very few were engaged in raising cotton. Slavery was largely confined to eastern areas near the Atlantic coast, and the slave population in the Carolinas and Georgia was not yet able to naturally reproduce its numbers.

By the time of Jefferson's death in 1826, a series of momentous revolutions had transformed the institution. One of these was demographic. During the seventeenth century, slaves had had few opportunities to establish stable family relationships. In the Chesapeake colonies and the Carolinas, two-thirds of all slaves were male, and most slaves lived on plantations with fewer than ten slaves. These units were so small and widely dispersed, the sex ratio was so skewed, that it was difficult for slaves to find spouses. A high death rate meant that many slaves did not live long enough to marry or, if they did, their marriages did not last very long. But by the 1720s in the Chesapeake and the 1750s and '60s in the South Carolina and Georgia Low Country, the slave population was naturally reproducing its numbers. Plantations, moreover, increased in size and efficiency as planters expanded their operations and imposed greater supervision on their slaves.

Another important change was religious. Out of a fear that baptism would change a slave's legal status, many early planters resisted the idea of converting slaves to Christianity. The black population was virtually untouched by Christianity until the religious revivals of the 1730s and 1740s. But by the early nineteenth century, slaveholders, adopting the view that Christianity would make slaves more submissive, orderly, and conscientious, actively encouraged missionary activities among slaves.

Slaves themselves found in Christianity a faith that could give them hope in an oppressive world. While Christianity has sometimes been called a religion of passivity, it proved impossible to purge it of its antislavery overtones—its promise of deliverance from bondage. Beginning in the 1740s and greatly accelerating in the early 1800s, many slaves converted to Christianity. In general, slaves did not join their masters' churches. Most became Baptists or Methodists. Important also is that between 1790 and 1860, 835,000 slaves were moved from Maryland, Virginia, and the Carolinas to Alabama, Mississippi, Louisiana, and Texas. We know that slaves were frequently sold apart from their families or separated from family members when they were moved to the Old Southwest. Finally, there was a transformation in moral values and sensibility. During the mid- and late eighteenth century, for the first time in history religious and secular groups condemned slavery as sinful and as a violation of natural rights. During the 1760s, the first movements in history began to denounce slavery. The earliest groups to oppose slavery were perfectionist religious sects like the Quakers who challenged all traditional authorities and wanted to live free from sin.

The American Revolution and Slavery

Leaders of the patriot cause repeatedly argued that British policies would make the colonists slaves of the British. The colonists' fears of mass enslavement derived in part from the highly visible example of racial slavery. A statement by George Washington in 1774 underscores the link between British tyranny and slavery. Washington explained that if the colonists failed aggressively to assert their rights, then the British ministry "shall make us as tame and abject slaves, as the blacks we rule over with such arbitrary sway."

Both the British and the colonists believed that slaves could serve an important role during the Revolution. In April 1775, Lord Dunmore, the royal governor of Virginia, threatened that he would free the colony's slaves if the colonists resorted to force against his authority. In November, he promised freedom to all slaves belonging to rebels who would join His Majesty's Troops. Some eight hundred slaves joined British forces, some wearing the emblem "Liberty to the Slaves." Meanwhile, an American diplomat, Silas Deane, hatched a secret plan to incite slave insurrections in Jamaica. Two South Carolinians, John Laurens and his father Henry, persuaded Congress to approve unanimously a plan to recruit an army of three thousand slave troops to stop a British invasion of South Carolina and Georgia. The federal government would compensate the slaves' owners and each black would, at the end of the war, be emancipated and receive fifty dollars. The South Carolina legislature rejected the plan. In the end, however, and in contrast to the later Latin American wars of independence and the United States Civil War, the conflict did not bring either side to risk a full-scale social revolution by issuing an emancipation proclamation.

As a result of the Revolution, a surprising number of slaves were manumitted, while thousands of others freed themselves by running away. Georgia lost about a third of its slaves and South Carolina lost twenty-five thousand. Despite these losses, slavery quickly recovered in the South. By 1810, South Carolina and Georgia had three times as many slaves as in 1770.

The Revolution had contradictory consequences for slavery. In the South, slavery ultimately became more firmly entrenched. In the North, in contrast, every state freed slaves as a result of court decisions or the enactment of gradual emancipation schemes. Yet even in the North, there was strong resistance to emancipation and freeing of slaves was accompanied by the emergence of a virulent form of racial prejudice.

Antebellum Slavery

During the last years of the eighteenth century, New World slavery seemed to be declining. As a result of the American and French revolutions, thousands of black slaves escaped slavery through revolt or simply by running away. Revolutionary ideals of liberty and equality encouraged many slave owners in the United States, the Caribbean, and Spanish America to emancipate their slaves. In the ten years after Virginia enacted a law allowing private manumissions, masters freed ten thousand slaves. A French traveler reported that people throughout the South "are constantly talking of abolishing slavery, of contriving some other means of cultivating their estates."

But slavery was not, in fact, on the road to extinction. During the early nineteenth century, it underwent a new boom, rapidly expanding in Brazil, Cuba, Trinidad, Guiana, the Windward Islands of the Caribbean, and new territories southwest of the Appalachian Mountains in the United States: into Georgia, Alabama, Mississippi, Louisiana, Arkansas, Missouri, and Texas. Eli Whitney's invention of the cotton gin gave slavery a new lease on life. Between 1792, when Whitney invented the cotton gin, and 1794, the price of slaves doubled. By 1825, field hands, who had brought $500 apiece in 1794, were worth $1,500. As the price of slaves grew, so, too, did their numbers. During the first decade of the nineteenth century, the number of slaves in the United States rose by thirty-three percent; during the following decade, the slave population grew another twenty-nine percent.

What Was Life Like Under Slavery?

Under southern law, slaves were considered chattel property. Like a domestic animal, they could be bought, sold, leased, and physically punished. Slaves were prohibited from owning property, testifying against whites in court, or traveling without a pass. Their marriages lacked legal sanction. In response to abolitionist attacks on slavery, southern legislatures enacted laws setting minimal standards for housing, food, and clothing—but these statutes went largely unenforced.

Prior to the Civil War, abolitionists charged that slaves were overworked, poorly clad, inadequately housed, and cruelly punished; that slavery was a highly profitable investment; and that far from being content, slaves longed for freedom. Apologists for slavery accused abolitionists of exaggerating slavery's evils, asserting that slaves were rarely whipped, that marriages were seldom broken by sale, and that most slaves were able to maintain stable family lives. They maintained that paternalism and public opinion protected slaves from cruelty; that slave insurrections were rare because most slaves were contented with bondage; that slavery was an economic burden that planters bore out of a sense of responsibility; and that slaves enjoyed a higher standard of living, a better diet and housing, and a greater life expectancy than many free urban workers in the North and in Europe. Recent historical research has largely confirmed the abolitionist indictment of slavery.

We now know that slaves suffered extremely high mortality. Half of all slave infants died during their first year of life, twice the rate of white babies. And while the death rate declined for those who survived their first year, it remained twice the white rate through age fourteen. This high infant and childhood death rate put at just twenty-one or twenty two the average life expectancy of a slave at birth, compared with forty to forty-three years for antebellum whites. Compared to whites, relatively few slaves lived into old age. Between 1830 and 1860, only ten percent of U.S. slaves were over fifty years old.

A major contributor to the high infant and child death rate was chronic undernourishment. Slave owners showed surprisingly little concern for slave mothers' health or diet during pregnancy, providing pregnant women with no extra rations and employing them in intensive field work even in the last week before they gave birth. Not surprisingly, slave mothers suffered high rates of spontaneous abortions, stillbirths, and deaths shortly after birth. Half of all slave infants weighed less than 5.5 pounds at birth, which we would today consider to be severely underweight.

Infants and children were badly malnourished. Most infants were weaned early, within three or four months of birth, and then fed gruel or porridge made of cornmeal. Around the age of three, they began to eat vegetables, soups, potatoes, molasses, grits, hominy, and cornbread. This diet lacked protein, thiamine, niacin, calcium, magnesium, and vitamin D. Slave children often suffered from night blindness, abdominal swellings, swollen muscles, bowed legs, skin lesions, and convulsions. These apparently stemmed from beriberi, pellagra, tetany, rickets, and kwashiorkor, diseases that are caused by protein and nutritional deficiencies. Deprived of an adequate diet, slave children were very small by modern standards. Their average height at age three was shorter than ninety-nine percent of twentieth-century American three-year-olds. At age seventeen, slave men were shorter than ninety-six percent of present-day seventeen-year-old men and slave women were shorter than eighty percent of contemporary women. Squalid living conditions aggravated health problems. Chickens, dogs, and pigs lived next to the slave quarters, and in consequence animal feces contaminated the area. Lacking privies, slaves had to urinate and defecate in the cover of nearby bushes. Such squalor contributed to high rates of diarrhea, dysentery, whooping cough, respiratory diseases, hepatitis, typhoid fever, and intestinal worms.

Slave Labor

It is a mistake to think that slave labor was simply unskilled brutish work. Cultivation of cotton, tobacco, rice, and sugar required careful, painstaking effort. On larger plantations, masters relied on slave carpenters, bricklayers, blacksmiths, wheelwrights, tanners, tailors, butchers, masons, coopers, cabinetmakers, metal workers, and silversmiths. Large numbers also worked as boatmen, waiters, cooks, drivers, housemaids, spinners, and weavers. At Monticello, Thomas Jefferson worked slave women in a small textile mill and a nail-making factory.

For the vast majority of slaves, however, slavery meant backbreaking field work, planting, cultivating, and harvesting cotton, hemp, rice, tobacco, or sugar cane. On a typical plantation, slaves worked ten or more hours a day, "from day clean to first dark," six days a week, with only the Sabbath off. At planting or harvesting time, planters required slaves to stay in the fields fifteen or sixteen hours a day. During the peak cotton picking or sugar harvesting season, eighteen-hour days were common. When they were not raising a cash crop, slaves grew other crops, such as corn or potatoes; cared for livestock; and cleared fields, cut wood, repaired buildings and fences. On cotton, sugar, and tobacco plantations, slaves worked together in gangs under the supervision of a supervisor or driver. On many rice and hemp plantations and on the coastal areas of South Carolina and Georgia, slave owners adopted the task system. Slaves had specific daily work assignments, and after they completed their tasks, their time was their own.

There is a tendency to think of slavery as an economically backward and inefficient institution. But recent research has shown that slavery, far from being an economic anachronism, was highly productive precisely because slaves could be forced to work far longer hours than free workers. Sugar plantations were the most innovative economic unit of their time in labor management and organization. They were the first true factories in the world and anticipated the assembly line and the factory system in their reliance on close supervision and division of tasks.

Slave masters extracted labor from virtually the entire slave community, young, old, healthy, and physically impaired. Children as young as three or four were put to work, usually in special "trash gangs" weeding fields, carrying drinking water, picking up trash, and helping in the kitchen. Young children also fed chickens and livestock, gathered wood chips for fuel, and drove cows to pasture. Around the age of eleven, boys began to perform adult field jobs. Between seven and twelve, boys and girls were put to work in intensive field work. Children made up about a third of the slave labor force. Older or physically handicapped slaves were put to work in cloth houses, spinning cotton, weaving cloth, and making clothes. Altogether, masters forced two-thirds of all slaves to work—twice the labor force participation rate among the free population, reflecting the high proportion of children, women, and the elderly toiling in cotton or rice fields.

Because slaves had no direct incentive to work hard, slave owners combined harsh penalties with positive incentives. Some masters denied disobedient slaves passes for visits off the plantation. Others confined recalcitrant slaves to private jails. Chains and shackles were widely used to control runaways. Whipping was a part of plantation discipline. But physical pain was not enough to elicit hard work. To stimulate productivity, some masters gave slaves small garden plots and permitted them to sell their produce. Others distributed gifts of food or money to productive slaves at the end of the year. Still other planters awarded prizes, holidays, and year-end bonuses to particularly productive slaves.

Not all slaves were field hands. During the 1850s, half a million slaves lived in southern towns and cities, where they worked in textile mills, iron works, tobacco factories, laundries, and shipyards. Other slaves labored as lumberjacks, as deckhands on riverboats, and in sawmills, gristmills, and quarries. Many were engaged in construction of roads and railroads. Even on plantations not all slaves were menial laborers. About 250,000 were craftsmen such as blacksmiths, shoemakers, or carpenters or held such domestic posts as coachman or house servant.

Slave Family Life

Slave marriages and family ties were not recognized by American law. Any owner was free to sell husbands from wives, parents from children, and brothers from sisters. In many cases, slave spouses lived apart. Many large slaveholders had numerous plantations and frequently shifted slaves, splitting families in the process.

Although some masters, like George Washington, were reluctant to buy or sell slaves, economic need or an owner's death often led to the separation of husbands from wives and parents from children. The most conservative estimates indicate that at least ten to twenty percent of slave marriages were destroyed by sale. The sale of children from parents was even more common. Over the course of a thirty-five-year lifetime, slaves had a fifty-fifty chance of being sold at least once and were likely to witness the sale of several members of their immediate family. Over a third of all slave children grew up in households from which sale or death had removed one or both parents. About a quarter of all slave children were raised in a single-parent household (nearly always with their mother) and another tenth were without either parent.

Even in instances in which marriages were not broken by sale, slave spouses often resided on separate plantations, owned by different individuals. On large plantations, one slave father in three had a different owner from his wife's, and could visit his family only at his master's discretion. On smaller holdings, divided ownership and households headed by the mother were even more common. Just one-third of the children on farms or plantations with fifteen or fewer slaves lived in a two-parent family, compared with two-thirds of the children on larger plantations. Because many planters prohibited marriages across plantations (and because slaves, like West Africans but unlike white southerners, did not marry first cousins), many slaves were unable to find a spouse. On the largest plantations, nearly twenty percent of the slaves who reached adulthood remained single throughout their lives.

Other obstacles stood in the way of an independent family life. Many slaves had to share their single-room cabins with relatives or other unrelated slaves. Even on model plantations, children between seven and ten were taken from their parents and sent to live in separate cabins. Slavery severely circumscribed the authority of slave parents. When a slave child named Jacob Stroyer was regularly beaten, his father told him: "Go back to your work and be a good boy, for I cannot do anything for you."

Of all the threats to slave family life, one of the most terrible was the sexual abuse of slave women. Some masters, like James H. Hammond, a congressman, governor, and United States senator from South Carolina, took slave mistresses and concubines. Hammond, whose wife bore him eight children, purchased an eighteen-year-old slave named Sally and her infant daughter, Louisa, in 1839. He made Sally his mistress, and fathered several children by her, and then when the daughter reached the age of twelve, fathered several children by her. Governor Francis Pickens of South Carolina and Confederate General Jubal Early each took slave mistresses. One ex-slave remembered that his master "would ship . . . husbands out of bed and get in with their wives." A survey of former slaves conducted in the 1930s revealed that 4.5 percent said that one of their parents had been white.

Yet African Americans managed to forge strong and durable family and kin ties within the institution of slavery. In spite of the refusal of southern law to recognize the legality of slave marriages, most slaves married and lived with the same spouse until death, and most slave children grew up in two-parent households. The strength of slave families is nowhere more evident than in the advertisements slave owners posted for runaway slaves. Over a third of the advertisements indicate that fugitives left an owner to visit a spouse, a child, or other relatives.

To sustain a sense of family identity, slaves often named their children after parents, grandparents, recently deceased relatives, and other kin. It used to be believed that masters assigned names to slaves or that slaves simply imitated their masters' system of naming. We now know that slaves were usually not named for owners. To be sure, some slaves were given classical names (like George Washington's slave Hercules). But many names reflected African practices. Many children received "day names" (after the day they were born) and "name-saking" (such as naming children after grandparents). Slaves passed down family names to their children, usually the name of an ancestor's owner rather than their current owner's.

Ties to an immediate family reached outward to an involved network of extended kin. Family destruction and dispersal created extended kinship networks stretching across whole counties. Whenever children were sold to neighboring plantations, grandparents, aunts, uncles, and cousins took on the functions of parents. When blood relatives were not present, strangers cared for children. Slave parents taught their children to call all adult slaves on the same plantation "aunt" or "uncle" and younger slaves "sister" or "brother." In this way, slave culture taught the young that they were members of a broader community in which all slaves had mutual obligations and responsibilities.

Slave Culture

As recently as 1964, the sociologist E. Franklin Frazier claimed that "the Negroes were practically stripped of their social heritage." This view is wrong. As brutal and destructive as the institution of slavery was, slaves were not defenseless victims. Through their families, religion, folklore, and music, as well as more direct forms of resistance, African Americans defied the debilitating effects of slavery and created a vital culture supportive of human dignity. Slaves were able to maintain much of their African traditions and created a new African-American culture that they successfully transmitted to their children. It has exerted a profound influence on white culture: on speech, religion, music, cuisine.

The American language is filled with Africanisms. Such words as bogus, bug, phony, yam, tote, gumbo, jamboree, jazz, and funky all have African roots. Our cuisine, too, is heavily influenced by African practices. Deep-fat frying, gumbos, and fricasees stem from West and Central Africa. Our music is heavily dependent on African traditions. Sea chanties and yodeling, as well as spirituals and the use of falsetto, were heavily influenced by African traditions. The frame construction of houses; the "call and response" pattern in sermons; the stress on the holy spirit and an emotional conversion experience—these too appear to derive at least partly from African customs. Finally, Africans had a critical role in the production of such crops as rice or sweet potatoes that the English had not previously encountered.

Religious and cultural traditions were essential to surviving the harshness and misery of life under slavery. Many slaves drew on African customs when they buried their dead. Conjurors adapted and blended African religious rites that made use of herbs and supernatural powers. Slaves also perpetuated a rich tradition of west and central African parables, proverbs, verbal games, and legends. They also retained in their folklore certain central figures. Cunning tricksters, often represented as tortoises, spiders, or rabbits, outwitted their more powerful enemies. During the late eighteenth and early nineteenth centuries, slaves embraced Christianity, but transformed it to meet their own needs. Slave religious beliefs, a mixture of Christianity and African traditions, provided slaves with the patience and hope necessary to endure slavery. Slave religion also upheld a vision of the spiritual equality of all human beings that strengthened their hopes of eventual deliverance from bondage. Spirituals, like "Go Down, Moses," with its refrain "let my people go," bespeak an identification with the Hebrew people who had overcome oppression and enslavement.

American Slavery in Comparative Perspective

Only about six percent of the slaves imported from Africa ended up in what is now the United States. The overwhelming majority went to Brazil or the West Indies, where they labored on plantations producing sugar, tobacco, coffee, and other subtropic products. Of the ten to fifteen million Africans who survived the voyage to the New World, over one-third landed in Brazil and between sixty and seventy percent ended up in Brazil or the sugar colonies of the Caribbean. Yet by 1860, approximately two-thirds of all New World slaves lived in the southern United States.

How did American slavery contrast with slavery in Latin America and the Caribbean? Was it more repressive or more benign? For a long time it was widely assumed that southern slavery was harsher and crueler than slavery in Latin America, where the Roman Catholic Church insisted that slaves had a right to marry, to seek relief from a cruel master, and to purchase their freedom. In contrast to the American South, there was no legal bar in Latin America to educating or freeing slaves; Spanish and Portuguese colonists were thought to be less tainted by racial prejudice than North Americans; and Latin American slavery was believed to be less subject to the pressures of a competitive capitalist economy.

This contrast between Latin American slavery and a harsher North American slavery appears to be grossly overdrawn. In practice, neither the Catholic Church nor the courts offered much protection to Latin American slaves. Cruel punishments were not unknown, such as tying slaves down and flogging them for nine to thirteen days. Slave owners in Latin America, like those in the American South, frequently sold slaves apart. Access to freedom was greater in Latin America, but in many cases masters freed sick, elderly, crippled, or simply unneeded slaves in order to relieve themselves of financial responsibilities. Death rates among slaves in the Caribbean were one-third higher than in the South and suicide appears to have been much more common. Sometimes Latin American slaves were forced to wear iron masks to keep them from eating dirt or drinking liquor. Unlike slaves in the South, West Indian slaves were expected to produce their own food in their "free time," and to care for the elderly and the infirm.

Among crucial differences between slavery in the Old South and that elsewhere in the Western Hemisphere perhaps the most obvious were demographic. The slave population in Brazil and the West Indies had a low proportion of female slaves, a tiny slave birthrate, and a high proportion of recent arrivals from Africa. In striking contrast, southern slaves had an equal sex ratio, a high birthrate, and a predominantly American-born population.

Slavery in the United States was especially distinctive in the ability of the slave population to increase its numbers by natural reproduction. In the Caribbean, Dutch Guiana, and Brazil, the slave death rate was so high and the birth rate so low that slaves could not sustain their population without imports from Africa. Rates of natural decrease ran as high as five percent a year. While the death rate of United States slaves was as high as that in Jamaica, the birth rate was eighty percent higher. The average number of children born to an early nineteenth-century southern slave woman was 9.2—twice as many as in the West Indies. By the mid-nineteenth century, slaves in the United States were therefore further removed from Africa than those in the Caribbean. While a majority of early nineteenth-century slaves in the British Caribbean and Brazil were born in Africa, in 1850 most United States slaves were third-, fourth-, or fifth-generation Americans. In addition, by the nineteenth century there were relatively few African-born slaves, which made it more difficult to maintain African practices in unmodified forms.

In the West Indies, slaves constituted eighty to ninety percent of the population, while in the United States South only about a third of the population were slaves. Plantation size also differed widely. In the Caribbean, slaves were held on much larger units, many plantations holding as many as five hundred slaves. In the American South only one slave owner held as many as a thousand slaves, and just 125 had over 250 slaves. Half of all slaves in the United States worked on units with twenty or fewer slaves; three-quarters had fewer than fifty.

These differences had important social implications. Slaves in the American South had much more contact with whites than did West Indian slaves. Slave owners lived on their plantations and slaves dealt with their owners regularly. Most planters placed plantation management, supply purchasing, and supervision in the hands of black drivers and foremen, and at least two-thirds of all slaves worked under the eye of black drivers. Absentee ownership was far more common in the West Indies, where planters relied heavily on paid managers and relied on a distinct class of free blacks and mulattoes to serve as intermediaries with the slave population. Standards of diet, housing, and medicine in the South may have exceeded those in the Caribbean, but southern masters also interfered more frequently in their personal lives. In the South, masters provided slaves with food, housing, and clothing; in the Caribbean, slaves had to raise their own food in their spare time.

Another important difference between Latin America and the United States involved the very concept of race. In Spanish and Portuguese America, an intricate system of racial classification emerged. The Spanish and Portuguese were much more tolerant of racial mixing, an attitude encouraged by a shortage of European women, and recognized a wide range of racial gradations, including black, mestizo, quadroon, and octoroon. The American South recognized essentially two races, white and black, and any discernible degree of African ancestry defined its possessor as black. It has been said, half-facetiously, that southerners are color blind, in the sense that individuals, despite their racial composition, are considered to be either white or black, while Latin Americans recognized degrees of blackness and whiteness.

A final difference between slavery in the United States and elsewhere in the Americas was that only in the South did slavery depend on the loyalty of non-slaveholding whites. In the South, three-quarters of white families owned no slaves. The key to maintaining their loyalty ultimately depended on appeals to racism.

Slave Revolts and Resistance

Slave resistance is a difficult subject to discuss. It is hard for us today to imagine how slavery could function as an efficient economic system in the face of slave resistance. On larger plantations, there were only about two adult white males to oversee fifty or more slaves. We like to think that if we were enslaved, we would actively resist the institution. As a popular anthem of the Civil Rights Era of the 1950s and 1960s put it: "Before I'd be a slave, I'd be buried in my grave." And although slave masters described their slave population as faithful, docile, and contented, slave owners in the South, Brazil, and the West Indies always feared slave revolt. In fact no enslaved people in history revolted as frequently as the New World slaves. Over two hundred examples of open rebellion or incipient slave conspiracies occurred in America between the early seventeenth and the mid-nineteenth centuries. Even when slaves did not resist their condition directly and openly, they sought autonomy in less dramatic ways.

Day-to-day resistance was the most common form of opposition to slavery. Breaking tools, feigning illness, staging slowdowns, and committing acts of arson and sabotage—all were forms of resistance and expressions of slaves' alienation from their masters. One North Carolina cook later recalled: "How many times I spit in the biscuits and peed in the coffee just to get back at them mean white folks."

Running away was another form of resistance. Most slaves ran away relatively short distances and were not trying permanently to escape from slavery. If not visiting a spouse or relative, they were temporarily withholding their labor as a form of economic bargaining and negotiation. Slavery involved a constant process of negotiation as slaves bargained over the pace of work, the amount of free time they would enjoy, monetary rewards, access to garden plots, and the freedom to practice burials, marriages, and religious ceremonies free from white oversight. Some fugitives did try to escape slavery permanently. While the idea of escaping slavery quickly brings to mind the Underground Railroad to the free states, in fact more than half of these long-distance runaways headed southward or to cities or to natural refuges like swamps. Often, runaways were relatively privileged slaves who had served as river boatmen or coachmen and were familiar with the outside world. Especially in the colonial period, fugitive slaves tried to form runaway communities known as "maroon colonies" located in swamps, mountains, or frontier regions. Some of these communities resisted capture for several decades. Many revolts were collective efforts to run away from slavery. In a famous 1739 revolt in colonial South Carolina known as the Stono Rebellion, slaves headed for refuge in Spanish Florida.

Probably the first slave revolt erupted in Hispaniola in 1522. During the early eighteenth century there were slave uprisings in Long Island in 1708 and in New York City in 1712. Slaves in South Carolina staged several insurrections, culminating in the Stono Rebellion in 1739, when they seized arms, killed whites, and burned houses. In 1740 and 1741, conspiracies were uncovered in Charleston and New York. During the late eighteenth century, slave revolts erupted in Guadeloupe, Grenada, Jamaica, Suriname, San Domingue (Haiti), Venezuela, and the Windward Islands and many fugitive slaves known as maroons, who fled to remote regions, carried on guerrilla campaigns (during the 1820s, a fugitive slave named Bob Ferebee led a band of fugitive slaves in guerrilla warfare in Virginia). During the early nineteenth century, major conspiracies or revolts against slavery took place in Richmond, Virginia, in 1800; in Louisiana in 1811; in Barbados in 1816; in Charleston, South Carolina, in 1822; in Demerara in 1823; and in Jamaica and in Southampton County, Virginia, in 1831.

Black religion made a major contribution to resistance to slavery. When Denmark Vesey sought to gain recruits for his plot to overthrow slavery in Charleston in 1822, one slave said, "he tries to prove . . . that slavery and bondage is against the Bible." Nat Turner's 1831 insurrection was inspired by a religious vision that revealed that "the time was fast approaching when the first should be last and the last should be first."

The main result of slave insurrections, throughout the Americas, was the mass executions of blacks. After a slave conspiracy was uncovered in New York City in 1741, eighteen slaves were hanged and thirteen were burned alive. After Denmark Vesey's conspiracy was uncovered, the authorities in Charleston hanged thirty-seven blacks. Following Nat Turner's insurrection, the local militia killed about one hundred blacks and twenty more slaves, including Turner, were later executed. In the South, the preconditions for successful rebellion did not exist, and tended to bring increased suffering and repression to the slave community.

Slave revolts were most likely when slaves outnumbered whites or plantations were large, when masters were absent, during periods of economic distress, and when large numbers of native-born Africans had been brought into an area at one time. That violent rebellion was rarer and smaller in scale in the American South than in Brazil or the Caribbean reflected the relatively small proportion of blacks to whites and of recent migrants from Africa to the native born. Another factor was that southern plantations were on average smaller. In Jamaica, slaves outnumbered whites by ten or eleven to one; in the South, a much larger white population was committed to suppressing rebellion. In general, Africans were more likely than New World-born slaves to participate in outright revolts. Not only did many Africans have combat experience prior to enslavement, but they also had fewer family and community ties that might inhibit violent insurrection.

The Economics of Slavery

During the years before the Civil War many northerners charged that slavery was incompatible with rapid economic growth. Despite clear evidence that slavery was profitable for individual planters, a growing number of people thought that slavery was inherently wasteful and inefficient, that it degraded labor, inhibited urbanization and mechanization, thwarted industrialization, and stifled progress. They associated slavery with economic backwardness, soil exhaustion, unproductive labor, indebtedness, and economic and social stagnation. The philosopher and poet Ralph Waldo Emerson said that "slavery is no scholar, no improver . . . it does not increase the white population; it does not improve the soil; everything goes to decay."

Much of the characterization was accurate. Like other slave societies, the South did not produce urban centers on a scale equal with those in the North. Virginia's largest city, Richmond, had a population of just 15,274 in 1850. That same year, Wilmington, North Carolina's largest city, had just 7,264 inhabitants. Southern cities were small because they failed to develop diversified economies. Unlike the cities of the North, southern cities rarely became centers of commerce, finance, or processing and manufacturing, and southern ports rarely engaged in international trade. By northern standards, the South's transportation network was primitive. Traveling the 1,460 miles from Baltimore to New Orleans in 1850 meant riding five different railroads, two stage coaches, and two steamboats. The South's educational system also lagged far behind the North's. In 1850, twenty percent of adult white southerners could not read or write, compared to a national figure of eight percent.

Does this mean that slavery was a declining institution? Was it doomed to extinction, even in the absence of civil war? The answer appears to be "no." In 1860, the South was more prosperous than any European nation except England, and had a higher per capita income than Italy on the eve of World War II.

Slave labor was efficient, productive, and adaptable to a variety of occupations, ranging from agriculture and mining to factory work. Slavery was the basis of the nation's most profitable industry. During the decades before the Civil War, slave-grown cotton accounted for over half the value of all United States exports, and provided virtually all the cotton used in the northern textile industry as well as seventy percent of the cotton used in British mills. A disproportionate share of the richest Americans, moreover, made their fortunes from slavery. In 1860, two out of every three Americans worth $100,000 or more lived in the South. Soaring slave prices during the 1850s suggests slave owners' confidence in the future.

Nevertheless, the South's political leaders had good reason for concern. Within the South, slave ownership was becoming concentrated into a smaller number of hands. The proportion of southern families owning slaves declined from thirty-six percent in 1830 to twenty-five percent in 1860. At the same time, slavery was sharply declining in the upper South. Between 1830 and 1860, the proportion of slaves in Missouri's population fell from 18 to 10 percent; in Kentucky, from twenty-four to nineteen percent; in Maryland, from twenty-three to thirteen percent. By the middle of the nineteenth century, slavery was becoming an exception in the New World, confined to Brazil, Cuba, Puerto Rico, a number of small Dutch colonies, and the American South. But the most important threat to slavery came from abolitionists, who denounced slavery as immoral.

Abolition

The growth of public opposition to slavery represents one of the most momentous moral transformations in history. As late as 1750, no church condemned slave ownership or slave trading. Britain, Denmark, France, Holland, Portugal, and Spain all openly participated in the slave trade. Beginning with the Quakers in the late 1750s, however, organized opposition to slavery quickly grew. In 1787, the Northwest Ordinance barred slavery from the territories north of the Ohio River; by 1804, the nine states north of Delaware had freed slaves or adopted gradual emancipation plans. In Haiti in 1791, nearly a half million slaves emancipated themselves by insurrection and revolutionary struggle. In 1807, Britain and the United States outlawed the African slave trade. The wars of national liberation in Spanish America ended slavery in Spain's mainland New World empire. In 1821, the region that now includes Ecuador, Colombia, and Venezuela adopted a gradual emancipation plan. Two years later, Chile agreed to emancipate its slave. In 1829, Mexico abolished slavery. In 1833, Britain emancipated 780,000 slaves, paying 20 million pounds sterling compensation to their owners. In 1848, Denmark and France freed slaves in their colonial empires. Slavery survived in Suriname and other Dutch New World colonies until 1863 and in the United States until 1865. The last New World slaves were emancipated in Cuba in 1886 and in Brazil in 1888.

Within the span of a century and a half, slavery, long regarded as an inevitable part of the social order, came to be seen as a violation of Christian morality and the natural, inalienable rights of man. The main impetus behind antislavery came from religion. New religious and humanitarian values contributed to a view of slavery as "the sum of all villainies," a satanic institution that gave rise to every imaginable sin: violence, despotism, racial prejudice, and sexual corruption.

Initially, many opponents of slavery supported colonization—the deportation of black Americans to Africa, the Caribbean, or Central America. But by the late 1820s, it was obvious that colonization was a wholly impractical solution to the problem of slavery. Each year the nation's slave population rose by 50,000, but in 1830, the American Colonization Society persuaded just 259 free blacks to migrate to Liberia, bringing to just 1,400 the total number of blacks colonized in Africa. In 1829, a twenty-five-year-old white Bostonian named William Lloyd Garrison denounced colonization as a cruel hoax designed to promote the racial purity of the North while doing nothing to end slavery in the South. He demanded immediate emancipation of slaves without compensation to their owners. Within six years, two hundred antislavery societies had sprouted up in the North, and had mounted a massive propaganda campaign against slavery.

The growth of militant abolitionism provoked a harsh public reaction. Mobs led by "gentlemen of property and standing" attacked the homes and businesses of abolitionist merchants, destroyed abolitionist printing presses, attacked black neighborhoods, and murdered the Reverend Elijah P. Lovejoy, the editor of an abolitionist newspaper. In the face of vicious attacks, the antislavery movement divided over questions of strategy and tactics. Radicals, led by Garrison, began to attack all forms of inequality and violence in American society, withdrew from churches that condoned slavery, demanded equal rights for women, and called for voluntary dissolution of the Union. Other abolitionists turned to politics as the most promising way to end slavery, helping to form the Liberty Party in 1840, the Free Soil Party in 1848, and the Republican Party in 1854.

By the late 1850s, a growing number of northerners had become convinced that slavery posed an intolerable threat to free labor and civil liberties. Many believed that an aggressive Slave Power had seized control of the federal government, incited revolution in Texas and war with Mexico, and was engaged in a systematic plan to extend slavery into the western territories. At the same time, an increasing number of southerners believed that antislavery radicals dominated northern politics and sought to bar slavery from the western territories and to undermine the institution in the states where it already existed.

The abolitionist John Brown's raid on the federal arsenal at Harpers Ferry in October 1859 produced shock waves throughout the South, producing fears of slave revolt and race war. When Abraham Lincoln was elected President in 1860, many white southerners were convinced that this represented the triumph of abolitionism in the North and thought they had no choice but to secede from the Union. The new President, however, was passionately committed to the preservation of the Union, and peaceful secession proved to be impossible.

The Experience of Liberation

African Americans took a pivotal part in their own liberation. During the first two years of the Civil War, federal officials refused to enlist black soldiers in the Union Army. But by early 1863, voluntary enlistments had fallen so sharply that the federal government instituted an unpopular military draft and decided to enroll black troops. Indeed, it was the availability of black troops that allowed President Lincoln to resist demands for a negotiated peace that might have retained slavery in the United States. Altogether, 186,000 black soldiers served in the Union Army and another

29,000 served in the Navy, accounting for nearly ten percent of all Union forces and 68,178 of the Union dead or missing. Three-fifths of all black troops were former slaves. The active participation of black troops made it inconceivable that African Americans would remain in slavery after the Civil War.

In 1863, at Fort Wagner in South Carolina and Port Hudson and Milliken's Bend in Louisiana, black troops proved their mettle in battle. But black troops also faced another battle: against discrimination in pay, promotions, and medical care. Despite promises of equal treatment, blacks were relegated to separate regiments commanded by white officers. Black soldiers received less pay than a white private, inferior benefits, and poorer food and equipment. While a white private was paid $13 a month in addition to a $3.50 clothing allowance, blacks received just $10 a month, out of which $3 was deducted for clothing. Until the end of the war, the government refused to commission black officers. Within the ranks, black troops faced repeated humiliations; most were employed in menial jobs and kept in rear-echelon assignments. Within the Union Army, they were punished by whipping (or were tied up by their thumbs); if captured by the Confederates, they faced execution. But despite these trials, black soldiers won the opportunity to fight and in 1864 the battle for equal pay. Drawing upon the education and training they received in the military, many black troops became community leaders during Reconstruction.

During the war, many southern slaves contributed to their own emancipation by deserting plantations and fleeing to Union lines. While slaves staged few insurrections during the war, the slave system began to unravel. Planters were stunned to see trusted house slaves and drivers lead field hands in deserting to the Union Army. For ex-slaves, emancipation was a moment of exhilaration, fear, and uncertainty. While some greeted the announcement of freedom with jubilation, others reacted with stunned silence. "You could hear a pin drop, everything was so quiet," a former slave recalled. Thousands of freedmen wandered the South, struggling desperately, but largely unsuccessfully, to reunite families forcibly separated by sale. A northern journalist met an ex-slave in North Carolina who had walked six hundred miles searching for his wife and children who had been sold four years before. Many couples, forbidden to marry during slavery, took the opportunity to formalize their unions, while others, who had lived apart from their families on separate plantations, were finally free to reside with their spouses. To display their emancipation, many freedmen changed their slave names, adopted new surnames, and insisted on being addressed as "mister" and "misses."

Shocked at seeing former slaves transformed into free women and men, southern whites complained of "betrayal" and "ingratitude." Revealing slave owners' capacity for self-deception, one former master complained that "those we loved best, and who loved us best—as we thought—were the first to leave us." In many parts of the South, the end of the war was followed by an outburst of white rage: whites whipped, clubbed, and murdered freed slaves. In contrast, the vast majority of former slaves refrained from vengeance against former masters. Instead, they struggled to achieve economic and political independence by forming separate black churches and schools, mutual aid societies, lodges, newspapers, and political organizations.

The Aftermath of Slavery

Except for Haiti, the American South was the only region in the Western Hemisphere in which slavery was overthrown by force of arms; the only place, except for Brazil, in which slave owners received no compensation for the loss of their slave property; and the only region, aside from Guadeloupe and Martinique, in which former slaves received civil and political rights. And it was the only post-emancipation society in which large slave owners were deprived of the right to hold public office and former slaves formed successful political alliances with whites.

Nevertheless, the abolition of slavery did not mean that former slaves had achieved full freedom. Throughout the Western Hemisphere, the end of slavery was followed by a period of reconstruction during which race relations were redefined and new systems of labor emerged. In former slave societies throughout the Americas, ex-slaves sought to free themselves from the gang system of labor on plantations and establish small, self-sufficient farms, while planters or local governments sought to restore as much of the old system as they could. The outcome, in many former slave societies, was the emergence of a caste system of race relations and a system of involuntary or forced labor, such as peonage, debt bondage, apprenticeship, contract laborers, indentured laborers, tenant farming, and sharecropping.

In every post-emancipation society, acute labor problems and a decline in productivity spurred efforts to revive plantation discipline. Even in Haiti, where black revolution had overthrown slavery, repeated attempts were made to restore the plantation system. On Caribbean islands—such as Antigua, Barbados, and St. Kitts— where land was totally controlled by white planters, the plantation system remained. In other areas—like British Guiana, Jamaica, or Trinidad—where former slaves were able to squat on unsettled land and set up subsistence farms, staple production fell sharply. To counteract the precipitous decline in sugar production, the British government imported into Guiana, Jamaica, Mauritius, Suriname, and Trinidad tens of thousands of "coolie" laborers from China, India, Java, and West Africa. In many plantation societies, governments sought to force former slaves back to work on plantations with strict vagrancy laws, coercive labor contracts, and regressive taxes. The story of Reconstruction in the American South embodies that broader concern with labor control.

Immediately following the war, all-white state legislatures passed "black codes" designed to force freed blacks to work on plantations, where they would be put to work in gangs. These codes denied blacks the right to purchase or even rent land. Vagrancy laws allowed authorities to arrest blacks "in idleness" and assign them to a chain gang or auction them off to a planter for as long as a year. Other statutes required blacks to have written proof of employment and barred them from leaving plantations. The Freedmen's Bureau, ostensibly designed to aid former slaves, helped to enforce laws against vagrancy and loitering and refused to allow ex-slaves to keep land that they had occupied during the war. One black army veteran asked: "If you call this Freedom, what did you call Slavery?"

Such efforts virtually to reenslave the freedmen led congressional Republicans to seize control of Reconstruction from President Andrew Johnson, deny congressional seats to representatives from the former Confederate states, pass the Civil Rights Act of 1866, and write the Fourteenth Amendment to the Constitution to extend citizenship rights to African Americans and guarantee them equal protection of the laws. In 1870, the country went even further by ratifying the Fifteenth Amendment, which extended voting rights to African-American men. But the most radical proposal advanced during Reconstruction—to confiscate plantations and redistribute portions of the land to the freedmen—was defeated. The freedmen, in alliance with carpetbaggers (northerners who had migrated to the South following the Civil War) and southern white Republicans known as scalawags, temporarily gained power in every former Confederate state except Virginia. Altogether, over six hundred blacks served as legislators in Reconstruction governments (though blacks comprised a majority only in the lower house of South Carolina's legislature). The Reconstruction governments drew up democratic state constitutions, expanded women's rights, provided debt relief, and established the South's first state-funded schools. During the 1870s, however, white terror tactics, northern apathy, and internal divisions within the southern Republican Party allowed white Democrats, known as Redeemers, to return to power in the South's state governments. The North's failure to enforce the Fourteenth and Fifteenth Amendments permitted racial segregation and disfranchisement in the South.

During and after Reconstruction, former slaves, along with many small white farmers, became trapped in a new system of economic exploitation—sharecropping. Lacking capital and land of their own, they had to work for large landowners. Initially, planters, with the support of the Freedmen's Bureau, sought to restore gang labor under the supervision of white overseers. The freedmen, who wanted autonomy and independence, refused to sign contracts that required gang labor. Ultimately, sharecropping emerged as a compromise. Instead of cultivating land in gangs supervised by overseers, landowners divided plantations into twenty- to fifty-acre plots suitable for farming by a single family. In exchange for land, a cabin, and supplies, sharecroppers agreed to raise a cash crop, usually cotton, and to give half of it to their landlord. High interest rates landlords and merchants charged for goods bought on credit transformed sharecropping into a system of economic dependency and poverty. The freedmen found that "freedom could make folks proud but it didn't make 'em rich."

Nevertheless, the sharecropping system did allow freedmen a degree of freedom and autonomy greater than that experienced under slavery. As a symbol of their newly-won independence, freedmen had teams of mules drag their former slave cabins away from the slave quarters into their own fields. Black wives and daughters sharply reduced their labor in the fields and instead devoted more time to home and children. For the first time, black families could divide their time between field work and housework in accordance with their own family priorities.

Chattel slavery had been defeated. The gang system of labor, enforced by the whip, was dead. Real gains had been won. But full freedom remained an unfulfilled promise.

*   *   *

In 1970, the countries of the Arabian peninsula became the last in the world to abolish legal slavery. Nevertheless, the buying and selling of human beings continues to flourish in many parts of the world. It has been rediscovered in Africa. Each year, an estimated one million Asian women and children, in Bangladesh,

Burma, India, Pakistan, Sri Lanka, Thailand, and elsewhere, are sold or auctioned into slavery to serve as prostitutes or child laborers. Methods of procurement have changed since the eighteenth century; instead of being kidnapped, slaves are bought in impoverished villages for a few hundred dollars. But slavery in its cruelty remains, chaining its victims to beds in brothels or at workbenches in sweatshops. The final chapter in the history of slavery remains unfinished.

Chapter 1

"Death's Gwineter Lay His Cold Icy Hands on Me":

ENSLAVEMENT

In 1441 a Portuguese sailor named Antam Goncalvez sailed south to what is now Morocco, carrying a cargo of sea lion skins and oil. During the voyage, Goncalvez reportedly expressed a desire to please Prince Henry of Portugal by bringing him African captives. While ashore, his crew wounded an African with a javelin and took him prisoner; and subsequently captured an African woman. Then the crew staged a raid, in which four Africans were killed and ten others were captured. The capture of these twelve African prisoners marked the beginning of the European slave trade with sub-Saharan Africa.

The number of Africans caught up in the Atlantic slave trade over the next four centuries remains unknown. The best estimates suggest that over nine-and-a-half million Africans were forcibly imported into the New World and that another two million died during the Middle Passage. But no one knows how many people died in Africa during wars in which slaves were seized, in the forced march to the coast, or in the coastal dungeons, pens, or barracoons where slaves were herded. The figure may well have been more than seven million, bringing the total number of Africans entrapped in the slave trade to more than eighteen million people.

As early as the mid-1450s, Europeans began to acquire West African slaves through trade rather than raids. By the seventeenth century, the English, French, Dutch, Danes, and Swedes had joined the Portuguese and Spanish in the African slave trade. Along the West African coast, European merchants established forts and trading posts—known as "factories" or "castles"—to serve as centers for collecting slaves.

Within West Africa, war, crop failure, drought, famine, politi-

cal instability, small-scale raiding, taxation, and judicial or religious punishment produced large numbers of slaves. War captives, condemned criminals, debtors, aliens, famine victims, and political dissidents—all might find themselves sold into slavery.

The slave trade was greatly encouraged by the low cost of slaves. Even though the price of slaves rose three- or four-fold during the eighteenth century, many Europeans were convinced that it was "cheaper to buy than to breed." Between the sixteenth and mid-eighteenth centuries, it was cheaper to import a slave from Africa than to raise a child to the age of fourteen. During the late seventeenth century, merchants in the Senegambia region of West Africa paid as little as one pound sterling for a young male, whom they sold to European traders for the equivalent of three-and-a-half pounds sterling, or eleven muskets, thirty-one gallons of brandy, or ninety-three pounds of wrought iron. Initially, many slaves were acquired from regions within fifty or a hundred miles of the West African coast. During the eighteenth century, however, rising prices led slavers to search for captives in interior regions, 500 to 1,000 miles inland.

The impact of the slave trade on West African society is almost impossible to calculate. The demographic consequences are the most obvious. While the slave trade probably did not drastically depopulate West Africa, it may well have caused sharp population declines in particular regions and it certainly kept the overall population growth rate low.

But the slave trade had other high social costs. Throughout West Africa, the slave trade fostered warfare, skewed local economies, expanded servitude within the region, and distorted class and political structures. While the slave trade enhanced the power, prestige, and wealth of particular West African rulers, merchants, and states, it contributed to economic stagnation and long-term political instability. The introduction of European guns and gunpowder reinforced political fragmentation, allowing particular states to grow at the expense of other states. Meanwhile, the influx of European textiles and manufactured goods undermined local West African industries.

Of course, the greatest cost of the slave trade was its human toll. The selections that follow document the African side of the Atlantic slave trade: capture, transit to the coast, and sale to Europeans. They disclose the human meaning of enslavement—as told by its victims.

1

Gomes Eannes de Azurara

"HOW ANTAM GONCALVEZ BROUGHT BACK THE FIRST CAPTIVES"

In 1441 a group of Portuguese traders led by Antam Goncalvez captured a number of African slaves, marking the beginning of the slave trade era. A chronicle published in 1453 describes this event.

More than half a century before Columbus "discovered" the New World, the Portuguese launched explorations along the African coast. Their initial objective was gold. But during the 1400s, the Portuguese began to capture slaves, usually unarmed fishermen, in coastal raids.

This raiding phase lasted little more than a decade. By the mid-1450s, it was clear that raiding was counterproductive. The West African coast was inaccessible to large oceangoing ships and the Portuguese had to launch longboats with eight- to twelve-man crews. African vessels with fifty men were able to defeat the Portuguese landing parties. By the 1460s, raiding was replaced by trading and commercial relations between the Portuguese and peoples along the African coast. One of the very few places where Europeans actually waged war to capture slaves was in the Portuguese colony of Angola.

How Antam Goncalvez brought back the first captives [in 1441]. . . . "O how fair a thing it would be if we who have come to this land for a cargo of such petty merchandise [skins and oils], were to meet with the good luck to bring the first captives before the face of our Prince. . . . I would fain go myself this next night with nine men of you (those who are most ready for the business), and prove a part of this land along the river, to see if I find any inhabitants; for I think we of right ought to meet with some, since

Source: Gomes Eannes de Azurara, *The Chronicle of the Discovery and Conquest of Guinea*, 1453.

43

'tis certain there are people here, who traffic with camels and other animals that bear their freights. . . . Since they have as yet no knowledge of us their gathering cannot be too large for us to try their strength; and, if God grant us to encounter them, the very least part of our victory will be the capture of one of them. . . ."

And as soon as it was night Antam Goncalvez chose nine men who seemed to him most fitted for the undertaking. . . . When they had gone a short part of the way, they saw a naked man following a camel. . . . But though he was only one, and saw the others that they were many; yet he had a mind to prove those arms of his right worthily and began to defend himself as best he could, shewing a bolder front than his strength warranted. But Affonso Goterres wounded him with a javelin, and this put the Moor in such fear that he threw down his arms like a beaten thing. . . . And as they were going on their way they saw a black Mooress come along (who was slave of those on the hill), and though some of our men were in favor of letting her pass to avoid a fresh skirmish, to which the enemy did not invite them—for, since they were in sight and their number more than doubled ours, they could not be of such faint hearts as to allow a chattel of theirs to be carried off—despite this, Antam Goncalvez bade them go at her; for if (he said) they scorned that encounter, it might make their foes pluck up courage against them. And now you see how the word of a captain prevaileth among men used to obey; for, following his will, they seized the Mooress.

2
John Barbot

"PREPOSSESSED OF THE OPINION . . . THAT THE EUROPEANS ARE FOND OF THEIR FLESH"

Over time, the slave trade dramatically increased in scale. Around 1500, the trade involved about five to six thousand slaves a year. By 1600, the number of slaves had increased to twenty to twenty-five thousand a year. In the period from 1750 to 1780, the figure had soared to sixty thousand

Source: John Barbot, "A Description of the Coasts of North and South Guinea," in Awnsham and John Churchill, eds., *Collection of Voyages and Travels* (London, 1732).

a year. In general, about three men were enslaved for every two women. About seventy percent of slaves were between 18 and 35. Thus most slaves were fully socialized adults who carried with them many skills (including military skills) and an adult's knowledge of their native culture and religion.

John Barbot, an agent for the French Royal African Company, made at least two voyages to the West Coast of Africa, in 1678 and 1682.

Those sold by the Blacks are for the most part prisoners of war, taken either in fight, or pursuit, or in the incursions they make into their enemies' territories; others stolen away by their own countrymen; and some there are, who will sell their own children, kindred, or neighbours. This has been often seen, and to compass it, they desire the person they intend to sell, to help them in carrying something to the factory by way of trade, and when there, the person so deluded, not understanding the language, is sold and deliver'd up as a slave, notwithstanding all his resistance, and exclaiming against the treachery. . . .

The kings are so absolute, that upon any slight pretense of offences committed by their subjects, they order them to be sold for slaves, without regard to rank, or possession. . . .

Abundance of little Blacks of both sexes are also stolen away by their neighbours, when found abroad on the roads, or in the woods; or else in the Cougans, or corn-fields, at the time of the year, when their parents keep them there all day, to scare away the devouring small birds, that come to feed on the millet, in swarms, as has been said above.

In times of dearth and famine, abundance of those people will sell themselves, for a maintenance, and to prevent starving. When I first arriv'd at Goerree, in December, 1681, I could have bought a great number, at very easy rates, if I could have found provisions to subsist them; so great was the dearth then, in that part of Nigritia.

To conclude, some slaves are also brought to these Blacks, from very remote inland countries, by way of trade, and sold for things of very inconsiderable value; but these slaves are generally poor and weak, by reason of the barbarous usage they have had in traveling so far, being continually beaten, and almost famish'd; so inhuman are the Blacks to one another. . . .

The trade of slaves is in a more peculiar manner the business of kings, rich men, and prime merchants, exclusive of the inferior sort of Blacks.

These slaves are severely and barbarously treated by their

masters, who subsist them poorly, and beat them inhumanly, as may be seen by the scabs and wounds on the bodies of many of them when sold to us. They scarce allow them the least rag to cover their nakedness, which they also take off from them when sold to Europeans; and they always go bare-headed. The wives and children of slaves, are also slaves to the master under whom they are married; and when dead, they never bury them, but cast out the bodies into some by place, to be devoured by birds, or beasts of prey.

This barbarous usage of those unfortunate wretches, makes it appear, that the fate of such as are bought and transported from the coast to America, or other parts of the world, by Europeans, is less deplorable, than that of those who end their days in their native country; for aboard ships all possible care is taken to preserve and subsist them for the interest of the owners, and when sold in America, the same motive ought to prevail with their masters to use them well, that they may live the longer, and do them more service. Not to mention the inestimable advantage they may reap, of becoming christians, and saving their souls, if they make a true use of their condition. . . .

Many of those slaves we transport from Guinea to America are prepossessed with the opinion, that they are carried like sheep to the slaughter, and that the Europeans are fond of their flesh; which notion so far prevails with some, as to make them fall into a deep melancholy and despair, and to refuse all sustenance, tho' never so much compelled and even beaten to oblige them to take some nourishment: notwithstanding all which, they will starve to death; whereof I have had several instances in my own slaves both aboard and at Guadalupe. And tho' I must say I am naturally compassionate, yet have I been necessitated sometimes to cause the teeth of those wretches to be broken, because they would not open their mouths, or be prevailed upon by any entreaties to feed themselves; and thus have forced some sustenance into their throats. . . .

As the slaves come down to Fida from the inland country, they are put into a booth, or prison, built for that purpose, near the beach, all of them together; and when the Europeans are to receive them, every part of every one of them, to the smallest member, men and women being all stark naked. Such as are allowed good and sound, are set on one side, and the others by themselves; which slaves so rejected are there called Mackrons, being above thirty five years of age, or defective in their limbs, eyes or teeth; or grown grey, or that have the venereal disease, or any other imperfection. These being set aside, each of the others, which have passed as good, is marked on the breast, with a red-hot iron, imprinting the mark of the French, English, or Dutch companies, that so each nation may distinguish their own, and to prevent their being chang'd by the natives for worse, as they are apt enough to do. In this particular, care is taken that the women, as tenderest, be not burnt too hard.

The branded slaves, after this, are returned to their former booth, where the factor is to subsist them at his own charge, which amounts to about two-pence a day for each of them, with bread and water, which is all their allowance. There they continue sometimes ten or fifteen days, till the sea is still enough to send them aboard; for very often it continues too boisterous for so long a time, unless in January, February and March, which is commonly the calmest season: and when it is so, the slaves are carried off by parcels, in bar-canoes, and put aboard the ships in the road. Before they enter the canoes, or come out of the booth, their former Black masters strip them of every rag they have, without distinction of men or women; to supply which, in orderly ships, each of them as they come aboard is allowed a piece of canvas, to wrap around their waist, which is very acceptable to those poor wretches. . . .

If there happens to be no stock of slaves at Fida, the factor must trust the Blacks with his goods, to the value of a hundred and fifty, or two hundred slaves; which goods they carry up into the inland, to buy slaves, at all the markets, for above two hundred leagues up the country, where they are kept like cattle in Europe; the slaves sold there being generally prisoners of war, taken from their enemies, like other booty, and perhaps some few sold by their own countrymen, in extreme want, or upon a famine; as also some as a punishment of heinous crimes: tho' many Europeans believe that parents sell their own children, men their wives and relations, which, if it ever happens, is so seldom, that it cannot justly be charged upon a whole nation, as a custom and common practice. . . .

One thing is to be taken notice of by sea-faring men, that this Fida and Ardra slaves are of all the others, the most apt to revolt aboard ships, by a conspiracy carried on amongst themselves; especially such as are brought down to Fida, from very remote inland countries, who easily draw others into their plot: for being used to see men's flesh eaten in their own country, and publick markets held for the purpose, they are very full of the notion, that we buy and transport them to the same purpose; and will therefore watch all opportunities to deliver themselves, by assaulting a ship's crew, and murdering them all, if possible: whereof, we have almost every year some instances, in one European ship or other, that is filled with slaves.

3
William Bosman

"IT IS THEIR COMMON PRACTICE TO ASSURE THE MERCHANT . . . THAT THEY HAVE A STOCK OF SLAVES, ONLY TO DRAW HIM ON SHORE"

The European trade for slaves generally took one of two forms: shipboard and factory. With shipboard trade, a captain would set at anchor off the African coast and sometimes land his cargo on shore. The factory trade took place in forts (or "castles") located along the coast. These "factories" usually began as secure places to store gold. Gradually, however, they were converted into compounds where slaves could be confined, bought, and sold.

The chief factor of the Dutch West India Company at Elmina Castle describes the process of procuring slaves.

It sometimes happens that when the in-land countries are at peace, there are no slaves to be got: So that the trade of this place is utterly uncertain. . . .

This nation [the Popo, a people who lived between Ponni and the river Volta on the Slave Coast] is more than ordinarily fraudulent and thievish. It is their common practice to assure the merchant or factor that they have a stock of slaves, only to draw him on shore; which having done they never part with him without having fleeced him, and besides detained him several months.

They [the natives of Whydah] are so diligent in the slave trade, that they are able to deliver one thousand slaves every month. . . . The first business of one of our factor[s] when he comes to Fida, is to satisfy the customs of the king and the great men, which amounts to about 100 pounds in Guinea value, as the good must yield there. After which we have free license to trade, which is published throughout the whole land by the cryer.

But yet before we can deal with any person, we are obliged to buy the king's whole stock of slaves at a set price; which is com-

Source: William Bosman, *A New and Accurate Description of the Coast of Guinea, Divided into the Gold, the Slave, and the Ivory Coasts*, 1705.

monly one third or one fourth higher than ordinary. After which we obtain free leave to deal with all his subjects of what rank soever. But if there happen to be no stock of slaves, the factor must then resolve to run the risk of trusting the inhabitants with goods to the value of one or two hundred slaves; which commodities they send into the inland country, in order to buy with them slaves at all markets, and that sometimes two hundred miles deep in the country: For you ought to be informed that markets of men are here kept in the same manner as those of beasts with us.

Not a few in our country fondly imagine that parents here sell their children, men their wives, and one brother the other: but those who think so deceive themselves; for this never happens on any other account but that of necessity, or some great crime. But most of the slaves that are offered to us are prisoners of war, which are sold by the victors as their booty.

When these slaves come to Fida, they are put in prison all together, and when we treat concerning buying them, they are all brought out together in a large plain; where, by our surgeons, whose province it is, they are thoroughly examined, even to the smallest member, and that naked too both men and women without the least distinction or modesty. Those which are approved as good arc set on one side; and the lame and faulty are set by as invalids. . . . These are such as are above five and thirty years old, or are maimed in the arms, legs, hands, or feet, have lost a tooth, are grey haired or have films over their eyes; as well as all those which are affected with any veneral distemper, or with several other diseases.

The invalids and the maimed being thrown out, as I have told you, the remainder are numbered, and it is entered who delivered them. In the mean while a burning iron, with the arms or name of the companies, lies in the fire; with which ours are marked on the breast.

This is done that we may distinguish them from the slaves of the English, French or others; (which are also marked with their mark) and to prevent the Negroes exchanging them for worse; at which they have a good hand.

I doubt not but this trade seems very barbarous to you, but since it is followed by mere necessity it must go on; but we yet take all possible care that they are not burned too hard, especially the women, who are more tender than the men.

We are seldom long detained in the buying of these slaves, because their price is established, the women being one fourth or fifth part cheaper than the men. . . .

When we have agreed with the owners of the slaves, they are

returned to their prison; where from that time forwards they are kept at our charge, cost us two pence a day a slave; which serves to subsist them, like our criminals, on bread and water: So that to save charges we send them on board our ships with the very first opportunity; before which their masters strip them of all they have on their backs; so that they come aboard stark naked as well women as men: in which condition they are obliged to continue, if the master of the Ship is not so charitable (which he commonly is) as to bestow something on them to cover their nakedness.

We are sometimes sufficiently plaqued with a parcel of slaves, which come from a far in-land country, who very innocently persuade one another, that we buy them only to fatten and afterwards eat them as a delicacy.

When we are so unhappy as to be pestered with many of this sort, they resolve and agree together (and bring over the rest of their party) to run away from the ship, kill the Europeans, and set the vessel a-shore; by which means they design to free themselves from being our food.

I have twice met with this misfortune; and the first time proved very unlucky to me, I not in the least suspecting it; but the up roar was timely quashed by the master of the ship and myself, by causing the abettor to be shot through the head, after which all was quiet.

But the second time it fell heavier on another ship, and that chiefly by the carelessness of the master, who having fished up the anchor of a departed English ship, had laid it in the hold where the male slaves were lodged; who, unknown to any of the ship's crew, possessed themselves of a hammer; with which, in a short time, they broke all their fetters in pieces upon the anchor: after this they came above deck and fell upon our men; some of whom they grievously wounded, and would certainly have mastered the ship, if a French and English ship had not very fortunately happened to lie by us; who perceiving by our firing a distress'd gun, that something was in disorder on board, immediately came to our assistance . . . and drove the slaves under deck: Notwithstanding which before all was appeased about twenty of them were killed.

4
Francis Moore

"SINCE THIS SLAVE TRADE HAS BEEN US'D, ALL PUNISHMENTS ARE CHANG'D INTO SLAVERY"

Enslavement generally took two forms. There was violent enslavement, as a result of wars and banditry. There was also legal enslavement, as punishment for legal or religious offenses. Over time, enslavement became the penalty for more and more legal and religious "crimes," including adultery. Increasingly, enslavement was extended not simply to a guilty party but to the person's entire family.

Moore, who was appointed in 1744 by the Royal African Company of England to serve at Fort James in the Gambia River, describes the process by which people were enslaved.

Besides the Slaves which the Merchants bring down, there are many bought along the River. These are either taken in War, as the former are, or else Men condemn'd for Crimes, or else People stolen, which is very frequent. The Company's Servants never buy any of the last, if they suspect it, without sending for the Alcade, or chief Men of the Place, and consulting with them about the Matter. Since this Slave Trade has been us'd, all Punishments are chang'd into Slavery; there being an Advantage on such Condemnations, they strain for Crimes very hard, in order to get the Benefit of selling the Criminal. Not only Murder, Theft and Adultery, are punish'd by selling the Criminal for a Slave, but every trifling Crime is punish'd in the same manner. . . .

There was a Man brought to me in Tomany, to be sold for having stolen a Tobacco pipe. I sent for the Alcade, and with much ado persuaded the Party grieved to accept of a Composition, and leave the Man free. . . .

Several of the Natives have many Slaves born in their Families: There is a whole Village near Brucoe of 200 People, who are the Wives, Slaves, or Children of one Man. And tho' in some Parts

Source: Francis Moore, *Travels into the Inland Parts of Africa, 1737* (1738).

of Africa they sell their Slaves born in the Family, yet in the River Gambia they think it is a very wicked thing and I never heard of but one that ever sold a Family-Slave, except for such Crimes as would have made them to be sold had they been free. If there are many Family slaves, and one of them commits a Crime, the Master cannot sell him without the joint Consent of the rest, for if he does, they will all run away, and be protected by the next Kingdom, to which they fly. The Slaves sold in the River, besides those brought by the Merchants, may amount in a Year to about 1000, more or less, according to the Wars upon the River. . . .

5
Ayabah Suleiman Diallo

"HE WAS NO COMMON SLAVE"

Any West African, regardless of status, might be enslaved. Ayabah Suleiman Diallo, who was born around 1701 to a family of Muslim clerics, was a well-educated merchant in the Senegambian region of West Africa, which had supplied Europe with beeswax, gold, gum, ivory, and small numbers of slaves since the fifteenth century. In 1730, he was kidnapped and transported to Maryland. In Maryland, he wrote a letter to his father, which came to the attention of James Oglethorpe, the founder of Georgia, who helped purchase his freedom and bring him to England, where he was known as Job ben Solomon.

In February, 1730, Job's father hearing of an English ship at Gambia River, sent him, with two servants to attend him, to sell two Negroes, and to buy paper, and other necessities; but desired him not to venture over the river, because the country of the Mandingoes, who are enemies . . . lies on the other side. Job not agreeing with Captain Pike . . . sent back the two servants to acquaint his father with it, and to let him know that he intended to go farther. Accordingly having agreed with another man, named

Source: Thomas Bluett, *Some Memoirs of the Life of Job, the Son of Solomon* (London, 1734).

Loumein Yoas, who understood the Mandingoe language, to go with him as his interpreter, he crossed the River Gambia, and disposed of his Negroes for some cows. As he was returning home, he stopped for some refreshment at the house of an old acquaintance; and the weather being hot, he hung up his arms in the house, while he refreshed himself. Those arms were very valuable; consisting of a gold-hilted sword, a gold knife, which they wear by their side, and a rich quiver of arrows, which King Sambo had made him a present of. It happened that a company of the Mandingoes, who live upon plunder, passing by at that time, and observing him unarmed, rushed in, to the number of seven or eight at once, at a back door, and pinioned Job, before he could get to his arms, together with his interpreter, who is a slave in Maryland still. They then shaved their heads and beards, which Job and his man resented as the highest indignity; tho' the Mandingoes meant no more by it, than to make them appear like Slaves taken in war. On the 27th of February, 1730, they carried them to Captain Pike at Gambia, who purchased them; and on the first of March they were put on board. Soon after Job found means to acquaint Captain Pike that he was the same person that came to trade with him a few days before, and after what manner he had been taken. Upon this Captain Pike gave him leave to redeem himself and his man; and Job sent to an acquaintance of his father's, near Gambia, who promised to send to Job's father, to inform him of what had happened, that he might take some course to have him set at liberty. But it being a fortnight's journey between that friend's house and his father's, and the ship sailing in about a week after, Job was brought with the rest of the slaves to Annapolis and Maryland, and delivered to Mr. Vachell Denton, factor to Mr. Hunt, before mentioned. Job heard since, by vessels that came from Gambia, that his father sent down several slaves, a little after Captain Pike sailed, in order to procure his redemption; and that Sambo, King of Futa, had made war upon the Mandingoes, and cut off great numbers of them, upon of the account of the injury they had done to his schoolfellow.

Mr. Vachell Denton sold Job to one Mr. Tolsey in Kent Island in Maryland, who put him to work in making tobacco; but he was soon convinced that Job had never been used to such labour. He every day showed more and more uneasiness under this exercise, and at last grew sick, being no way able to bear it; so that his master was obliged to find easier work for him, and therefore put him to tend the cattle. Job would often leave the cattle, and withdraw into the woods to pray; but a white boy frequently watched him, and whilst he was at his devotion would mock him, and throw dirt in his face. This very much disturbed Job, and added considerably to his other misfortunes; all which were increased by his ignorance of the English language, which prevented him from complaining, or telling his case to any person about him. Grown in some measure desperate, by reason of his present hardship, he resolved to travel at a venture; thinking he might possibly be taken up by some master, who would use him better or otherwise meet with some lucky accident, to divert or abate his grief. Accordingly, he travelled thro' the woods, till he came to the County of Kent, upon Delaware Bay, now esteemed part of Pensilvania; altho' it is properly a part of Maryland, and belongs to my Lord Baltimore. There is a law in force, throughout the colonies of Virginia, Maryland, Pensilvania, etc. as far as Boston in New England, viz. that any Negroe, or white servant who is not known in the county, or has no pass, may be secured by any person, and kept in the common gaol, till the master of such servant shall fetch him. Therefore Job being able to give no account of himself, was put in prison there.

This happened about the beginning of June, 1731 when I, who was attending the courts there, and had heard of Job, went with several gentlemen to the gaoler's house, being a tavern, and desired to see him. He was brought into the tavern to us, but could not speak one word of English. Upon our taking and making signs to him, he wrote a line or two before us, and when he read it, pronounced the words Allah and Mahommed; by which, and his refusing a glass of wine we offered him, we perceived he was a Mahomedtan, but could not imagine of what country he was, or how he got thither; for by his affable carriage, and the easy composure of his countenance, we could perceive he was no common slave.

When Job had been some time confined, an old Negroe man, who lived in that neighbourhood, and could speak the Jalloff language, which Job also understood, went to him, and conversed with him. By this Negroe the keeper was informed to whom Job belonged, and what was the cause of his leaving his master. The keeper thereupon wrote to his master, who soon after fetched him home, and was much kinder to him than before; allowing him a place to pray in, and some other conveniences, in order to make his slavery as easy as possible. Yet slavery and confinement was by no means agreeable to Job, who had never been used to it; he therefore wrote a letter in Arabick to his father, acquainting him with his misfortunes, hoping he might yet find means to redeem him. This letter he sent to Mr. Vachell Denton, desiring it might be sent to Africa by Captain Pike; but he being gone to England, Mr. Denton sent the letter inclosed to Mr. Hunt, in order to be sent to Africa by Captain Pike from England; but Captain Pike had sailed for Africa before the letter came to Mr. Hunt, who therefore kept it in his own hands, till he should have a proper opportunity of sending it. It happened that this letter was seen by James Oglethorpe, Esq. [an English philanthropist who found the of colony of Georgia as a haven for debtors], who, according to his usual goodness and generosity, took compassion on Job, and gave his bond to Mr. Hunt for the payment of a certain sum, upon the delivery of Job here in England. Mr. Hunt upon this sent to Mr. Denton, who purchased him again of his master for the same money which Mr. Denton had formerly received for him; his master being very willing to part with him, as finding him no ways fit for his business.

6
Olaudah Equiano

"THEY . . . CARRY OFF AS MANY AS THEY CAN SEIZE"

Along with war, banditry was a major source of slaves. It is important to recognize that banditry was usually an outgrowth of war. War disrupted civic order. Long protracted wars and civil wars were especially likely to produce conditions of public disorder and corruption. These conflicts produced bands of demobilized soldiers who sometimes became permanent armed gangs who supported themselves by engaging in robbery and other illegal activities, including the slave trade.

Olaudah Equiano, an Ibo from Nigeria, was just eleven years old when he was kidnapped into slavery. He was held captive in West Africa for seven months and then sold to British slavers, who shipped him to Barbados and then took him to Virginia. After serving a British naval officer, he was sold to a Quaker merchant from Philadelphia who allowed him to purchase his freedom in 1766. In later life, he played an active role in the movement to abolish the slave trade.

My father, besides many slaves, had a numerous family, of which seven lived to grow up, including myself and a sister, who

Source: *The Interesting Narrative of the Life of Olaudah Equiano or Gustavus Vassa the African* (London, 1789).

was the only daughter. As I was the youngest of the sons, I became, of course, the greatest favourite of my mother, and was always with her; and she used to take particular pains to form my mind. I was trained up from my earliest years in the arts of agriculture and war; and my mother adorned me with emblems, after the manner of our greatest warriors. In this way I grew up till I was turned the age of eleven, when an end was put to my happiness in the following manner:—Generally, when the grown people in the neighbourhood were gone far in the fields to labour, the children assembled together in some of the neighborhood's premises to play; and commonly some of us used to get up a tree to look out for any assailant, or kidnapper, that might come upon us; for they sometimes took those opportunities of our parents' absence, to attack and carry off as many as they could seize. One day, as I was watching at the top of a tree in our yard, I saw one of those people come into the yard of our next neighbour but one, to kidnap, there being many stout young people in it. Immediately, on this, I gave the alarm of the rogue, and he was surrounded by the stoutest of them, who entangled him with cords, so that he could not escape till some of the grown people came and secured him. But alas! ere long, it was my fate to be thus attacked, and to be carried off, when none of the grown people were nigh. One day, when all our people were gone out to their works as usual, and only I and my dear sister were left to mind the house, two men and a woman got over our walls, and in a moment seized us both; and, without giving us time to cry out, or make resistance, they stopped our mouths, and ran off with us into the nearest wood. Here they tied our hands, and continued to carry us as far as they could, till night came on, when we reached a small house, where the robbers halted for refreshment, and spent the night. We were then unbound; but were unable to take any food; and, being quite overpowered by fatigue and grief, our only relief was some sleep, which allayed our misfortune for a short time.

7
Captain William Littleton

"DO YOU KNOW OF ANY WARS BEING CARRIED ON FOR THE PURPOSE OF OBTAINING SLAVES TO SELL TO THE EUROPEANS?"

Enslavement was generally an outgrowth of war. This raises the question of whether West and Central African nations went to war in order to capture slaves. The answer appears to be no. Wars were fought primarily for diplomatic and political reasons. Nations recognized that waging wars simply to acquire slaves was dangerous, since even powerful nations like Dahomey could not be certain of winning every war they fought. Nevertheless, it is clear that the nature of African warfare changed in the seventeenth and eighteenth centuries in order to maximize the capture of people who could be sold as slaves. By selling war captives, a nation could permanently deprive its adversaries of their productive adult male population.

In this selection, a Parliamentary commission asks a slave ship captain about whether slave traders intentionally instigate warfare in order to obtain slaves.

Counsel called in.
The Counsel for the Petitions from Liverpool proceeded in their
    Evidence, and called Captain WILLIAM LITTLETON

Have you been at Gambia?
Yes.
In what capacity did you go?
As Mate.
In what Year?
In 1762.
How long did you continue there?
Eleven Years—trading there as a Merchant.

Source: *Committee of the Whole House, to consider further of the Circumstances of the Slave Trade, complained of in the several Petitions which were presented to the House in the last Session of Parliament, relative to the State of the African Slave Trade* [1789].

In the course of your trade did you go up the river Gambia?

Yes.

Was you acquainted with the Language of the country?

Sufficiently so to do my business with the natives.

Are you acquainted with their manners and customs?

Tolerably so—as much as a man could be who resided chiefly on board his vessel.

Is Slavery known in that Country as a general condition?

Yes.

Do the Freemen keep many Slaves?

Some do.

How are the Slaves obtained, which are sold to the Europeans?

By various modes—a great proportion of them from the Black traders, who are Mahometans, and traverse the interior part of the Country to get Slaves.

Do you know of any wars being carried on for the purpose of obtaining slaves to sell to the Europeans?

I never heard of any carried on for that purpose. The wars have always originated from their own dissensions.

Are wars beneficial, or otherwise, to the Slave trade carried on by the Europeans?

Wars in the vicinity of the trading ports are always injurious to the trade in articles of every kind; and I have been told by the Black Merchants that they have gone 3 or 400 miles to avoid those countries where wars existed.

Do you know of the practice of kidnapping Slaves, or that they are taken by fraud or violence, by Blacks or Whites?

I never heard that a Whiteman ever kidnapped a Slave; if he did, it would put a total end to that man's trading—I never hear of such a thing—I speak of the river Gambia only, I don't know what is done on the other parts of the Coast—I never heard that of any of the natives in that part where I resided and did business.—If they made any attempt of that kind, they would be sold them selves.

Have you ever heard of any parties going out armed at night to take Slaves?

Never, but against their enemies, with whom they were at open war.

8
Mungo Park

"THE COMMODITIES EXPORTED TO THE GAMBIA . . . CONSIST CHIEFLY OF FIRE-ARMS AND AMMUNITION, IRON WARE, SPIRITUOUS LIQUORS, TOBACCO"

Park, the Scottish explorer of the Niger River, was born in 1771 and died in 1806, near Bussa on the Niger, now in Nigeria. In the following passages, he describes the slave trade and indicates that in this exchange power did not lie exclusively with Europeans.

The kingdom of Barra, in which the town of Jillifree [a British trading post on the north bank of the Gambia River; Alex Haley claimed that his ancestor Kunte Kinte came from here] is situated, produces great plenty of the necessaries of life; but the chief trade of the inhabitants is in salt; which commodity they carry up the river in canoes as high as Barraconda, and bring down in return Indian corn, cotton cloths, elephants' teeth, small quantities of gold dust, &c. The number of canoes and people constantly employed in this trade, make the King of Barra more formidable to Europeans than any other chieftain on the rivers and this circumstance probably encouraged him to establish those exorbitant duties, which traders of all nations are obliged to pay at entry, amounting to nearly £20. on every vessel, great and small. These duties or customs, are generally collected in person by the Alkaid, or Governor of Jillifree, and he is attended on these occasions by a numerous train of dependants, among whom are found many who, by their frequent intercourse with the English, have acquired a smattering of our language but they are commonly very noisy, and very troublesome begging for every thing they fancy with such earnestness and importunity, that traders, in order to get quit of them, are frequently obliged to grant their requests. . . .

The commodities exported to the Gambia from Europe consist chiefly of fire-arms and ammunition, iron ware, spirituous

Source: Mungo Park, *Travels in the Interior Districts of Africa*, 1797.

liquors, tobacco, cotton caps, a small quantity of broad cloth, and a few articles of the manufacture of Manchester; a small assortment of India goods, with some glass beads, amber, and other trifles: for which are taken in exchange slaves, gold-dust, ivory, beeswax, and hides. Slaves are the chief article, but the whole number which at this time are annually exported from the Gambia by all nations, is supposed to be under one thousand.

Most of these unfortunate victims are brought to the Coast in periodical caravans; many of them from very remote inland countries; for the language which they speak is not understood by the inhabitants of the maritime districts. In a subsequent part of my work I shall give the best information I have been able to collect concerning the manner in which they are obtained. On their arrival at the Coast, if immediate opportunity offers of selling them to advantage, they are distributed among the neighbouring villages, until a slave ship arrives, or until they can be sold to black traders, who sometimes purchase on speculation. In the meanwhile, the poor wretches are kept constantly fettered, two and two of them being chained together, and employed in the labours of the field: and I am sorry to add, are very scantily fed, as well as harshly treated. The price of a slave varies according to the number of purchasers from Europe, and the arrival of caravans from the interior; but in general I reckon, that a young and healthy male, from 16 to 25 years of age, may be estimated on the spot from 8 to £20. sterling.

9
Venture Smith

"I THEN HAD A ROPE PUT ABOUT MY NECK"

Kidnapped at the age of six, Venture Smith was sold to the steward on a slave ship and brought to Connecticut. At the age of thirty-one, after several changes of ownership, he purchased his freedom with money that he earned by hiring out his labor and "cleaning musk-rats and minks, raising potatoes and carrots, and by fishing in the night, and

Source: *A Narrative of the Life and Adventures of Venture, A Native of Africa* (New London, Conn., 1798; expanded ed., Hamden, Conn., 1896).

*at odd spells." In order to purchase his wife and sons, he
fished, sailed on a whaler, ferried wood from Long Island
to Rhode Island, and raised watermelons. Later, he actually became a slaveholder, purchasing at least three slaves.
At his death at the age of seventy-seven in 1805 in East
Haddam, Connecticut, he left a hundred-acre farm and
three houses.*

I was born in Dukandarra, in Guinea, about the year 1729. My
father's name was Saungm Furro, Prince of the tribe of Dukandara.
My father had three wives. Polygamy was not uncommon in that
country, especially among the rich, as every man was allowed to
keep as many wives as he could maintain. . . .

The first thing worthy of notice which I remember was, a con-
tention between my father and mother, on account of my father
marrying his third wife without the consent of his first and eldest,
which was contrary to the custom generally observed among my
countrymen. In consequence of this rupture, my mother left her
husband and country, and travelled away with her three children to
the eastward. I was then five years old. . . . After five days travel . . .
my mother was pleased to stop and seek a refuge for me. She left
me at the house of a very rich farmer. I was then, as I should judge,
not less than one hundred and forty miles from my native place,
separated from all my relations and acquaintance. . . .

My father sent a man and horse after me. After settling with
my guardian for keeping me, he took me away and went for home.
It was then about one year since my mother brought me here.
Nothing remarkable occurred to us on our journey until we arrived
safe home.

I found then that the difference between my parents had been
made up previous to their sending for me. On my return, I was
received both by my father and mother with great joy and affection,
and was once more restored to my paternal dwelling in peace and
happiness. I was then about six years old.

Not more than six weeks had passed after my return before a
message was brought by an inhabitant of the place where I lived the
preceding year to my father, that that place had been invaded by a
numerous army from a nation not far distant, furnished with musi-
cal instrument, and all kinds of arms then in use; that they were
instigated by some white nation who equipped and sent them to
subdue and possess the country; that his nation had made no
preparation for war, having been for a long time in profound peace;
that they could not defend themselves against such a formidable

train of invaders, and must therefore necessarily evacuate their lands to the fierce enemy, and fly to the protection of some chief; and that if he would permit them they would come under his rule and protection when they had to retreat from their own possessions. He was a kind and merciful prince, and therefore consented to these proposals. . . .

He gave them every privilege and all the protection his government could afford. But they had not been there longer than four days before news came to them that the invaders had laid waste their country, and were coming speedily to destroy them in my father's territories. This affrighted them, and therefore they immediately pushed off to the southward, into the unknown countries there, and were never more heard of.

Two days after their retreat, the report turned out to be but too true. A detachment from the enemy came to my father and informed him, that the whole army was encamped not far out of his dominions, and would invade the territory and deprive his people of their liberties and rights, if he did not comply with the following terms. These were to pay them a large sum of money, three hundred fat cattle, and a great number of goats, sheep, asses, etc.

My father told the messenger he would comply rather than that his subjects should be deprived of their rights and privileges, which he was not then in circumstances to defend from so sudden an invasion. Upon turning out those articles, the enemy pledged their faith and honor that they would not attack him. On these he relied and therefore thought it unnecessary to be on his guard against the enemy. But their pledges of faith and honor proved no better than those of other unprincipled hostile nations; for a few days after a certain relation of the king came and informed him, that the enemy who sent terms of accommodation to him and received tribute to their satisfaction, yet meditated an attack upon his subjects by surprise and that probably they would commence their attack in less than one day, and concluded with advising him, as he was not prepared for war, to order a speedy retreat of his family and subjects. He complied with this advice.

The same night which was fixed upon to retreat, my father and his family set off about the break of day. The king and his two younger wives went in one company, and my mother and her children in another. We left our dwellings in succession, and my father's company went on first. We directed our course for a large shrub plain, some distance off, where we intended to conceal ourselves from the approaching enemy, until we could refresh ourselves a little. But we presently found that our retreat was not secure. For having struck up a little fire for the purpose of cooking victuals, the enemy who happened to be encamped a little distance off, had sent out a scouting party who discovered us by the smoke of the fire, just as we were extinguishing it, and about to eat. As soon as we had finished eating, my father discovered the party, and immediately began to discharge arrows at them. This was what I first saw, and it alarmed both me and the women, who being unable to make any resistance, immediately betook ourselves to the tall thick reeds not far off, and left the old king to fight alone. For some time I beheld him from the reeds defending himself with great courage and firmness, till at last he was obliged to surrender himself into their hands.

They then came to us in the reeds, and the very first salute I had from them was a violent blow on the back part of the head with the fore part of a gun, and at the same time a grasp round the neck. I then had a rope put about my neck, as had all the women in the thicket with me, and were immediately led to my father, who was likewise pinioned and haltered for leading. In this condition we were all led to the camp. The women and myself being pretty submissive, had tolerable treatment from the enemy, while my father was closely interrogated respecting his money which they knew he must have. But as he gave them no account of it, he was instantly cut and pounded on his body with great inhumanity, that he might be induced by the torture he suffered to make the discovery. All this availed not in the least to make him give up his money, but he despised all the tortures which they inflicted, until the continued exercise and increase of torment, obliged him to sink and expire He thus died without informing his enemies where his money lay. I saw him while he was thus tortured to death. The shocking scene is to this day fresh in my mind, and I have often been overcome while thinking on it. . . .

The army of the enemy was large, I should suppose consisting of about six thousand men. Their leader was called Baukurre. After destroying the old prince, they decamped and immediately marched toward the sea, lying to the west, taking with them myself and the women prisoners. In the march a scouting party was detached from the main army. To the leader of this party I was made waiter, having to carry his gun, etc. As we were a scouting we came across a herd of fat cattle, consisting of about thirty in number. These we set upon, and immediately wrested from their keepers, and afterwards converted them into food for the army. The enemy had remarkable success in destroying the country wherever they went. For as far as they had penetrated, they laid the habitations waste and captured the people. The distance they had now brought me was about four hundred miles. All the march I had very hard tasks imposed on me, which I must perform on pain of punishment. I was obliged to carry on my head a large glat stone used for grinding our corn, weighing as I should suppose, as much as twenty-five pounds; besides victuals, mat and cooking utensils. Though I was pretty large and stout at my age, yet these burdens were very grievous to me, being only six years and a half old.

We were then come to a place called Malagasco. When we entered the place we could not see the least appearance of either houses or inhabitants, but upon stricter search found, that instead of houses above ground they had dens in the sides of hillocks, contiguous to ponds and streams of water. In these we perceived they had all hid themselves, as I supposed they usually did on such occasions. In order to compel them to surrender, the enemy contrived to smoke them out with faggots. These they put to the entrance of the caves and set them on fire. While they were engaged in this business, to their great surprise some of them were desperately wounded with arrows which fell from above on them. This mystery they soon found out. They perceived that the enemy discharged these arrows through holes on top of the dens, directly into the air. Their weight brought them back, point downwards on their enemies heads, whilst they were smoking the inhabitants out. The points of their arrows were poisoned, but their enemy had an antidote for it, which they instantly applied to the wounded part. The smoke at last obliged the people to give themselves up. They came out of their caves, first putting the palms of their hands together, and immediately after extended their arms, crossed at their wrists, ready to be bound and pinioned. . . .

The invaders then pinioned the prisoners of all ages and sexes indiscriminately, took their flocks and all their effects, and moved on their way towards the sea. On the march the prisoners were treated with clemency, on account of their being submissive and humble. Having come to the next tribe, the enemy laid siege and immediately took men, women, children, flocks, and all their valuable effects. They then went on to the next district which was contiguous to the sea, called in Africa, Anamaboo. The enemies' provisions were then almost spent, as well as their strength. The inhabitants knowing what conduct they had pursued, and what were their present intentions, improved the favorable opportunity, attacked them, and took enemy, prisoners, flocks and all their effects. I was then taken a second time. All of us were then put into the castle [a European slave trading post], and kept for market. On a certain time I and other prisoners were put on board a canoe, under our master, and rowed away to a vessel belonging to Rhode Island, commanded by Captain Collingwood, and the mate Thomas

Mumford. While we were going to the vessel, our master told us all to appear to the best possible advantage for sale. I was bought on board by one Robert Mumford, steward of said vessel, for four gallons of rum, and a piece of calico, and called Venture, on account of his having purchased me with his own private venture. Thus I came by my name. All the slaves that were bought for that vessel's cargo, were two hundred and sixty.

Slave ship by Mahlon Blaine in John W. Vandercook BLACK MAJESTY, Harper, 1928, p. 16.

Chapter 2

"God's A-Gwineter Trouble de Water":

THE MIDDLE PASSAGE

When the British frigate North Star *stopped and boarded a slave ship in the south Atlantic in 1829—two decades after the United States and Britain outlawed the Atlantic slave trade—the crew found conditions aboard the slaver almost unspeakably horrible. Its cargo consisted of 505 African men and women. Another fifty-five had been tossed overboard during seventeen days at sea. The slaves "were all enclosed under grated hatchways, between decks. The space was so low that they sat between each others' legs, and stowed so close together, that there was no possibility of lying down, or at all changing their position, by night or by day. . . . They were all branded like sheep . . . burnt with a red hot iron. . . ." Each captive, chained by the neck and legs, had just one square foot of sitting space.*

No aspect of the Atlantic slave trade aroused more passionate denunciation than the Middle Passage—the transoceanic voyage to the New World. On many ships, slaves were crowded almost beyond belief. Typically, slaves had less than half the space provided for convicts aboard prison ships. A parliamentary inquiry concluded that conditions aboard the British slaver Brookes *were fairly typical. To carry its cargo of 451 slaves, every man was allowed a space just 6' long, 16" wide, and 2' 7" high; every woman, a space 5' 10" long and 16" wide; every boy, 5' by 14"; every girl, 4' 6" by 12". But on at least one voyage, the ship carried as many as 609 slaves.*

Average death rates were extraordinary, running as high as 168 deaths for every 1,000 slaves leaving the African coast. Average child mortality was even higher. Some voyages were particularly deadly. The British slaver Hero *lost 360 slaves—over half its slaves—mainly from smallpox; the* Briton *lost half its 375 slaves.*

The major cause of death was ameobic dysentery—"the bloody flux"—caused by contaminated food and water supplies, reflecting the low level of sanitation aboard the ships. Other killers included small pox, measles, and other communicable diseases. In addition, many slaves died in shipboard revolts, attacks by pirates, and shipwrecks, or from suicide.

1

James Barbot, Jr.

"PREMEDITATED A REVOLT"

The death rate on slave ships was closely connected to the length of the voyage. Once the voyage exceeded a month, slave mortality rose steeply. The biggest problem was the shortage of drinking water and resulting dehydration.

James Barbot, Jr., a sailor aboard the English slaver Don Carlos, *describes a slave uprising that took place aboard the vessel.*

About one in the afternoon, after dinner, we, according to custom caused them, one by one, to go down between decks, to have each his pint of water; most of them were yet above deck, many of them provided with knives, which we had indiscreetly given them two or three days before, as not suspecting the least attempt of this nature from them; others had pieces of iron they had torn off our forecastle door, as having premeditated a revolt, and seeing all the ship's company, at best but weak and many quite sick, they had also broken off the shackles from several of their companions feet, which served them, as well as billets they had provided themselves with, and all other things they could lay hands on, which they imagin'd might be of use for this enterprize. Thus arm'd, they fell in crouds and parcels on our men, upon the deck unawares, and stabb'd one of the stoutest of us all, who receiv'd fourteen or fifteen wounds of their knives, and so expir'd. Next they assaulted our boatswain, and cut one of his legs so round the bone, that he could not move, the nerves being cut through; others cut our cook's throat to the pipe, and others wounded three of the sailors, and threw one of them over-board in that condition, from the forecastle into the sea; who, however, by good providence, got hold of the bowline of the fore-sail, and sav'd himself . . . we stood in arms, firing on the revolted slaves, of whom we kill'd some, and wounded many: which so terrif'd the rest, that they gave way, dispersing themselves some one way and some another between decks, and

---

Source: James Barbot, Jr., "A Supplement to the Description of the Coasts of North and South Guinea," in Awnsham and John Churchill, *Collection of Voyages and Travels* (London, 1732).

under the fore-castle; and many of the most mutinous, leapt over board, and drown'd themselves in the ocean with much resolution, shewing no manner of concern for life. Thus we lost twenty seven or twenty eight slaves, either kill'd by us, or drown'd; and having master'd them, caused all to go betwixt decks, giving them good words. The next day we had them all again upon deck, where they unanimously declar'd, the Menbombe slaves had been the con-trivers of the mutiny, and for an example we caused about thirty of the ringleaders to be very severely whipt by all our men that were capable of doing that office. . . .

I have observ'd, that the great mortality, which so often hap-pens in slave-ships, proceeds as well from taking in too many, as from want of knowing how to manage them aboard. . . .

As to the management of our slaves aboard, we lodge the two sexes apart, by means of a strong partition at the main mast; the forepart is for men, the other behind the mast for the women. If it be in large ships carrying five or six hundred slaves, the deck in such ships ought to be at least five and a half or six foot high, which is very requisite for driving a continual trade of slaves: for the greater height it has, the more airy and convenient it is for such a considerable number of human creatures; and consequently far the more healthy for them, and fitter to look after them. We build a sort of half-deck along the sides with deals and spars provided for that purpose in Europe, that half-deck extending no father than the sides of our scuttles and so the slaves lie in two rows, one above the other, and as close together as they can be crouded. . . .

The planks, or deals, contract some dampness more or less, either from the deck being so often wash'd to keep it clean and sweet, or from the rain that gets in now and then through the scut-tles or other openings, and even from the very sweat of the slaves; which being so crouded in a low place, is perpetual, and occasions many distempers, or at best great inconveniences dangerous to their health. . . .

It has been observ'd before, that some slaves fancy they are carry'd to be eaten, which make them desperate; and others are so on account of their captivity: so that if care be not taken, they will mutiny and destroy the ship's crue in hopes to get away.

To prevent such misfortunes, we use to visit them daily, nar-rowly searching every corner between decks, to see whether they have not found means, to gather any pieces of iron, or wood, or knives, about the ship, notwithstanding the great care we take not to leave any tools or nails, or other things in the way: which, how-ever, cannot be always so exactly observ'd, where so many people are in the narrow compass of a ship.

We cause as many of our men as is convenient to lie in the quarter-deck and gun-room, and our principal officers in the great cabin, where we keep all our small arms in a readiness, with sentinels constantly at the doors and avenues to it; being thus ready to disappoint any attempts our slave might make on a sudden.

These precautions contribute very much to keep them in awe; and if all those who carry slaves duly observ'd them, we should not hear of so many revolts as have happen'd. Where I was concern'd, we always kept our slaves in such order, that we did not perceive the least inclination in any of them to revolt, or mutiny, and lost very few of our number in the voyage.

It is true, we allow'd them much more liberty, and us'd them with more tenderness than most other Europeans would think prudent to do; as, to have them all upon deck every day in good weather; to take their meals twice a-day, at fix'd hours, that is, at ten in the morning, and at five at night; which being ended, we made the men go down again between the decks; for the women were almost entirely at their own discretion, to be upon deck as long as they pleas'd, nay even many of the males had the same liberty by turns, successively; few or none being fetter'd or kept in shackles, and that only on account of some disturbances, or injuries, offer'd to their fellow captives, as will unavoidably happen among a numerous croud of such savage people. Besides, we allow'd each of them betwixt their meals a handful of Indian wheat and Mandioca, and now and then short pipes and tobacco to smoak upon deck by turns, and some coconuts; and to the women a piece of coarse cloth to cover them, and the same to many of the men, which we took care they did wash from time to time, to prevent vermin, which they are very subject to; and because it look'd sweeter and more agreeable. Toward the evening they diverted themselves on the deck, as they thought fit, some conversing together, others dancing, singing, and sporting after their manner, which pleased them highly, and often made us pastime; especially the female sex, who being apart from the males, on the quarter-deck, and many of them young sprightly maidens, full of jollity and good-humour, afforded us abundance of recreation; as did several little fine boys, which we mostly kept to attend on us about the ship.

We mess'd the slaves twice a day, as I have observed; the first meal was of our large beans boil'd, with a certain quantity of Muscovy lard. . . . The other meal was of pease, or of Indian wheat, and sometimes meal of Mandioca . . . boiled with either lard, or suet, or grease by turns: and sometimes with palm-oil and malaguette or Guinea pepper. I found they had much better stomachs for beans, and it is a proper fattening food for captives. . . .

At each meal we allow'd every slave a full coconut shell of water, and from time to time a dram of brandy, to strengthen their stomachs. . . .

Much more might be said relating to the preservation and maintenance of slaves in such voyages, which I leave to the prudence of the officers that govern aboard, if they value their own reputation and their owners' advantage; and shall only add these few particulars, that tho' we ought to be circumspect in watching the slaves narrowly, to prevent or disappoint their ill designs for our own conservation, yet must we not be too severe and haughty with them, but on the contrary, caress and humor them in every reasonable thing. Some commanders, of a morose peevish temper are perpetually beating and curbing them, even without the least offence, and will not suffer any upon deck but when unavoidable to ease themselves does require; under pretence it hinders the work of the ship and sailors and that they are troublesome by their nasty nauseous stench, or their noise; which makes those poor wretches desperate, and besides their falling into distempers thro' melancholy, often is the occasion of their destroying themselves.

Such officers should consider, those unfortunate creatures are men as well as themselves, tho' of a different colour, and pagans; and that they ought to do to others as they would be done by in like circumstances. . . .

2

Captain William Snelgrave

"WE WERE OBLIGED TO SECURE THEM VERY WELL IN IRONS AND WATCH THEM NARROWLY: YET THEY NEVERTHELESS MUTINIED"

The overall profitability of slave trading was surprisingly low. One reason was the high slave mortality rate. It usually took a captain several voyages before he learned how

Source: William Snelgrave, *New Account of some p[arts] of guinea and the slave trade, containing, I. The history of the late conquest of the kingdom of Whidaw by the king of Dahome. II. The manner how the Negroes become slaves. III. A relation of the author's being taken by pirates, and the many dangers he underwent,* 1734.

to reduce the death rate (and to prevent mutinies). But most captains made so little on their first voyage, that they did not undertake another.

In this selection, William Snelgrave, a slave ship captain, describes the precautions that slavers must take in order to prevent shipboard rebellions.

I have seen several Voyages when there has been no attempt made by our negroes to mutiny; which, I believe, was owing chiefly to their being kindly used and to my Officers' Care in keeping a good Watch. But sometimes we meet with stout stubborn People amongst them, who are never to be made easy; and these are generally some of the Cormantines, a Nation of the Gold Coast. I went in the year 1721, in the *Henry* of London, a Voyage to that part of the Coast, and bought a good many of these People. We were obliged to secure them very well in Irons and watch them narrowly: Yet they nevertheless mutinied, tho' they had little prospect of succeeding. I lay at that time near a place called Muntford on the Gold Coast, having near five hundred Negroes on board, three hundred of which were Men. Our Ship's Company consisted of fifty white People, all in health: And I had very good Officers; so that I was very easy in all respects.

After we had secured these People, I called the Linguists and ordered them to bid the Men-Negroes between Decks be quiet (for there was a great noise amongst them). On their being silent, I asked "What had induced them to mutiny?" They answered, "I was a great Rogue to buy them, in order to carry them away from their own Country, and that they were resolved to regain their Liberty if possible." I replied, "That they had forfeited their Freedom before I bought them, either by Crimes or by being taken in War, according to the Custom of their Country; and they being now my Property, I was resolved to let them feel my Resentment if they abused my Kindness: Asking at the same time, Whether they had been ill used by the white Men, or had they wanted for any thing the Ship afforded?" To this they replied, "They had nothing to complain of." Then I observed to them, "That if they should gain their Point and escape to the Shore, it would be no Advantage to them, because their Countrymen would catch them and sell them to other Ships." This served my purpose, and they seemed to be convinced of their Fault, begging, "I would forgive them, and promising for the future to be obedient and never mutiny again, if I would not punish them this time." This I readily granted, and so they went to sleep. When Daylight came we called the Men Negroes up on Deck, and examining their Irons found them all secure. So this Affair happily ended, which I was very glad of; for these People are the stoutest and most sensible Negroes on the Coast: Neither are they so weak as to imagine as others do that we buy them to eat them; being satisfied we carry them to work in our Plantations as they do in their own Country.

However a few days after this we discovered they were plotting again, and preparing to mutiny. For some of the Ringleaders proposed to one of our Linguists, If he could procure them an Ax they would cut the Cables the Ship rid by [was anchored to] in the night; and so on her driving (as they imagined) ashore they should get out of our hands and then would become his Servants as long as they lived.

For the better understanding of this I must observe here that these Linguists are Natives and Freemen of the Country, whom we hire on account of their speaking good English during the time we remain trading on the Coast; and they are likewise Brokers between us and the black Merchants.

This Linguist was so honest as to acquaint me with what had been proposed to him, and advised me to keep a strict Watch over the Slaves: For tho' he had represented to them the same as I had done on their mutinying before, that they would all be catch'd again and sold to other Ships, in case they could carry their Point and get on Shore, yet it had no effect upon them.

This gave me a good deal of Uneasiness. For I knew several Voyages had proved unsuccessful by Mutinies; as they occasioned either the total loss of the Ships and the white Men's Lives; or at least by rendering it absolutely necessary to kill or wound a great number of the Slaves in order to prevent a total Destruction. Moreover, I knew many of these Cormantine Negroes despised Punishment and even Death itself: It having often happened at Barbadoes and other Islands that on their being any ways hardly dealt with, to break them of their Stubbornness in refusing to work, twenty or more have hang'd themselves at a time in a Plantation.

3
Olaudah Equiano

"A MULTITUDE OF BLACK PEOPLE . . . CHAINED TOGETHER"

Olaudah Equiano vividly recounts the shock and isolation that he felt during the Middle Passage to Barbados and his fear that the European slavers would eat him.

Their complexions, differing so much from ours, their long hair and the language they spoke, which was different from any I had ever heard, united to confirm me in this belief. Indeed, such were the horrors of my views and fears at the moment, that if ten thousand worlds had been my own, I would have freely parted with them all to have exchanged my condition with that of the meanest slave of my own country. When I looked around the ship and saw a large furnace of copper boiling, and a multitude of black people of every description chained together, every one of their countenances expressing dejection and sorrow, I no longer doubted my fate. Quite overpowered with horror and anguish, I fell motionless on the deck and fainted. When I recovered a little, I found some black people about me, and I believe some were those who had brought me on board and had been receiving their pay. They talked to me in order to cheer me up, but all in vain. I asked them if we were not to be eaten by those white men with horrible looks, red faces and long hair. They told me I was not.

I took a little down my palate, which, instead of reviving me as they thought it would, threw me into the greatest consternation at the strange feeling it produced, having never tasted such liquor before. Soon after this, the blacks who had brought me on board went off and left me abandoned to despair.

I now saw myself deprived of all chance of returning to my native country or even the least glimpse of hope of gaining the shore, which I now considered as friendly. I even wished for my former slavery in preference to my present situation, which was filled with horrors of every kind.

There I received such a salutation in my nostrils as I had never

Source: *The Interesting Narrative of the Life of Olaudah Equiano or Gustavus Vassa the African* (London, 1789).

experienced in my life. With the loathesomeness of the stench and the crying together, I became so sick and low that I was not able to eat, nor had I the least desire to taste anything. I now wished for the last friend, Death, to relieve me.

Soon, to my grief, two of the white men offered me eatables and on my refusing to eat, one of them held me fast by the hands and laid me across the windlass and tied my feet while the other flogged me severely. I had never experienced anything of this kind before. If I could have gotten over the nettings, I would have jumped over the side, but I could not. The crew used to watch very closely those of us who were not chained down to the decks, lest we should leap into the water. I have seen some of these poor African prisoners most severely cut for attempting to do so, and hourly whipped for not eating. This indeed was often the case with myself.

I inquired of these what was to be done with us. They gave me to understand we were to be carried to these white people's country to work for them. I then was a little revived, and thought if it were no worse than working, my situation was not so desperate. But still I feared that I should be put to death, the white people looked and acted in so savage a manner. I have never seen among my people such instances of brutal cruelty, and this not only shown towards us blacks, but also to some of the whites themselves.

One white man in particular I saw, when we were permitted to be on deck, flogged so unmercifully with a large rope near the foremast that he died in consequence of it, and they tossed him over the side as they would have done a brute. This made me fear these people the more, and I expected nothing less than to be treated in the same manner.

I asked them if these people had no country, but lived in this hollow place? They told me they did not but came from a distant land. "Then," said I, "how comes it that in all our country we never heard of them?"

They told me because they lived so far off. I then asked where were their women? Had they any like themselves? I was told they had.

"And why do we not see them" I asked. They answered, "Because they were left behind."

I asked how the vessel would go? They told me they could not tell, but there was cloth put upon the masts by the help of the ropes I saw, and then vessels went on, and the white men had some spell or magic they put in the water when they liked in order to stop the vessel when they liked.

I was exceedingly amazed at this account, and really thought they were spirits. I therefore wished much to be from amongst them, for I expected they would sacrifice me. But my wishes were in vain—for we were so quartered that it was impossible for us to make our escape.

At last, when the ship we were in had got in all her cargo, they made ready with many fearful noises, and we were all put under deck, so that we could not see how they managed the vessel.

The stench of the hold while we were on the coast was so intolerably loathsome, that it was dangerous to remain there for any time . . . some of us had been permitted to stay on the deck for the fresh air. But now that the whole ship's cargo were confined together, it became absolutely pestilential. The closeness of the place and the heat of the climate, added to the number of the ship, which was so crowded that each had scarcely room to turn himself, almost suffocated us.

This produced copious perspirations so that the air became unfit for respiration from a variety of loathsome smells, and brought on a sickness among the slaves, of which many died—thus falling victims of the improvident avarice, as I may call it, of their purchasers. This wretched situation was again aggravated by the galling of the chains, which now became insupportable, and the filth of the necessary tubs [toilets] into which the children often fell and were almost suffocated. The shrieks of the women and the groans of the dying rendered the whole a scene of horror almost inconceivable.

Happily perhaps for myself, I was soon reduced so low that it was necessary to keep me almost always on deck and from my extreme youth I was not put into fetters. In this situation I expected every hour to share the fate of my companions, some of whom were almost daily brought upon the deck at the point of death, which I began to hope would soon put an end to my miseries. Often did I think many of the inhabitants of the deep much more happy than myself. I envied them the freedom they enjoyed, and as often wished I could change my condition for theirs. Every circumstance I met with, served only to render my state more painful and heightened my apprehensions and my opinion of the cruelty of the whites.

One day, when we had a smooth sea and moderate wind, two of my wearied countrymen who were chained together (I was near them at the time), preferring death to such a life of misery, somehow made through the nettings and jumped into the sea. Immediately another quite dejected fellow, who on account of his illness was suffered to be out of irons, followed their example. I believe many more would very soon have done the same if they had not been prevented by the ship's crew, who were instantly alarmed.

Those of us that were the most active were in a moment put down under the deck, and there was such a noise and confusion among the people of the ship as I never heard before to stop her and get the boat out to go after the slaves. However, two of the wretches were drowned, but they got the other and afterwards flogged him unmercifully for thus attempting to prefer death to slavery.

I can now relate hardships which are inseparable from this accursed trade. Many a time we were near suffocation from the want of fresh air, which we were often without for whole days together. This, and the stench of the necessary tubs, carried off many.

4

Alexander Falconbridge

"THE MEN NEGROES . . . ARE . . . FASTENED TOGETHER . . . BY HANDCUFFS"

Alexander Falconbridge, a surgeon aboard slave ships and later the governor of a British colony for freed slaves in Sierra Leone, offers a vivid account of the Middle Passage.

From the time of the arrival of the ships to their departure, which is usually about three months, scarce a day passes without some Negroes being purchased and carried on board; sometimes in small and sometimes in large numbers. The whole number taken on board depends on circumstances. In a voyage I once made, our stock of merchandise was exhausted in the purchase of about 380 Negroes, which was expected to have procured 500. . . .

The unhappy wretches thus disposed of are bought by the black traders at fairs, which are held for that purpose, at the distance of upwards of two hundred miles from the sea coast; and these fairs are said to be supplied from an interior part of the country. Many Negroes, upon being questioned relative to the places of their nativity, have asserted that they have travelled during the rev-

Source: Alexander Falconbridge, *An Account of the Slave Trade on the Coast of Africa* (London, 1788).

olution of several moons (their usual method of calculating time) before they have reached the places where they were purchased by the black traders.

At these fairs, which are held at uncertain periods, but generally every six weeks, several thousands are frequently exposed to sale who had been collected from all parts of the country for a very considerable distance around. . . . During one of my voyages, the black traders brought down, in different canoes, from twelve to fifteen hundred Negroes who had been purchased at one fair. They consisted chiefly of men and boys, the women seldom exceeding a third of the whole number. From forty to two hundred Negroes are generally purchased at a time by the black traders, according to the opulence of the buyer, and consist of all ages, from a month to sixty years and upwards. Scarcely any age or situation is deemed an exception, the price being proportionable. Women sometimes form a part of them, who happen to be so far advanced in their pregnancy as to be delivered during their journey from the fairs to the coast; and I have frequently seen instances of deliveries on board ship. . . .

When the Negroes, whom the black traders have to dispose of, are shown to the European purchasers, they first examine them relative to their age. They then minutely inspect their persons and inquire into the state of their health; if they are inflicted with any disease or are deformed or have bad eyes or teeth; if they are lame or weak in the joints or distorted in the back or of a slender make or narrow in the chest; in short, if they have been ill or are afflicted in any manner so as to render them incapable of much labor. If any of the foregoing defects are discovered in them they are rejected. But if approved of, they are generally taken on board the ship the same evening. The purchaser has liberty to return on the following morning, but not afterwards, such as upon re-examination are found exceptionable. . . .

Near the mainmast a partition is constructed of boards which reaches athwart the ship. This division is called a barricado. It is about eight feet in height and is made to project about two feet over the sides of the ship. In this barricado there is a door at which a sentinel is placed during the time the Negroes are permitted to come upon the deck. It serves to keep the different sexes apart; and as there are small holes in it, where blunderbusses are fixed and sometimes a cannon, it is found very convenient for quelling the insurrections that now and then happen. . . .

The men Negroes, on being brought aboard the ship, are immediately fastened together, two and two, by handcuffs on their wrists and by irons riveted on their legs. They are then sent down between the decks and placed in an apartment partitioned off for that purpose. The women also are placed in a separate apartment between the decks, but without being ironed. An adjoining room on the same deck is appointed for the boys. Thus they are all placed in different apartments.

But at the same time, however, they are frequently stowed so close, as to admit of no other position than lying on their sides. Nor will the height between decks, unless directly under the grating, permit the indulgence of an erect posture; especially where there are platforms, which is generally the case. These platforms are a kind of shelf, about eight or nine feet in breadth, extending from the side of the ship toward the centre. They are placed nearly midway between the decks, at the distance of two or three feet from each deck. Upon these the Negroes are stowed in the same manner as they are on the deck underneath.

In each of the apartments are placed three or four large buckets, of a conical form, nearly two feet in diameter at the bottom and only one foot at the top and in depth of about twenty-eight inches, to which, when necessary, the Negroes have recourse. It often happens that those who are placed at a distance from the buckets, in endeavoring to get to them, tumble over their companions, in consequence of their being shackled. These accidents, although unavoidable, are productive of continual quarrels in which some of them are always bruised. In this distressed situation, unable to proceed and prevented from getting to the tubs, they desist from the attempt; and as the necessities of nature are not to be resisted, ease themselves as they lie. This becomes a fresh source of boils and disturbances and tends to render the condition of the poor captive wretches still more uncomfortable. The nuisance arising from these circumstances is not infrequently increased by the tubs being too small for the purpose intended and their being emptied but once every day. The rule for doing so, however, varies in different ships according to the attention paid to the health and convenience of the slaves by the captain.

About eight o'clock in the morning the Negroes are generally brought upon deck. Their irons being examined, a long chain, which is locked to a ring-bolt fixed in the deck, is run through the rings of the shackles of the men and then locked to another ring-bolt fixed also in the deck. By this means fifty or sixty and sometimes more are fastened to one chain in order to prevent them from rising or endeavoring to escape. If the weather proves favorable they are permitted to remain in that situation till four or five in the afternoon when they are disengaged from the chain and sent below.

The diet of the Negroes while on board, consists chiefly of horse beans boiled to the consistency of a pulp; of boiled yams and rice and sometimes a small quantity of beef or pork. The latter are frequently taken from the provisions laid in for the sailors. They sometimes make use of a sauce composed of palm-oil mixed with flour, water and pepper, which the sailors call slabber-sauce. Yams are the favorite food of the Eboe [Ibo] or Bight Negroes, and rice or corn of those from the Gold or Windward Coast; each preferring the produce of their native soil. . . .

They are commonly fed twice a day; about eight o'clock in the morning and four in the afternoon. In most ships they are only fed with their own food once a day. Their food is served up to them in tubs about the size of a small water bucket. They are placed round these tubs, in companies of ten to each tub, out of which they feed themselves with wooden spoons. These they soon lose and when they are not allowed others they feed themselves with their hands. In favorable weather they are fed upon deck but in bad weather their food is given them below. Numberless quarrels take place among them during their meals; more especially when they are put upon short allowance, which frequently happens if the passage from the coast of Guinea to the West Indies islands proves of unusual length. In that case, the weak are obliged to be content with a very scanty portion. Their allowance of water is about half a pint each at every meal. It is handed round in a bucket and given to each Negro in a pannekin, a small utensil with a straight handle, somewhat similar to a sauce boat. However, when the ships approach the islands with a favourable breeze, the slaves are no longer restricted.

Upon the Negroes refusing to take sustenance, I have seen coals of fire, glowing hot, put on a shovel and placed so near their lips as to scorch and burn them. And this has been accompanied with threats of forcing them to swallow the coals if they any longer persisted in refusing to eat. These means have generally had the desired effect. I have also been credibly informed that a certain captain in the slave-trade, poured melted lead on such of his Negroes as obstinately refused their food.

Exercise being deemed necessary for the preservation of their health they are sometimes obliged to dance when the weather will permit their coming on deck. If they go about it reluctantly or do not move with agility, they are flogged; a person standing by them all the time with a cat-o'-nine-tails in his hands for the purpose. Their music, upon these occasions, consists of a drum, sometimes with only one head; and when that is worn out they make use of the bottom of one of the tubs before described. The poor wretches are frequently compelled to sing also; but when they do so, their songs are generally, as may naturally be expected, melancholy lamentations of their exile from their native country.

The women are furnished with beads for the purpose of affording them some diversion. But this end is generally defeated by the squabbles which are occasioned in consequence of their stealing from each other.

On board some ships the common sailors are allowed to have intercourse with such of the black women whose consent they can procure. And some of them have been known to take the inconstancy of their paramours so much to heart as to leap overboard and drown themselves. The officers are permitted to indulge their passions among them at pleasure and sometimes are guilty of such excesses as disgrace human nature. . . .

The hardships and inconveniences suffered by the Negroes during the passage are scarcely to be enumerated or conceived. They are far more violently affected by seasickness than Europeans. It frequently terminates in death, especially among the women. But the exclusion of fresh air is among the most intolerable. For the purpose of admitting this needful refreshment, most of the ships in the slave trade are provided, between the decks, with five or sick air-ports on each side of the ship of about five inches in length and four in breadth. In addition, some ships, but not one in twenty, have what they denominate wind-sails. But whenever the sea is rough and the rain heavy it becomes necessary to shut these and every other conveyance by which the air is admitted. The fresh air being thus excluded, the Negroes' rooms soon grow intolerable hot. The confined air, rendered noxious by the effluvia exhaled from their bodies and being repeatedly breathed, soon produces fevers and fluxes which generally carries off great numbers of them.

During the voyages I made, I was frequently witness to the fatal effects of this exclusion of fresh air. I will give one instance, as it serves to convey some idea, though a very faint one, of their terrible sufferings. . . . Some wet and blowing weather having occasioned the port-holes to be shut and the grating to be covered, fluxes and fevers among the Negroes ensued. While they were in this situation, I frequently went down among them till at length their room became so extremely hot as to be only bearable for a very short time. But the excessive heat was not the only thing that rendered their situation intolerable. The deck, that is the floor of their rooms, was so covered with the blood and mucus which had proceeded from them in consequence of the flux, that it resembled a slaughter-house. It is not in the power of the human imagination to picture a situation more dreadful or disgusting. Numbers of the slaves having fainted, they were carried upon deck where several of them died and the rest with great difficulty were restored. . . .

As very few of the Negroes can so far brook the loss of their liberty and the hardships they endure, they are ever on the watch to take advantage of the least negligence in their oppressors. Insurrections are frequently the consequence; which are seldom expressed without much bloodshed. Sometimes these are successful and the whole ship's company is cut off. They are likewise always ready to seize every opportunity for committing some acts of desperation to free themselves from their miserable state and notwithstanding the restraints which are laid, they often succeed.

Chapter 3

"Weary Traveler":

ARRIVAL IN THE NEW WORLD

In 1806, a year before the United States and Britain outlawed the African slave trade, George Pickard, an English physician, witnessed the sale of a newly-arrived boatload of enslaved Africans in the West Indies. To the white settlers, he wrote, "it seemed a day of feasting and hilarity, but to the poor Africans it was a period of heavy grief and affliction; for they were to be sold as beasts of burden—torn from each other—and widely dispersed."

The terrors of the Middle Passage were followed by another series of shocks. The "unpitied sable beings" were put on public auction. The purchasers, observed Pickard, "handled and inspected them, with as little concern as if they had been examining cattle." "They turned them about, felt them, viewed their shapes and limbs, and looked into their mouths, made them jump and throw out their arms, and subjected them to all the means of trial as if dealing for a horse or other brute animal."

Family ties were often disregarded by the purchasers. One slave, Pickard wrote, told to stand up, refused, and "sunk his chin upon his breast and hung his head." He pointed to an African woman, "held up two fingers to the auctioneer, and implored the multitude in anxious suppliant gestures . . . which seemed to say—'Let us be sold together.'"

85

1
Olaudah Equiano

"DREAD AND TREMBLING"

Olaudah Equiano offers a firsthand account of his arrival in the West Indies in 1756.

As the vessel drew nearer, we plainly saw the harbor and other ships of different kinds and sizes and we soon anchored amongst them off Bridgetown. Many merchants and planters came on board. . . . They put us in separate parcels and examined us attentively. They also made us jump, and pointed to the land, signifying we were to go there. We thought by this we should be eaten by these ugly men, as they appeared to us. When soon after we were all put down under the deck again, there was much dread and trembling among us and nothing but bitter cries to be heard all the night from the apprehensions. At last the white people got some old slaves from the land to pacify us. They told us we were not to be eaten, but to work, and were soon to go on land, where we should see many of our country people. This report eased us much, and sure enough, soon after we landed, there came to us Africans of all languages.

We were conducted immediately to the merchant's yard, where we were all pent up together, like so many sheep in a fold, without regard to sex or age. As every object was new to me, everything I saw filled me with surprise. What struck me first was that the houses were built with bricks and stories, and in every respect different from those I had seen in Africa, but I was still more astonished to see people on horseback. I did not know what this could mean, and indeed I thought these people were full of nothing but magical arts. While I was in this astonishment, one of my fellow prisoners spoke to a countryman of his about the horses who said they were the same kind they had in their country. I understood

Source: *The Interesting Narrative of the Life of Olaudah Equiano or Gustavus Vassa the African* (London, 1789).

87

them, though they were from a distant part of Africa and I thought
it odd I had not seen any horses there; but afterwards when I came
to converse with different Africans, I found they had many horses
amongst them, and much larger than those I then saw.

We were not many days in the merchant's custody, before we
were sold after their usual manner. . . . On a signal given, (as the
beat of a drum), buyers rush at once into the yard where the slaves
are confined, and make a choice of that parcel they like best. The
noise and clamor with which this is attended, and the eagerness
visible in the countenances of the buyers, serve not a little to increase the apprehension of terrified Africans. . . . In this manner,
without scruple, are relations and friends separated, most of them
never to see each other again. I remember in the vessel in which I
was brought over . . . there were several brothers who, in the sale,
were sold in different lots; and it was very moving on this occasion,
to see and hear their cries in parting.

2
Alexander Falconbridge

"VARIOUS DECEPTIONS ARE USED IN THE DISPOSAL OF SICK SLAVES"

*Alexander Falconbridge describes the reaction of enslaved
Africans to their sale.*

When the ships arrive in the West Indies (the chief mart for
this inhuman merchandize), the slaves are disposed as I have before observed by different methods. Sometimes the mode of disposal is that of selling them by what is termed a scramble, and a
day is soon fixed for that purpose. Previously the sick or refused
slaves, of which there are frequently many, are usually conveyed on
shore and sold at a tavern, by vendue or public auction. These in
general are purchased . . . upon speculation, at so low a price as five
or six dollars a head. I was informed by a mulatto woman that she
purchased a sick slave at Grenada, upon speculation, for the small

Source: Alexander Falconbridge, *An Account of the Slave Trade on the Coast of Africa*
(London, 1788).

sum of one dollar, as the poor wretch was apparently dying of the flux. It seldom happens that any who are carried ashore in the emaciated state to which they are generally reduced by that disorder long survive after their landing. I once saw sixteen conveyed on shore and sold in the foregoing manner, the whole of whom died before I left the island. Sometimes the captains march their slaves through the town at which they intend to dispose of them, and then place them in rows where they are examined and purchased.

The mode of selling them by scramble having fallen under my observation the oftenest, I shall be more particular in describing it. Being some years ago, at one of the islands in the West Indies, I was witness to a sale by scramble, where about 250 Negroes were sold. Upon this occasion all the Negroes scrambled for bear an equal price; which is agreed upon between the captains and the purchasers before the sale begins. On a day appointed, the Negroes were landed and placed together in a large yard belonging to the merchants to whom the ship was consigned. As soon as the hour agreed on arrived, the doors of the yard were suddenly thrown open and in rushed a considerable number of purchasers, with all the ferocity of brutes. Some instantly seized such of the Negroes as they could conveniently lay hold of with their hands. Others being prepared with several handkerchiefs tied together, encircled as many as they were able. While others, by means of a rope, effected the same purpose. It is scarcely possible to describe the confusion of which this mode of selling is productive. It likewise causes much animosity among the purchasers who not infrequently fall out and quarrel with each other. The poor astonished Negroes were so terrified by these proceedings, that several of them, through fear climbed over the walls of the courtyard and ran wild about the town, but were soon hunted down and retaken. . . .

Various deceptions are used in the disposal of sick slaves and many of these must excite in every humane mind the liveliest sensations of horror. I have been well informed that a Liverpool captain boasted of his having cheated some Jews by the following stratagem. A lot of slaves afflicted with the flux, being about to be landed for sale, he directed the ship's surgeons to stop the anus of each of them with oakum. Thus prepared they were landed and taken to the accustomed place of sale, where, being unable to stand but for a very short time, they were usually permitted to sit. The buyers, when they examined them, oblige them to stand up in order to see if there be any discharge; and when they do not perceive this appearance they consider it as a symptom of recovery. In the present instance, such an appearance being prevented, the bargain was struck and the slaves were accordingly sold. But it was not long before discovery ensued. The excruciating pain which the prevention of a discharge of such an acrimonious nature occasioned, not being able to be borne by the poor wretches, the temporary obstruction was removed and the deluded purchasers were speedily convinced of the imposition.

Chapter 4

"We Raise de Wheat, Dey Gib Us de Corn":

CONDITIONS OF LIFE

In 1852, the New York Times commissioned Frederick Law Olmsted to travel through the Cotton Kingdom and conduct an objective investigation of slavery. His assignment: to assess slaves' working conditions, the type of food they ate, the use of the whip by masters and overseers, and the amount of free time available to slaves. For fourteen months, Olmsted crisscrossed the South on horseback, stagecoach, and train; then, between 1856 and 1860, he published three volumes of his observations. He depicted slavery as a wasteful and inefficient system, which degraded labor, exhausted soil, and deprived slaves of any incentives to work hard. He charged that planters, fearful of sabotage or carelessness, provided slaves with only simple, heavy implements, and depicted slave labor as crude, brutish work.

Historians now know that Olmsted's portrait of slavery was seriously distorted. Far from being inefficient, slave labor was highly productive. While cultivating cotton, rice, and tobacco was hard, backbreaking work, it also required a high degree of care and skill. Moreover, many slaves served as skilled craftsmen, working as blacksmiths, butchers, carpenters, coopers, bricklayers, metal workers, tanners, weavers, and wheelwrights.

This section's selections offer graphic portraits of life under slavery. From these eyewitness accounts of slavery, it is possible to reach our own conclusions about slaves' working conditions and their diet, clothing, and housing.

1
Solomon Northrup

"THERE IS NO SUCH THING AS REST"

Solomon Northrup was a free black who was kidnapped in New York and sold into slavery for twelve years. He was finally returned to freedom through the efforts of New York's governor. In the following selection he describes how cotton was raised on his Louisiana plantation.

The hands are required to be in the cotton field as soon as it is light in the morning, and, with the exception of ten or fifteen minutes, which is given them at noon to swallow their allowance of cold bacon, they are not permitted to be a moment idle until it is too dark to see, and when the moon is full, they often times labor till the middle of the night. They do not dare to stop even at dinner time, nor return to the quarters, however late it be, until the order to halt is given by the driver.

The day's work over in the field, the baskets are "toted," or in other words, carried to the gin-house, where the cotton is weighed. No matter how fatigued and weary he may be—no matter how much he longs for sleep and rest—a slave never approaches the gin-house with his basket of cotton but with fear. If it falls short in weight—if he has not performed the full task appointed him, he knows that he must suffer. And if he has exceeded it by ten or twenty pounds, in all probability his master will measure the next day's task accordingly. So, whether he has too little or too much, his approach to the gin-house is always with fear and trembling. Most frequently they have too little, and therefore it is they who are not anxious to leave the field. After weighing, follow the whippings; and then the baskets are carried to the cotton house, and their contents stored away like hay, all hands being sent in to tramp it down. If the cotton is not dry, instead of taking it to the gin-house at once, it is laid upon platforms, two feet high, and some three times as

Source: *Twelve Years a Slave: Narrative of Solomon Northrup* (Auburn, N.Y., 1853).

wide, covered with boards or plank, with narrow walks running between them.

This done, the labor of the day is not yet ended, by any means. Each one must then attend to his respective chores. One feeds the mules, another the swine—another cuts the wood, and so forth; besides, the packing is all done by candle light. Finally, at a late hour, they reach the quarters, sleepy and overcome with the long day's toil. Then a fire must be kindled in the cabin, the corn ground in the small hand-mill, and supper, and dinner for the next day in the field, prepared. All that is allowed them is corn and bacon, which is given out at the corncrib and smoke-house every Sunday morning. Each one receives, as his weekly allowance, three and a half pounds of bacon, and corn enough to make a peck of meal. That is all—no tea, coffee, sugar, and with the exception of a very scanty sprinkling now and then, no salt. . . .

An hour before daylight the horn is blown. Then the slaves arouse, prepare their breakfast, fill a gourd with water, in another deposit their dinner of cold bacon and corn cake, and hurry to the field again. It is an offense invariably followed by a flogging, to be found at the quarters after daybreak. Then the fears and labors of another day begin; and until its close there is no such thing as rest. . . .

In the month of January, generally, the fourth and last picking is completed. Then commences the harvesting of corn. . . . Ploughing, planting, picking cotton, gathering the corn, and pulling and burning stalks, occupies the whole of the four seasons of the year. Drawing and cutting wood, pressing cotton, fattening and killing hogs are but incidental labors.

2
Charles Ball

"THE GENERAL FEATURES OF SLAVERY ARE THE SAME EVERYWHERE"

For forty years, Charles Ball toiled as a slave in Maryland, South Carolina, and Georgia, and, according to his autobiography, managed to escape twice. In the following selection, he describes the regimen on a tobacco plantation.

Source: Charles Ball, *Fifty Years in Chains; or, the Life of an American Slave* (New York, 1858).

In Maryland and Virginia, although the slaves are treated with so much rigour, and oftimes with so much cruelty, I have seen instances of the greatest tenderness of feeling on the part of their owners. I, myself, had three masters in Maryland, and I cannot say now, even after having resided so many years in a a state where slavery is not tolerated, that either of them (except the last, who sold me to the Georgians, and was an unfeeling man,) used me worse than they had a moral right to do, regarding me merely as an article of property, and not entitled to any rights as a man, political or civil. My mistresses, in Maryland, were all good women; and the mistress of my wife, in whose kitchen I spent my Sundays and many of my nights, for several years, was a lady of most benevolent and kindly feelings. She was a true friend to me, and I shall always venerate her memory. . . .

If the proprietors of the soil in Maryland and Virginia, were skillful cultivators—had their lands in good condition—and kept no more slaves on each estate, than would be sufficient to work the soil in a proper manner, and kept up the repairs of the place—the condition of the coloured people would not be, by any means, a comparatively unhappy one. I am convinced, that in nine cases in ten, the hardships and suffering of the coloured population of lower Virginia, are attributable to the poverty and distress of its owners. In many instances, an estate scarcely yields enough to feed and clothe the slaves in a comfortable manner, without allowing anything for the support of the master and family; but it is obvious, that the family must first be supported, and the slaves must be content with the surplus—and this, on a poor, old, worn out tobacco plantation, is often very small, and wholly inadequate to the comfortable sustenance of the hands, as they are called. There, in many places, nothing is allowed to the poor Negro, but his peck of corn per week, without the sauce of a salt herring, or even a little salt itself. . . .

The general features of slavery are the same everywhere; but the utmost rigour of the system, is only to be met with, on the cotton plantations of Carolina and Georgia, or in the rice fields which skirt the deep swamps and morasses of the southern rivers. In the tobacco fields of Maryland and Virginia, great cruelties are practiced—not so frequently by the owners, as by the overseers of the slaves; but yet, the tasks are not so excessive as in the cotton region, nor is the press of labour so incessant throughout the year. It is true, that from the period when the tobacco plants are set in the field, there is no resting time until it is housed; but it is planted out about the first of May, and must be cut and taken out of the field before the frost comes. After it is hung and dried, the labor of stripping and preparing it for the hogshead in leaf, or of manufacturing it into twist, is comparatively a work of leisure and ease. Besides, on almost every plantation the hands are able to complete the work of preparing the tobacco by January, and sometimes earlier; so that the winter months, form some sort of respite from the toils of the year. The people are obliged, it is true, to occupy themselves in cutting wood for the house, making rails and repairing fences, and in clearing new land, to raise the tobacco plants for the next year; but as there is usually time enough, and to spare, for the completion of all this work, before the season arrives for setting the plants in the field; the men are seldom flogged much, unless they are very lazy or negligent, and the women are allowed to remain in the house, in the very cold, snowy, or rainy weather. . . .

In Maryland I never knew a mistress or a young mistress, who would not listen to the complaints of the slaves. It is true, we were always obliged to approach the door of the mansion, with our hats in our hands, and the most subdued and beseeching language in our mouths—but, in return, we generally received words of kindness, and very often a redress of our grievances; though I have known very great ladies, who would never grant any request from the plantation hands, but always referred them and their petitions to their master, under a pretence, that they could not meddle with things that did not belong to the house. The mistresses of the great families, generally gave mild language to the slaves; though they sometimes sent for the overseer and had them severely flogged; but I have never heard any mistress, in either Maryland or Virginia, indulge in the low, vulgar and profane vituperations, of which I was myself the object, in Georgia, for many years, whenever I came into the presence of my mistress. Flogging—though often severe and excruciating in Maryland, is not practiced with the order, regularity and system, to which it is often reduced in the South. On the Potomac, if a slave gives offence, he is generally chastised on the spot, in the field where he is at work, as the overseer always carried a whip—sometimes a twisted cow-hide, sometimes a kind of horse-whip, and very often a simple hickory switch or gad, cut in the adjoining woods. For stealing meat, or other provisions, or for any of the higher offences, the slaves are stripped, tied up by the hands—sometimes by the thumbs—and whipped at the quarter— but many times, on a large tobacco plantation, there is not more than one of these regular whippings in a week—though on others, where the master happens to be a bad man, or a drunkard—the back of the unhappy Maryland slaves, is seamed with scars from his neck to his hips.

3
Josiah Henson

"WE LODGED IN LOG HUTS"

*Josiah Henson spent thirty years on a plantation in Mont-
gomery County, Maryland, before he escaped slavery and
became a Methodist preacher, abolitionist, lecturer, and
founder of a cooperative colony of former slaves in Canada. His memoirs, published in 1849, provided Harriet
Beecher Stowe with her model of Uncle Tom.*

My earliest employments were, to carry buckets of water to
the men at work, and to hold a horse-plough, used for weeding
between the rows of corn. As I grew older and taller, I was en-
trusted with the care of master's saddle-horse. Then a hoe was put
into my hands, and I was soon required to do the day's work of a
man; and it was not long before I could do it, at least as well as my
associates in misery.

A description of the everyday life of a slave on a southern
plantation illustrates the character and habits of the slave and the
slaveholder, created and perpetuated by their relative position. The
principal food of those upon my master's plantation consisted of
corn-meal and salt herrings; to which was added in summer a little
buttermilk, and the few vegetables which each might raise for himself and his family, on the little piece of ground which was assigned
to him for the purpose, called a truck-patch.

In ordinary times we had two regular meals in a day: breakfast at twelve o'clock, after laboring from daylight, and supper
when the work of the remainder of the day was over. In harvest
season we had three. Our dress was of tow-cloth; for the children,
nothing but a shirt; for the older ones a pair of pantaloons or a
gown in addition, according to the sex. Besides these, in the winter
a round jacket or overcoat, a wool-hat once in two or three years,
for the males, and a pair of coarse shoes once a year.

We lodged in log huts, and on the bare ground. Wooden floors
were an unknown luxury. In a single room were huddled, like cattle, ten or a dozen persons, men, women, and children. All ideas of

Source: *"Uncle Tom's Story of His Life": An Autobiography of the Rev. Josiah Henson*
(London, 1877).

refinement and decency were, of course, out of the question. We had neither bedsteads, nor furniture of any description. Our beds were collections of straw and old rags, thrown down in the corners and boxed in with boards; a single blanket the only covering. Our favourite way of sleeping, however, was on a plank, our heads raised on an old jacket and our feet toasting before the smouldering fire. The wind whistled and the rain and snow blew in through the cracks, and the damp earth soaked in the moisture till the floor was miry as a pig-sty. Such were our houses. In these wretched hovels were we penned at night, and fed by day; here were the children born and the sick—neglected.

4

Francis Henderson

"MY . . . BEDSTEAD CONSISTED OF A BOARD WIDE ENOUGH TO SLEEP ON"

Francis Henderson was nineteen when he managed to escape from a slave plantation outside of Washington, D.C., in 1841. Here, he describes conditions on his plantation.

Our houses were but log huts—the tops partly open—ground floor—rain would come through. My aunt was quite an old woman, and had been sick several years; in rains I have seen her moving from one part of the house to the other, and rolling her bedclothes about to try to keep dry—everything would be dirty and muddy. I lived in the house with my aunt. My bed and bedstead consisted of a board wide enough to sleep on—one end on a stool, the other placed near the fire. My pillow consisted of my jacket—my covering was whatever I could get. My bedtick was the board itself. And this was the way the single men slept—but we were comfortable in this way of sleeping, being used to it. I only remember having but one blanket from my owners up to the age of nineteen, when I ran away.

Our allowance was given weekly—a peck of sifted corn meal,

Source: Benjamin Drew, *A North-Side View of Slavery* (Boston, 1856).

a dozen and a half herrings, two and a half pounds of pork. Some of the boys would eat this up in three days—then they had to steal, or they could not perform their daily tasks. They would visit the hog-pen, sheep-pen, and granaries. I do not remember one slave but who stole some things—they were driven to it as a matter of necessity. I myself did this—many a time have I, with others, run among the stumps in chase of a sheep, that we might have something to eat. . . . In regard to cooking, sometimes many have to cook at one fire, and before all could get to the fire to bake hoe cakes, the overseer's horn would sound: then they must go at any rate. Many a time I have gone along eating a piece of bread and meat, or herring broiled on the coals—I never sat down at a table to eat except at harvest time, all the time I was a slave. In harvest time, the cooking is done at the great house, as the hands they have are wanted in the field. This was more like people, and we liked it, for we sat down then at meals. In the summer we had one pair of linen trousers given us—nothing else; every fall, one pair of woolen pantaloons, one woolen jacket, and two cotton shirts.

My master had four sons in his family. They all left except one, who remained to be a driver. He would often come to the field and accuse the slave of having taken so and so. If we denied it, he would whip the grown up ones to make them own it. Many a time, when we didn't know he was anywhere around, he would be in the woods watching us—first thing we would know, he would be sitting on the fence looking down upon us, and if any had been idle, the young master would visit him with blows. I have known him to kick my aunt, an old woman who had raised and nursed him, and I have seen him punish my sisters awfully with hickories from the woods.

The slaves are watched by the patrols, who ride about to try to catch them off the quarters, especially at the house of a free person of color. I have known the slaves to stretch clothes lines across the street, high enough to let the horse pass, but not the rider; then the boys would run, and the patrols in full chase would be thrown off by running against the lines. The patrols are poor white men, who live by plundering and stealing, getting rewards for runaways, and setting up little shops on the public roads. They will take whatever the slaves steal, paying in money, whiskey, or whatever the slaves want. They take pigs, sheep, wheat, corn—anything that's raised they encourage the slaves to steal: these they take to market next day. It's all speculation—all a matter of self-interest, and when the slaves run away, these same traders catch them if they can, to get the reward. If the slave threatens to expose his traffic, he does not care—for the slave's word is good for nothing—it would not be taken.

5
Jacob Stroyer

"MOST OF THE CABINS . . . WERE BUILT . . . TO CONTAIN TWO FAMILIES"

One of fifteen children, Jacob Stroyer was born on a plantation twenty-eight miles from Columbia, South Carolina, in 1849. After the Civil War he became an African Methodist Episcopal minister, serving in Salem, Massachusetts.

Most of the cabins in the time of slavery were built so as to contain two families; some had partitions, while others had none. When there were no partitions each family would fit up its own part as it could; sometimes they got old boards and nailed them up, stuffing the cracks with rags; when they could not get boards they hung up old clothes. When the family increased the children all slept together, both boys and girls, until one got married; then a part of another cabin was assigned to that one, but the rest would have to remain with their mother and father, as in childhood, unless they could get with some of their relatives or friends who had small families, or unless they were sold; but of course the rules of modesty were held in some degrees by the slaves, while it could not be expected that they could entertain the highest degree of it, on account of their condition. A portion of the time the young men slept in the apartment known as the kitchen, and the young women slept in the room with their mother and father. The two families had to use one fireplace. One who was accustomed to the way in which the slaves lived in their cabins could tell as soon as he entered whether they were friendly or not, for when they did not agree the fires of the two families did not meet on the hearth, but there was a vacancy between them, that was a sign of disagreement. In a case of this kind, when either of the families stole a hog, cow or sheep from the master, he had to carry it to some of his family, for fear of being betrayed by the other family. On one occasion a man, who lived with one unfriendly, stole a hog, killed it and carried some of the meat home. He was seen by some one of the other

Source: Jacob Stroyer, *My Life in the South* (enlarged edition; Salem, Mass., 1898).

family, who reported him to the overseer, and he gave the man a severe whipping. . . .

No doubt you would like to know how the slaves could sleep in their cabins in summer, when it was so very warm. When it was too warm for them to sleep comfortably, they all slept under trees until it grew too cool, that is along in the month of October. Then they took up their beds and walked.

6

James Martin

"THE SLAVES ARE PUT IN STALLS LIKE . . . CATTLE"

James Martin, born on a Virginia plantation in 1847, was ninety years old when he was interviewed by the Works Progress Administration in 1937. After the Civil War he moved to Texas, where he served in the 9th U.S. Cavalry and later worked as a cowboy. Here, he describes a slave auction.

The slaves are put in stalls like the pens they use for cattle—a man and his wife with a child on each arm. And there's a curtain, sometimes just a sheet over the front of the stall, so the bidders can't see the "stock" too soon. The overseer's standin' just outside with a big black snake whip and a pepperbox pistol in his belt. Across the square a little piece, there's a big platform with steps leadin' to it.

Then, they pulls up the curtain, and the bidders is crowdin' around. Them in back can't see, so the overseer drives the slaves out to the platform, and he tells the ages of the slaves and what they can do. They have white gloves there, and one of the bidders takes a pair of gloves and rubs his fingers over a man's teeth, and he says to the overseer, "You call this buck twenty years old? Why there's cut worms in his teeth. He's forty years old, if he's a day." So they knock this buck down for a thousand dollars. They calls the men "bucks" and the women "wenches."

Source: George P. Rawick, ed., *The American Slave: A Composite Autobiography* (Westport, Conn., 1972), Texas Narr., Vol. 5, 62–65.

When the slaves is on the platform—what they calls the "block"—the overseer yells, "Tom or Jason, show the bidders how you walk." Then, the slave steps across the platform, and the biddin' starts.

At these slave auctions, the overseer yells, "Say, you bucks and wenches, get in your hole. Come out here." Then, he makes 'em hop, he makes 'em trot, he makes 'em jump. "How much," he yells, "for this buck? A thousand? Eleven hundred? Twelve hundred dollars?" Then the bidders makes offers accordin' to size and build.

Cart-boy by Porte Crayon [David Hunter Strother]
in THE OLD SOUTH ILLUSTRATED, Harper, 1857,
p. 146.

Chapter 5

"Like a Motherless Child":

CHILDHOOD

As they remembered their lives in bondage, former slaves invariably recalled a moment in their childhood when they were first forced to confront the harsh realities of slavery. For one former Louisiana slave that moment came when her mistress whipped her for saying "to missis, 'My mother sent me.' We were not allowed to call our mammies 'mother.' It was too near the way of the white folks." For other ex-slaves, the shock of recognition came upon seeing their parents whipped or upon confronting the fact that their parents were unable to protect them from punishment from a master or an overseer.

For a Virginia slave known only as Charles, the crucial moment came when his white playmates first began to treat him as a slave. His master's son recalled that moment. "It is customary in nearly all households in the South for the white and black children connected with each other to play together," he wrote. "The trial . . . comes when the young Negroes who have hitherto been on this democratic footing with the young whites are presently deserted by their . . . companions, who enter upon school-life . . . ceasing to associate with their swarthy comrades any longer, meet them in the future with the air of the master." Charles responded with bitterness and defiance. He set fire to the family's house and was subsequently sold to the deep South.

1
Jacob Stroyer

"I CANNOT DO ANYTHING FOR YOU"

In the following selection, Jacob Stroyer describes growing up under slavery. Note the ways that some slave children sought to imitate the behavior of their white owners and the ways that slave owners undermined the authority of slave parents.

Gilbert was a cruel [slave] boy. He used to strip his fellow Negroes while in the woods, and whip them two or three times a week, so that their backs were all scarred, and threatened them with severer punishments if they told; this state of things had been going on for quite a while. As I was a favorite with Gilbert, I always managed to escape a whipping, with the promise of keeping the secret of the punishment of the rest. . . . But finally, one day, Gilbert said to me, "Take," as he used to call me, "you am a good boy, but I'm gwine to wip you some to-day, as I wip dem toder boys." Of course I was required to strip off my only garment, which was an Osnaburg linen shirt, worn by both sexes of the Negro children in the summer. As I stood trembling before my merciless superior, who had a switch in his hand, thousands of thoughts went through my little mind as to how to get rid of the whipping. I finally fell upon a plan which I hoped would save me from a punishment that was near at hand. . . . I commenced reluctantly to take off my shirt, at the same time pleading with Gilbert, who paid no attention to my prayer. . . . Having satisfied myself that no mercy was to be found with Gilbert, I drew my shirt off and threw it over his head, and bounded forward on a run in the direction of the sound of the [nearby] carpenters. By the time he got from the entanglement of my garment, I had quite a little start of him. . . . As I got near to the carpenters, one of them ran and met me, into whose arms I jumped. The man into whose arms I ran was Uncle Benjamin, my

Source: Jacob Stroyer, *My Life in the South* (enlarged edition; Salem, Mass., 1898).

mother's uncle. . . . I told him that Gilbert had been in the habit of stripping the boys and whipping them two or three times a week, when we went into the woods, and threatened them with greater punishment if they told. . . . Gilbert was brought to trial, severely whipped, and they made him beg all the children to pardon him for his treatment to them.

[My] father . . . used to take care of horses and mules. I was around with him in the barn yard when but a very small boy; of course that gave me an early relish for the occupation of hostler, and I soon made known my preference to Col. Singleton, who was a sportsman, and an owner of fine horses. And, although I was too small to work, the Colonel granted my request; hence I was allowed to be numbered among those who took care of the fine horses and learned to ride. But I soon found that my new occupation demanded a little more than I cared for.

It was not long after I had entered my new work before they put me upon the back of a horse which threw me to the ground almost as soon as I had reached his back. It hurt me a little, but that was not the worst of it, for when I got up there was a man standing near with a switch in hand, and he immediately began to beat me. Although I was a very bad boy, this was the first time I had been whipped by anyone except father and mother, so I cried out in a tone of voice as if I would say, this is the first and last whipping you will give me when father gets hold of you.

When I had got away from him I ran to father with all my might, but soon found my expectation blasted, as father very coolly said to me, "Go back to your work and be a good boy, for I cannot do anything for you." But that did not satisfy me, so on I went to mother with my complaint and she came out to the man who had whipped me; he was a groom, a white man master had hired to train the horses. Mother and he began to talk, then he took a whip and started for her, and she ran from him, talking all the time. I ran back and forth between mother and him until he stopped beating her. After the fight between the groom and mother, he took me back to the stable yard and gave me a severe flogging. And, although mother failed to help me at first, still I had faith that when he had taken me back to the stable yard, and commenced whipping me, she would come and stop him, but I looked in vain, for she did not come.

Then the idea first came to me that I, with my dear father and mother and the rest of my fellow Negroes, were doomed to cruel treatment through life, and was defenseless. But when I found that father and mother could not save me from punishment, as they themselves had to submit to the same treatment, I concluded to appeal to the sympathy of the groom, who seemed to have full control over me; but my pitiful cries never touched his sympathy. . . .

One day, about two weeks after Boney Young [the white man who trained horses for Col. Singleton] and mother had the conflict, he called me to him. . . . When I got to him he said, "Go and bring me the switch, sir." I answered, "yes, sir," and off I went and brought him one . . . [and] he gave me a first-class flogging. . . .

When I went home to father and mother, I said to them, "Mr. Young is whipping me too much now, I shall not stand it, I shall fight him." Father said to me, "You must not do that, because if you do he will say that your mother and I advised you to do it, and it will make it hard for your mother and me, as well as for yourself. You must do as I told you, my son: do your work the best you can, and do not say anything." I said to father, "But I don't know what I have done that he should whip me; he does not tell me what wrong I have done, he simply calls me to him and whips me when he gets ready." Father said, "I can do nothing more than to pray to the Lord to hasten the time when these things shall be done away; that is all I can do. . . ."

2
James W. C. Pennington

"THE WANT OF PARENTAL CARE AND ATTENTION"

In 1849, James W. C. Pennington, the minister of a Presbyterian Church in New York City and the recipient of a degree from the University of Heidelberg in Germany, published a narrative of his life that revealed the astonishing news that he was a fugitive slave and a former blacksmith from Maryland. In his account of his life, Pennington offers the following reflections on the impact of slavery upon slave children.

Source: *The Fugitive Blacksmith or, Events in the History of James W. C. Pennington* (2nd ed.; London, 1849).

My feelings are always outraged when I hear [ministers] speak of "kind masters,"—"Christian masters,"—"the mildest form of slavery,"—"well fed and clothed slaves," as extenuations of slavery; I am satisfied they either mean to pervert the truth, or they do not know what they say. The being of slavery, its soul and body, lives and moves in the chattel principle, the property principle, the bill of sale principle; the cart-whip, starvation, and nakedness, are its inevitable consequences to a greater or less extent, warring with the dispositions of men. . . .

Another evil of slavery [is] . . . the want of parental care and attention. My parents were not able to give any attention to their children during the day. I often suffered much from hunger and other similar causes. To estimate the sad state of a slave child, you must look at it as a helpless human being thrown upon the world without the benefit of its natural guardians. It is thrown into the world without a social circle to flee to for hope, shelter, comfort, or instruction. The social circle, with all its heaven-ordained blessings, is of the utmost importance to the tender child; but of this, the slave child, however tender and delicate, is robbed.

There is another source of evil to slave children, which I cannot forbear to mention here, as one which early embittered my life,—I mean the tyranny of the master's children. My master had two sons, about the ages and sizes of my older brother and myself. We were not only required to recognize these young sirs as our young masters, but they felt themselves to be such; and, in consequence of this feeling, they sought to treat us with the same air of authority that their father did the older slaves.

Another evil of slavery that I felt severely about this time, was the tyranny and abuse of the overseers. These men seem to look with an evil eye upon children. I was once visiting a menagerie, and being struck with the fact, that the lion was comparatively indifferent to every one around his cage, while he eyed with peculiar keenness a little boy I had; the keeper informed me that such was always the case. Such is true of those human beings in the slave states, called overseers. They seem to take pleasure in torturing the children of slaves, long before they are large enough to be put at the hoe, and consequently under the whip.

We had an overseer, named Blackstone; he was an extremely cruel man to the working hands. He always carried a long hickory whip, a kind of pole. He kept three or four of these in order that he might not at any time be without one.

I once found one of these hickories lying in the yard, and supposing that he had thrown it away, I picked it up, and boy-like, was using it for a horse; he came from the field, and seeing me with it, fell upon me with the one he then had in his hand, and flogged me most cruelly. From that, I lived in constant dread of that man; and he would show how much he delighted in cruelty by chasing me from my play with threats and imprecations. I have lain for hours in a wood, or behind a fence, to hide from his eye. . . .

When I was nine years of age, myself and my brother were hired out from home; my brother was placed with a pump-maker, and I was placed with a stone-mason. We were both in a town some six miles from home. As the men with whom we lived were not slaveholders, we enjoyed some relief from the peculiar evils of slavery. Each of us lived in a family where there was no other Negro.

The slaveholders in that state [Maryland] often hire the children of their slaves out to non-slaveholders, not only because they save themselves the expense of taking care of them, but in this way they get among their slaves useful trades. They put a bright slave-boy with a tradesman, until he gets such a knowledge of the trade as to be able to do his own work, and then he takes him home. I remained with the stonemason until I was eleven years of age: at this time I was taken home. This was another serious period in my childhood; I was separated from my older brother, to whom I was much attached; he continued at his place, and not only learned the trade to great perfection, but finally became the property of the man with whom he lived, so that our separation was permanent, as we never lived nearer after, than six miles.

3
Lunsford Lane

"I DISCOVERED THE DIFFERENCE BETWEEN MYSELF AND MY MASTER'S WHITE CHILDREN"

Lunsford Lane, who grew up on a plantation near Raleigh, North Carolina, manufactured pipes and tobacco and succeeded in saving enough money to buy his own freedom and purchase his wife and seven children. Here he describes his experiences as a slave child.

Source: *The Narrative of Lunsford Lane* (Boston, 1842).

My father was a slave to a near neighbor. The apartment where I was born and where I spent my childhood and youth was called "the kitchen," situated some fifteen or twenty rods from the "great house." Here the house servants lodged and lived, and here the meals were prepared for the people in the mansion. . . .

My infancy was spent upon the floor, in a rough cradle, or sometimes in my mother's arms. My early boyhood in playing with the other boys and girls, colored and white, in the yard, and occasionally doing such little matters of labor as one of so young years could. I knew no difference between myself and the white children; nor did they seem to know any in turn. Sometimes my master would come out and give a biscuit to me, and another to one of his own white boys; but I did not perceive the difference between us. I had no brothers or sisters, but there were other colored families living in the same kitchen, and the children playing in the same yard with me and my mother. . . .

When I began to work, I discovered the difference between myself and my master's white children. They began to order me about, and were told to do so by my master and mistress. I found, too, that they had learned to read, while I was not permitted to have a book in my hand. To be in possession of anything written or printed, was regarded as an offence. And then there was the fear that I might be sold away from those who were dear to me, and conveyed to the far South. I had learned that being a slave I was subject to the worst (to us) of all calamities; and I knew of others in similar situations to myself, thus sold away. My friends were not numerous; but in proportion as they were few they were dear; and the thought that I might be separated from them forever, was like that of having the heart wrenched from its socket; while the idea of being conveyed to the far South, seemed infinitely worse than the terrors of death.

Chapter 6

"Nobody Knows de Trouble I See":

FAMILY

A former slave reacted bitterly to the remark that his former master had been kind to his slaves. "Kind! I was dat man's slave; and he sold my wife, and he sold my two chill'en . . . Kind!, yes, he gib me corn enough, and he gib me pork enough, and he neber gib me one lick wid de whip, but whar's my wife?—whar's my chill'en? Take away de pork, I say; take away de corn, I can work and raise dese for myself; but gib me back de wife of my bosom, and gib me back my poor chill'on as was sold away."

Nothing provided greater ammunition for critics of slavery than the outrages committed on slave families. Southern law did not recognize or protect slave marriages or slave family ties. Slave owners were free to sell husbands from wives and parents from children and to sexually exploit slave wives or daughters.

Certainly, many owners believed that it was in their own self-interest to encourage stable family lives. They knew that stable families raised slave morale, reduced the likelihood of slaves running away, and encouraged a high slave birthrate. Thus, many slaveholders promoted stable families by participating in slave marriage ceremonies, providing slave families with separate garden plots, prohibiting divorce, and severely punishing adultery.

But slave owners also regarded slaves as a form of property that might be sold at any time. In conducting marriages, slaveholders pointedly omitted any words that indicated that slave unions were perpetual. A former slave noted that masters would never say "'What God done jined, cain't no man pull asunder.'" Instead, they "jus' say, 'Now you married.'" A slave preacher thought slave owners should conclude the ceremony with the words: "till death or buckra [master] do you part."

Many slave spouses resided on separate farms or plantations. Millie Barber's parents lived five miles apart, and her father could

111

only visit his family if he received permission from his owner. As she later recalled: "My pa have to git a pass to come to see my mammy. He come sometimes widout de pass. Patrollers catch him way up de chimney hidin' one night; they stripped him right befo' mammy and give him thirty-nine lashes." After purchasing new slaves, some masters required them to take new husbands or wives. A former Louisiana slave, Stephen Jordon, described the anguish that this could cause: "I myself had my wife on another plantation. The woman my master gave me had a husband on another plantation. Every thing was mixed up. My other wife had two children for me, but the woman master gave me had no children. We were put in the same cabin, but both of us cried, me for my old wife and she for her old husband."

Despite the possibility of disruption, slaves were intensely committed to their families. To perpetuate a sense of family identity, slave parents named their children after ancestors or relatives. The strength of slave family ties is also suggested by the number of advertisements for runaway slaves that indicate that the fugitives were seeking to visit family members who lived on separate plantations.

Surviving slave letters provide a graphic record of the strength of slave families. After learning that he was going to be sold away from his family, a slave named Abream Scriven wrote to his wife: "My dear wife for you and my Children my pen cannot Express the griffe I feel parted from you all. . . . I remain your truly husband until Death." A Tennessee slave, named George Pleasant, expressed similar sentiments to his wife, who lived in North Carolina: "I hope with Gods helpe that I may be abble to rejoys with you on the earth and In heaven lets meet when [God] will."

1

Laura Spicer

"IT NEVER WAS OUR WISH TO BE SEPARATED"

When he and his wife were sold apart, Laura Spicer's husband remarried, thinking that he would never see her again. After the Civil War, however, Laura found him, prompting anguish and confusion.

I don't know whether I have told you Laura Spicer's story. She was sold from her husband some years ago, and he, hearing she was dead, married again. He has had a wavering inclination to again unite his fortunes with hers; and she has received a letter from him in which he said, "I read you letters over and over again. I keep them always in my pocket. If you are married I don't ever want to see you again." And yet, in some of his letters, he says, "I would much rather you would get married to some good man, for every time I gits a letter from you it tears me all to pieces. The reason why I have not written you before, in a long time, is because your letters disturbed me so very much. You know I love my children. I treats them good as a Father can treat his children; and I do a good deal of it for you. I was sorry to hear that Lewellyn, my poor little son, have had such bad health. I would come and see you, but I know you could not bear it. I want to see you and I don't want to see you. I love you just as well as I did the last day I saw you, and it will not do for you and I to meet. I am married, and my wife have two children, and if you and I meets it would make a very dissatisfied family."

Some of the children are with the mother and the father writes, "Send me some of the children's hair in a separate paper with their names on the paper. Will you please git married, as long as I am married. My dear, you know the Lord know both of our

---

Source: Unsigned and undated letter (1869?) in the Chase Papers, American Antiquarian Society, Worcester, Massachusetts.

113

hearts. You know it never was our wishes to be separated from each other, and it never was our fault. Oh, I can see you so plain, at any-time, I had rather anything to have happened to me most than ever have been parted from you and the children. As I am, I do not know which I love best, you or Anna. If I was to die, today or tomorrow, I do not think I would die satisfied till you tell me you will try and marry some good, smart man that will take good care of you and the children; and do it because you love me; and not because I think more of the wife I have got than I do of you. The woman is not born that feels as near to me as you do. You feel this day like myself. Tell them [the children] they must remember they have a good father and one that cares for them and one that thinks about them every day. —My heart did ache when reading your very kind and interesting letter. Laura I do not think that I have changed any at all since I saw you last—I thinks of you and my children every day of my life. Laura I do love you the same. My love to you never have failed. Laura, truly, I have got another wife, and I am very sorry, that I am. You feels and seems to me as much like my dear loving wife, as you ever did Laura.

2
Josiah Henson

"THE OVERSEER . . . SENT MY MOTHER AWAY . . . TO A RETIRED PLACE"

Nothing aroused greater fury within the slave commu-
nity than the sexual abuse of slave women. Josiah Henson
describes his father's reaction to an overseer's attempt to
molest his mother.

I was born June 15th, 1789, in Charles County, Maryland, on a farm belonging to Mr. Francis Newman, about a mile from Port Tobacco. My mother was a slave of Dr. Josiah McPherson, but hired to the Mr. Newman to whom my father belonged. The only

Source: Josiah Henson, *Uncle Tom's Story of His Life: An Autobiography of the Rev. Josiah Henson* (London, 1877).

incident I can remember which occurred while my mother continued on Mr. Newman's farm, was the appearance one day of my father with his head bloody and his back lacerated. He was beside himself with mingled rage and suffering. The explanation I picked up from the conversation of others only partially explained the matter to my mind; but as I grew older I understood it all. It seemed the overseer had sent my mother away from the other field hands to a retired place, and after trying persuasion in vain, had resorted to force to accomplish a brutal purpose. Her screams aroused my father at his distant work, and running up, he found his wife struggling with the man. Furious at the sight, he sprung upon him like a tiger. In a moment the overseer was down, and, mastered by rage, my father would have killed him but for the entreaties of my mother, and the overseer's own promise that nothing should ever be said of the matter. The promise was kept—like most promises of the cowardly and debased—as long as the danger lasted.

The laws of the state provide means and opportunities for revenge so ample, that miscreants like him never fail to improve them. "A nigger has struck a white man"; that is enough to set a whole county on fire; no question is asked about the provocation. The authorities were soon in pursuit of my father. The fact of the sacrilegious act of lifting a hand against the sacred temple of a white man's body . . . this was all it was necessary to establish. And the penalty followed: one hundred lashes on the bare back, and to have the right ear nailed to the whipping-post, and then severed from the body. For a time my father kept out of the way, hiding in the woods, and at night venturing into some cabin in search of food. But at length the strict watch set baffled all his efforts. His supplies cut off, he was fairly starved out, and compelled by hunger to come back and give himself up.

The day for the execution of the penalty was appointed. The Negroes from the neighboring plantations were summoned, for their moral improvement, to witness the scene. A powerful blacksmith named Hewes laid on the stripes. Fifty were given, during which the cries of my father might be heard a mile, and then a pause ensued. True, he had struck a white man, but as valuable property he must not be damaged. Judicious men felt his pulse. Oh! he could stand the whole. Again and again the thong fell on his lacerated back. His cries grew fainter and fainter, till a feeble groan was the only response to his final blows. His head was then thrust against the post, and his right ear fastened to it with a tack; a swift pass of a knife, and the bleeding member was left sticking to the place. Then came a hurrah from the degraded crowd, and the exclamation, "That's what he's got for striking a white man." A few said, "it's a damned shame"; but the majority regarded it as but a proper tribute to their offended majesty. . . .

Previous to this affair my father, from all I can learn, had been a good-humored and light-hearted man, the ringleader in all fun at corn-huskings and Christmas buffoonery. His banjo was the life of the farm, and all night long at a merry-making would he play on it while the other Negroes danced. But from this hour he became utterly changed. Sullen, morose, and dogged, nothing could be done with him. The milk of human kindness in his heart was turned to gall. He brooded over his wrongs. No fear or threats of being sold to the far south—the greatest of all terrors to the Maryland slave—would render him tractable. So off he was sent to Alabama. What was his fate neither my mother nor I have ever learned. . . .

For two or three years my mother and her young family of six children had resided on [Dr. McPherson's] estate; and we had been in the main very happy. . . .

Our term of happy union as one family was now, alas! at an end. Mournful as was the Doctor's death to his friends it was a far greater calamity to us. The estate and the slaves must be sold and the proceeds divided among the heirs. We were but property—not a mother, and the children God had given her.

Common as are slave-auctions in the southern states, and naturally as a slave may look forward to the time when he will be put upon the block, still the full misery of the event—of the scenes which precede and succeed it—is never understood till the actual experience comes. The first sad announcement that the sale is to be; the knowledge that all ties of the past are to be sundered; the frantic terror at the idea of being "sent south"; the almost certainty that one member of a family will be torn from another; the anxious scanning of purchasers' faces; the agony at parting, often forever, with husband, wife, child—these must be seen and felt to be fully understood. Young as I was then, the iron entered into my soul. The remembrance of breaking up of McPherson's estate is photographed in its minutest features in my mind. The crowd collected around the stand, the huddling group of Negroes, the examination of muscle, teeth, the exhibition of agility, the look of the autioneer, the agony of my mother—I can shut my eyes and see them all.

My brothers and sisters were bid off first, and one by one, while my mother, paralyzed by grief, held me by the hand. Her turn came, and she was bought by Isaac Riley of Montgomery County. Then I was offered to the assembled purchasers. My mother, half distracted by the thought of parting forever from all her children, pushed through the crowd, while the bidding for me was going on, to the spot where Riley was standing. She fell at his feet and clung to his knees, entreating him in tones that a mother only could command, to buy her baby as well as herself, and spare to her one, at least of her little ones. Will it, can it be believed that this man, thus appealed to, was capable not merely of turning a deaf ear to her supplication, but of disengaging himself from her with such violent blows and kicks, as to reduce her to the necessity of creeping out of his reach, and mingling the groan of bodily suffering with the sob of a breaking heart? As she crawled away from the brutal man I heard her sob out, "Oh, Lord Jesus, how long, how long shall I suffer this way!" I must have been then between five and six years old. I seem to see and hear my poor weeping mother now. This was one of my earliest observations of men; an experience which I only shared with thousands of my race, the bitterness of which to any individual who suffers it cannot be diminished by the frequency of its recurrence, while it is dark enough to overshadow the whole after-life with something blacker than a funeral pall.

3
Lewis Clarke

"THERE IS BUT LITTLE . . . SCRUPLE ABOUT SEPARATING FAMILIES"

Lewis Clarke, the son of a Scottish weaver and a slave mother, was born in Kentucky in 1815. Despite an agreement that she was to be freed upon her husband's death, Clarke's mother and her nine children remained in slavery. After he learned that he was going to be sold in New Orleans, Clarke successfully fled through Ohio across Lake Erie to Canada in 1841. In an account of his life published in 1846, he provided answers to questions he was frequently asked about the impact of slavery upon slave families.

Source: *Interesting Memoirs and Documents Relating to American Slavery, and the Glorious Struggle Now Making for Complete Emancipation* (London, 1846).

[Question] Are families often separated? How many such cases have you personally known?

[Answer]—I never knew a whole family to live together till all were grown up in my life. There is almost always, in every family, some one or more keen and bright, or else sullen and stubborn slave, whose influence they are afraid of on the rest of the family, and such a one must take a walking ticket to the south.

There are other causes of separation. The death of a large owner is the occasion usually of many families being broken up. Bankruptcy is another cause of separation, and the hard-heartedness of a majority of slave-holders another and a more fruitful cause than either or all the rest. Generally there is but little more scruple about separating families than there is with a man who keeps sheep in selling off the lambs in the fall. On one plantation where I lived, there was an old slave named Paris. He was from fifty to sixty years old, and a very honest and apparently pious slave. A slave-trader came along one day, to gather hands for the south. The old master ordered the waiter or coachman to take Paris into the back room pluck out all his gray hairs, rub his face with a greasy towel, and then had him brought forward and sold for a young man. His wife consented to go with him, upon a promise from the trader that they should be sold together, with their youngest child, which she carried in her arms. They left two behind them, who were only from four to six or eight years of age. The speculator collected his drove, started for the market, and, before he left the state, he sold that infant child to pay one of his tavern bills, and took the balance in cash. . . .

[Question] Have you ever known a slave mother to kill her own children?

[Answer] There was a slave mother near where I lived, who took her child into the cellar and killed it. She did it to prevent being separated from her child. Another slave mother took her three children and threw them into a well, and then jumped in with them, and they were all drowned. Other instances I have frequently heard of. At the death of many and many a slave child, I have seen the two feelings struggling in the bosom of a mother—joy, that it was beyond the reach of the slave monsters, and the natural grief of a mother over her child. In the presence of the master, grief seems to predominate; when away from them, they rejoice that there is one whom the slave-killer will never torment.

Chapter 7

"Go Home to My Lord and Be Free":

RELIGION

Some slaveholders were quite open in their belief that religion could serve as a valuable mechanism of social control, instilling submissiveness and conscientiousness within slaves. One 1845 pamphlet asserted that Christianity could promote "good will," "meekness," "patience," "truth and faithfulness." But Christian religion also had another face, emphasizing judgment, equality, and liberation. As one white observer in Georgia commented, the slaves believe "that in the life to come there will also be white people and black people; but then the white people will be slaves, and they shall have the dominion over them."

During the seventeenth century, slave owners were reluctant to Christianize their slaves for fear that baptized slaves would have to be set free. They also worried that the Christian notion of the spiritual equality of all human beings would lead slaves to demand their freedom. Many slaves rejected Christianity because, as one white observer put it, a "Fondness they have for their old Heathenish Rites, and the strong Prejudice they must have against Teachers from among those, whom they serve so unwillingly."

By the second quarter of the eighteenth century, a growing number of slaveholders concluded that Christianity would make slaves more docile and conscientious, by placing them "under strong Obligations to perform [their] duties with the greatest Diligence and Fidelity . . . from a Sense of Duty to God, and the Belief and Expectation of a future account." The process of converting slaves to Christianity began in earnest during the Great Awakening of the 1730s and 1740s and then accelerated in the late eighteenth century.

Within the Baptist and Methodist churches, slaves began to create a hybrid African-American form of Christianity, blending Chris-

tian rituals and beliefs with elements of West African culture. The result, as Albert J. Raboteau has shown, was a religion with its own distinctive forms of preaching and worship, characterized by rhythmic sermons, "shouting" and other ecstatic behavior induced by spiritual possession, and forms of singing and dancing influenced by slaves' African traditions.

On individual plantations, slaves held informal or secret prayer meetings, apart from the influence of their masters. Here slave preachers conducted baptisms, weddings, and funerals, and slaves sang spirituals, which blended Christian hymns and psalms with African styles and gave expression to the slaves' intense desire for freedom and transcendence. Slave religion, in turn, co-existed alongside folk traditions with African roots, like witchcraft, herbalism, and conjure (which involved supernatural spells and charms) that addressed needs unmet by Protestant Christianity.

1

Olaudah Equiano

"THE STRONG ANALOGY . . . IN THE MANNERS . . . OF MY COUNTRYMEN, AND THOSE OF THE JEWS"

Religion played a central role in the cultures of West Africa. In this extract from his memoirs, Olaudah Equiano describes Ibo religion in eastern Nigeria and observes that certain aspects of African religious belief resemble those found in Judaism and Christianity.

As to religion, the natives believe that there is one Creator of all things, and that he lives in the sun, and is girded round with a belt, that he may never eat or drink; but according to some, he smokes a pipe, which is our own favorite luxury. They believe he governs events, especially our deaths or captivity; but, as for the doctrine of eternity, I do not remember to have ever heard of it: some however believe in the transmigration of souls in a certain degree. Those spirits, which are not transmigrated, such as their dear friends or relations, they believe always attend them, and guard them from the bad spirits of their foes. For this reason, they always, before eating, as I have observed, put some small portion of the meat, and pour some of their drink, on the ground for them; and they often make oblations of the blood of beasts or fowls at their graves. I was very fond of my mother, and almost constantly with her. When she went to make these oblations at her mother's tomb, which was a kind of small solitary thatched house, I sometimes attended her. There she made her libations, and spent most of the night in cries and lamentation. . . .

We compute the year from the day on which the sun crosses the line; and, on its setting that evening, there is a general shout throughout the land; at least, I can speak from my own knowledge,

Source: *The Interesting Narrative of the Life of Olaudah Equiano or Gustavus Vassa the African* (London, 1789).

121

throughout our vicinity. The people at the same time made a great noise with rattles not unlike the basket rattles used by children here, though much larger, and hold up their hands to heaven for a blessing. It is then the greatest offerings are made; and those children whom our wise men foretell will be fortunate are then presented to different people. . . . They have many offerings, particularly at full moons, generally two at harvest, before the fruits are taken out of the ground; and, when any young animals are killed, sometimes they offer up part of them as a sacrifice. . . .

We practiced circumcision like the Jews, and made offerings and feasts on that occasion in the same manner as they did. Like them also our children were named from some event, some circumstance, or fancied foreboding, at the time of their birth. I was named Olaudah, which, in our language, signifies vicissitude, or fortune also; one favored, and having a loud voice, and well spoken. I remember we never polluted the name of the object of our adoration; on the contrary, it was always mentioned with the greatest reverence; and we were totally unacquainted with swearing, and all those terms of abuse and reproach which find their way so readily and copiously into the language of more civilized people. The only expressions of that kind I remember were "May you rot, or may you swell, or may a beast take you."

I have before remarked, that the natives of this part of Africa are extremely cleanly. This necessary habit of decency was with us a part of religion, and therefore we had many purifications and washings. . . . Those that touched the dead at any time were obliged to wash and purify themselves before they could enter a dwelling house. Every woman too, at certain times, was forbidden to come into a dwelling-house, or touch any person, or anything we eat. I was so fond of my mother I could not keep from her, or avoid touching her at some of those periods, in consequence of which I was obliged to be kept out with her in a little house made for that purpose, till offering was made, and then we were purified.

Though we had no places of public worship, we had priests and magicians, or wise men. I do not remember whether they had different offices, or whether they were united in the same persons, but they were held in great reverence by the people. They calculated our time and foretold events. . . . They wore their beards; and, when they died, they were succeeded by their sons. Most of their implements and things of value were interred along with them. Pipes and tobacco were also put into the grave with the corpse, which was always perfumed and ornamented; and animals were offered in sacrifice to them. None accompanied their funerals, but those of the same profession or tribe. These buried them after sunset, and always returned from the grave by a different way from that which they went.

These magicians were also our doctors or physicians. They practiced bleeding by cupping; and were very successful in healing wounds and expelling poisons. They had likewise some extraordinary method of discovering jealousy, theft, and poisoning; the success of which no doubt they derived from the unbounded influence over the credulity and superstition of the people. I do not remember what those methods were, except that as to poisoning. I recollect an instance or two, which I hope it will not be deemed impertinent here to insert, as it may serve as a kind of specimen of the rest, and is still used by the Negroes in the West Indies. A young woman had been poisoned, but it was not known by whom: the doctor ordered the corpse to be taken up by some persons, and carried to the grave. As soon as the bearers had raised it on their shoulders, they seemed seized with some sudden impulse, and ran to and fro, unable to stop themselves. At last, after having passed through a number of thorns and prickly bushes unhurt, the corpse fell from them close to a house, and defaced it in the fall; and the owner being taken up, he immediately confessed the poisoning. . . .

Such is the imperfect sketch my memory has furnished me with of the manner and customs of a people among whom I first drew my breath. And here I cannot forbear suggesting what has long struck me very forcibly, namely, the strong analogy which even by this sketch, imperfect as it is, appears to prevail in the manners and customs of my countrymen, and those of the Jews, before they reached the Land of Promise. . . . Like the Israelites in their primitive state, our government was conducted by our chiefs, our judges, our wise men, and elders; and the head of a family with us enjoyed a similar authority over his household with that which is ascribed to Abraham and the other patriarchs. The law of retaliation obtained almost universally with us as with them: and even their religion appeared to have shed upon us a ray of its glory, though broken and spent in its passage, or eclipsed by the cloud with which time, tradition, and ignorance, might have enveloped it: for we had our circumcision (a rule I believe peculiar to that people): we had also our sacrifices and burnt-offerings, our washings and purifications, on the same occasion as they had.

2

Charles Ball

"I ASSISTED . . . TO INTER THE INFANT"

*During the early nineteenth century, some slaves contin-
ued to draw upon West African religious customs in bury-
ing the dead. In this selection, Charles Ball, a slave in western Maryland, describes a slave funeral.*

I assisted her and her husband to inter the infant . . . and its
father buried with it, a small bow and several arrows; a little bag of
parched meal; a miniature canoe, about a foot long, and a little
paddle, (with which he said it would cross the ocean to his own
country) a small stick, with an iron nail, sharpened and fastened
into one end of it; and a piece of white muslim, with several curi-
ous and strange figures painted on it in blue and red, by which, he
said, his relations and countrymen would know the infant to be
his son, and would receive it accordingly, on its arrival amongst
them. . . . He cut a lock of hair from his head, threw it upon the
dead infant, and closed the grave with his own hands. He then told
us the God of his country was looking at him, and was pleased with
what he had done.

Source: Charles Ball, *Slavery in the United States: A Narrative of the Life and Adventures of Charles Ball, A Black Man* (New York, 1837).

3

Peter Randolph

"THE SLAVES ASSEMBLE IN
THE SWAMPS"

*Peter Randolph, who grew up in slavery on a plantation in
Prince George County, Virginia, received his freedom in
1847 following his owner's death, and then served as an*

Source: Peter Randolph, *Slave Cabin to the Pulpit* (Boston, 1893).

antislavery agent, a newspaper editor, and as a Baptist minister in the North and in Canada. Following the Civil War, he served as minister in the Ryland or Old African Baptist Church in Richmond, Virginia. This selection describes the disparity between the version of Christianity that masters taught to the slaves and the version that slaves taught to themselves.

Many say the Negroes receive religious education—that Sabbath worship is instituted for them as for others, and were it not for slavery, they would die in their sins—that really, the institution of slavery is a benevolent missionary enterprise. Yes, they are preached to, and I will give my readers some faint glimpses of these preachers, and their doctrines and practices.

In Prince George County there were two meeting-houses intended for public worship. Both were occupied by the Baptist denomination. These houses were built by William and George Harrison, brothers . . . that their slaves might go there on the Sabbath and receive instruction, such as slave-holding ministers would give. The prominent preaching to the slaves was, "'Servants, obey your masters.' Do not steal or lie, for this is very wrong. Such conduct is sinning against the Holy Ghost, and is base ingratitude to your kind masters, who feed, clothe and protect you. . . ." I should think, when making such statements, the slaveholders would feel the rebuke of the Apostle and fall down and be carried out from the face of day, as were Ananias and Sapphira, when they betrayed the trust committed to them, or refused to bear true testimony in regard to that trust.

There was another church, about fourteen miles from the one just mentioned. It was called "Brandon's church," and there the white Baptists worshiped. . . .

There was one Brother Shell who used to preach. One Sabbath, while exhorting the poor, impenitent, hard-hearted, ungrateful slaves, so much beloved by their masters, to repentance and prayerfulness, while entreating them to lead good lives, that they might escape the wrath (of the lash) to come, some of his crocodile tears overflowed his cheek. . . . But, my readers, Monday morning, Brother Shell was afflicted with his old malady, hardness of heart, so that he was obliged to catch one of the sisters by the throat, and give her a terrible flogging.

The like of this is the preaching, and these are the men that spread the Gospel among the slaves. Ah! such a Gospel had better be buried in oblivion, for it makes more heathens than Christians.

Such preachers ought to be forbidden by the laws of the land ever to mock again at the blessed religion of Jesus, which was sent as a light to the world. . . .

Not being allowed to hold meetings on the plantation, the slaves assemble in the swamps, out of reach of the patrols. They have an understanding among themselves as to the time and place of getting together. This is often done by the first one arriving breaking boughs from the trees, and bending them in the direction of the selected spot. Arrangements are then made for conducting the exercises. They first ask each other how they feel, the state of their minds, etc. The male members then select a certain space, in separate groups, for their division of the meeting. Preaching in order, by the brethren; then praying and singing all round, until they generally feel quite happy. The speaker usually commences by calling himself unworthy, and talks very slowly, until, feeling the spirit, he grows excited, and in a short time, there fall to the ground twenty or thirty men and women under its influence. Enlightened people call it excitement; but I wish the same was felt by everybody, so far as they are sincere.

The slave forgets all his sufferings, except to remind others of the trials during the past week, exclaiming: "Thank God, I shall not live here always!" Then they pass from one to another, shaking hands, and bidding each other farewell, promising, should they meet no more on earth, to strive and meet in heaven, where all is joy, happiness and liberty. As they separate, they sing a parting hymn of praise.

Sometimes the slaves meet in an old log-cabin, when they find it necessary to keep a watch. If discovered, they escape, if possible; but those who are caught often get whipped. Some are willing to be punished thus for Jesus' sake. Most of the songs used in worship are composed by the slaves themselves, and describe their own sufferings. Thus:

"Oh, that I had a bosom friend,
To tell my secrets to,
One always to depend upon
In everything I do!"

"How do I wander, up and down!
I seem a stranger, quite undone;
None to lend an ear to my complaint,
No one to cheer me, though I faint."

Some of the slaves sing—

> "No more rain, no more snow,
> No more cowskin on my back!"

Then they change it by singing—

> "Glory be to God that rules on high."

In some places, if the slaves are caught praying to God, they are whipped more than if they had committed a great crime. The slave holders will allow the slaves to dance, but do not want them to pray to God. Sometimes, when a slave, on being whipped, calls upon God, he is forbidden to do so, under threat of having his throat cut, or brains blown out. Oh, reader! this seems very hard— that slaves cannot call on their Maker, when the case most needs it. Sometimes the poor slave takes courage to ask his master to let him pray, and is driven away, with the answer, that if discovered praying, his back will pay the bill.

4

Henry Bibb

"MANY . . . BELIEVE IN WHAT THEY CALL CONJURATION"

Henry Bibb, born to a white father and a slave mother in Shelby County, Kentucky, in 1815, was held in slavery in Kentucky, Louisiana, and in present-day Arkansas. In 1837, he escaped through Ohio and Michigan into Canada. In this selection, he describes slaves' notions of conjure that existed alongside Christianity.

In 1833, I had some very serious religious impressions, and there was quite a number of slaves in that neighborhood, who felt

Source: *Narrative of the Life and Adventures of Henry Bibb, An American Slave* (New York, 1849).

very desirous to be taught to read the Bible. There was a Miss Davis, a poor white girl, who offered to teach a Sabbath School for the slaves, notwithstanding public opinion and the law was opposed to it. Books were furnished and she commenced the school; but the news soon got to our owners that she was teaching us to read. This caused quite an excitement in the neighborhood. Patrols were appointed to go and break it up the next Sabbath. They were determined that we should not have a Sabbath School in operation. For slaves this was called an incendiary movement.

The Sabbath is not regarded by a large number of the slaves as a day of rest. They have no schools to go to; no moral nor religious instruction at all in many localities where there are hundreds of slaves. Hence they resort to some kind of amusement. Those who make no profession of religion, resort to the woods in large numbers on that day to gamble, fight, get drunk, and break the Sabbath. This is often encouraged by slaveholders. When they wish to have a little sport of that kind, they go among the slaves and give them whiskey, to see them dance, "pat juber," sing and play on the banjo. Then get them to wrestling, fighting, jumping, running foot races, and butting each other like sheep. This is urged on by giving them whiskey; making bets on them; laying chips on one slave's head, and daring another to tip it off with his hand; and if he tipped it off, it would be called an insult, and cause a fight. Before fighting, the parties choose their seconds to stand by them while fighting; a ring or a circle is formed to fight in, and no one is allowed to enter the ring while they are fighting, but their seconds, and the white gentlemen. They are not allowed to fight a duel, nor to use weapons of any kind. The blows are made by kicking, knocking, and butting with their heads; they grab each other by their ears, and jam their heads together like sheep. If they are likely to hurt each other very bad, their masters would rap them with their walking canes, and make them stop. After fighting they make friends, shake hands, and take a dram together, and there is no more of it.

But this is all principally for want of moral instruction. This is where they have no Sabbath Schools; no one to read the Bible to them; no one to preach the gospel who is competent to expound the Scriptures, except slaveholders. And the slaves, with but few exceptions, have no confidence at all in their preaching, because they preach a pro-slavery doctrine. They say, "Servants be obedient to your masters;—and he that knoweth his master's will and doeth it not, shall be beaten, with many stripes;—" means that God will send them to hell, if they disobey their masters. This kind of preaching has driven thousands into infidelity. They view themselves as suffering unjustly under the lash, without friends, without protection of law or gospel, and the green-eyed monster tyranny staring them in the face. They know that they are destined to die in that wretched condition, unless they are delivered by the arm of Omnipotence. And they cannot believe or trust in such a religion, as above named. . . .

There is much superstition among the slaves. Many of them believe in what they call "conjuration," tricking, and witchcraft; and some of them pretend to understand the art, and say that by it they can prevent their masters from exercising their will over their slaves. Such are often applied to by others, to give them power to prevent their masters from flogging them. The remedy is most generally some kind of bitter root; they are directed to chew it and spit towards their masters when they are angry with the slaves. At other times they prepare certain kinds of powders, to sprinkle about their masters' dwellings. This is all done for the purpose of defending themselves in some peaceable manner, although I am satisfied that there is no virtue at all in it. . . .

[A conjurer] said if I would pay him a small sum, he would prevent my being flogged. After I had paid him, he mixed up some alum, salt and other stuff into a powder, and said I must sprinkle it about my master, if he should offer to strike me; this would prevent him. He also gave me some kind of bitter root to chew, and spit towards him, which would certainly prevent my being flogged. According to order I used his remedy, and for some cause I was let pass without being flogged that time.

I had then great faith in conjuration and witchcraft. I was led to believe that I could do almost as I pleased, without being flogged. So on the next Sabbath my conjuration was fully tested by my going off, and staying away until Monday morning, without permission. When I returned home, my master declared that he would punish me for going off; but I did not believe that he could do it, while I had this root and dust; and as he approached me, I commenced talking saucy to him. But he soon convinced me that there was no virtue in them. He became so enraged at me for saucing him, that he grasped a handful of switches and punished me severely, in spite of all my roots and powders. . . .

I wanted to be well thought of by [young women], and would go to great lengths to gain their affection. I had been taught by the old superstitious slaves, to believe in conjuration, and it was hard for me to give up the notion, for all I had been deceived by them. One of these conjurers, for a small sum, agreed to teach me to make any girl love me that I wished. After I had paid him, he told me to get a bull frog, and take a certain bone out of the frog, dry it, and when I got a chance I must step up to any girl whom I wished to make love me, and scratch her somewhere on her naked skin with this bone, and she would be certain to love me, and would follow me in spite of herself; no matter who she might be engaged to, nor who she might be walking with.

So I got me a bone for a certain girl, whom I knew to be under the influence of another young man. I happened to meet her in the company of her lover, one Sunday evening, walking out; so when I got a chance, I fetched her a tremendous rasp across her neck with this bone, which made her jump. But in place of making her love me, it only made her angry with me. She felt more like running after me to retaliate on me for thus abusing her, than she felt like loving me.

Chapter 8

"Oppressed So Hard They Could Not Stand":

PUNISHMENT

Dr. John Wesley Monette, an apologist for slavery, rejected the charge that whipping slaves was cruel and barbaric. He acknowledged that to anyone unacquainted with the lash, "hearing the loud sharp crack of the whip upon the naked skin, would almost tremble for the life of the poor sufferer." But, he assured his readers, there was no reason for anxiety. "After hearing fifty or one hundred stripes thus being laid on," one would "find the skin not broken, and not a drop of blood drawn from him!" Indeed, he insisted, a buckskin whip's end was so soft that one "could scarcely hurt a child with it." He acknowledged that a lashing "stings, or 'hurts' the skin smartly," but, he added, it "does not bruise it." Though slave owners tried to disguise it, most relied on physical punishment to force slaves to toil for long hours and meager rewards.

Though slave owners, like Monette, tried to deny—or obscure—the cruelty of slavery, the fact remains that slave management was based on fear.

A Georgia slave owner maintained that "the surest and best method of managing Negroes, is to love them." "If we love our horse . . . he will become gentle, docile and obedient," he observed. "Why will it not have the same effect upon slaves." Many slaveholders offered a variety of rewards and incentives; they gave slaves small garden patches on which they could raise their own crops, distributed gifts, and offered cash bonuses and special holidays to particularly diligent slaves. A few masters actually made profit-sharing agreements with slaves.

Yet even the most humane masters balanced the hope of reward with the threat of punishment. A slave owner might deny disobedient or unproductive slaves passes off of the plantation or reduce their rations. One Maryland planter forced a slave to eat worms that she had failed to pick off of a tobacco plant. One farmer described his approach to discipline: "I do not punish often, but I seldom let an offense pass." He disciplined children by "pulling an ear, or a sound box." He placed adults in solitary confinement within a windowless "hewed log house, with a good substantial door, lock and key."

Ultimately a master's authority rested on the threat of physical pain. To discipline slaves, plantation owners set up private jails, confined slaves in stocks, and shackled them with chains and iron collars. It was the whip, however, that became the defining symbol of slavery. A Louisiana planter declared that "the highest punishment must not exceed 100 lashes in one day and to that extent only in extreme cases. In general 15 to 20 lashes will be a sufficient flogging."

1
Frederick Douglass

"MATTERS FOR WHICH A SLAVE MAY BE WHIPPED"

Perhaps the nineteenth century's staunchest advocate of equal rights, Frederick Douglass was born into slavery on Maryland's eastern shore in 1818, the son of a slave woman and an unknown white man. While toiling as a ship's caulker, he taught himself to read. After he escaped from slavery at the age of twenty, he became the abolitionist movement's most effective orator and published an influential antislavery newspaper, The North Star. In this excerpt from one of his three autobiographies, he describes the circumstances that prompted slave owners to whip slaves.

A mere look, word, or motion,—a mistake, accident, or want of power,—are all matters for which a slave may be whipped at any time. Does a slave look dissatisfied? It is said, he has the devil in him, and it must be whipped out. Does he speak loudly when spoken to by his master? Then he is getting high-minded, and should be taken down a button-hole lower. Does he forget to pull off his hat at the approach of a white person? Then he is wanting in reverence, and should be whipped for it. Does he ever venture to vindicate his conduct, when censured for it? Then he is guilty of impudence,—one of the greatest crimes of which a slave can be guilty. Does he ever venture to suggest a different mode of doing things from that pointed out by his master? He is indeed presumptuous, and getting above himself. . . .

Source: *Narrative of the Life of Frederick Douglass, An American Slave* (3rd. English ed., Leeds, 1846).

2
John Brown

"FIXED BELLS AND HORNS ON MY HEAD"

John Brown, who was born into slavery in Southampton County, Virginia, and later toiled in Georgia and Louisiana, describes the methods of discipline employed by one of his owners.

To prevent my running any more, Stevens fixed bells and horns on my head. This is not by any means an uncommon punishment. I have seen many slaves wearing them. A circle of iron, having a hinge behind, with a staple and padlock before, which hang under the chin, is fastened round the neck. Another circle of iron fits quite close round the crown of the head. The two are held together in this position by three rods of iron, which are fixed in each circle. These rods, or horns, stick out three feet above the head, and have a bell attached to each. The bells and horns do not weigh less than twelve to fourteen pounds. When Stevens had fixed this ornament on my head, he turned me loose, and told me I might run off now if I liked.

I wore the bells and horns, day and night, for three months, and I do not think any description I could give of my sufferings during this time would convey anything approaching to a faint idea of them. Let alone that their weight made my head and neck ache dreadfully, especially when I stooped to my work. At night I could not lie down to rest, because the horns prevented my stretching myself, or even curling myself up; so I was obliged to sleep crouching. Of course it was impossible for me to attempt to remove them, or to get away, though I still held to my resolution to make another venture as soon as I could see my way of doing it.

Source: John Brown, *Slave Life in Georgia: A Narrative of the Life, Sufferings, and Escape of John Brown, A Fugitive Slave, Now in England* (London, 1855).

3
William Wells Brown

"I WAS TIED UP IN THE SMOKEHOUSE"

One of the nation's first black novelists and historians, William Wells Brown was born in Lexington, Kentucky, in 1816 and raised in Missouri. After serving as a slave driver, he was hired out to transport slaves to the New Orleans slave market, but managed to escape. Here, he describes the punishments he encountered while a slave in Missouri.

My mother was hired out in the city, and I was also hired out there to Major Freeland, who kept a public house. He was formerly from Virginia, and was a horse-racer, cock-fighter, gambler, and withal an inveterate drunkard. There were ten or twelve servants in the house, and when he was present, it was cut and slash—knock down and drag out. In his fits of anger, he would take up a chair, and throw it at a servant; and in his more rational moments, when he wished to chastise one, he would tie them up in the smokehouse, and whip them; after which, he would cause a fire to be made of tobacco stems, and smoke them. This he called "Virginia play."

I complained to my master of the treatment which I received from Major Freeland; but it made no difference. He cared nothing about it, so long as he received the money for my labor. After living with Major Freeland five or six months, I ran away, and went into the woods back of the city; and when night came on, I made my way to my master's farm, knowing that if Mr. Haskell, the overseer, should discover me, I should be again carried back to Major Freeland; so I kept in the woods. One day, while in the woods, I heard the barking and howling of dogs, and in a short time they came so near that I knew them to be the bloodhounds of Major Benjamin O'Fallon. He kept five or six, to hunt runaway slaves with.

As soon as I was convinced that it was them, I knew there was no chance of escape. I took refuge in the top of a tree and the hounds were soon at its base, and there remained until the hunters came up in a half or three quarters of an hour afterwards. There were two men with the dogs, who, as soon as they came up, ordered me to descend. I came down, was tied, and taken to St. Louis jail.

Source: *Narrative of William W. Brown, A Fugitive Slave* (Boston, 1847).

Major Freeland soon made his appearance, and took me out, and ordered me to follow him, which I did. After we returned home I was tied up in the smokehouse, and was very severely whipped. After the major had flogged me to his satisfaction, he sent out his son Robert, a young man eighteen or twenty years of age, to see that I was well smoked. He made a fire of tobacco stems, which soon set me to coughing and sneezing. This, Robert told me, was the way his father used to do to his slaves in Virginia. After giving me what they conceived to be a decent smoking, I was untied and again set to work.

4

Moses Roper

"AMONG THE INSTRUMENTS OF TORTURE EMPLOYED"

Moses Roper, who was born into slavery in Caswell County, North Carolina, lived in North and South Carolina and in Georgia before he successfully fled to the North and then to England. In this selection from his autobiography, he describes the punishment he faced after he tried unsuccessfully to run away.

My master gave me a hearty dinner, the best he ever did give me; but it was to keep me from dying before he had given me all the flogging he intended. After dinner he took me up to the log-house, stripped me quite naked, fasted a rail up very high, tied my hands to the rail, fastened my feet together, put a rail between my feet, and stood on the end of it to hold me down; the two sons then gave me fifty lashes, the son-in-law another fifty, and Mr. Gooch himself fifty more.

While doing this his wife came out, and begged him not to kill me, the first act of sympathy I ever noticed in her. When I called for water, they brought a pail-full and threw it over my back ploughed up by the lashes. After this, they took me to the black-

Source: Moses Roper, *Narrative of the Adventures and Escape of Moses Roper* (London, 1837).

smith's shop, got two large bars of iron, which they bent around my feet, each bar weighing twenty pounds, and put a heavy log-chain on my neck. . . .

Among the instruments of torture employed, I here describe one:—This is a machine used for packing and pressing cotton. By it he hung me up by the hands, a horse, and at times, a man moving round the screw and carrying it up and down, and pressing the block into a box into which the cotton is put. At this time he hung me up for a quarter of an hour. I was carried up ten feet from the ground. . . . After this torture, I stayed with him several months, and did my work very well. It was about the beginning of 1832, when he took off my irons, and being in dread of him, he having threatened me with more punishment, I attempted again to escape from him. At this time I got into North Carolina: but a reward having been offered for me, a Mr. Robinson caught me, and chained me to a chair, upon which he sat up with me all night, and next day proceeded home with me. This was Saturday. Mr. Gooch had gone to church, several miles from his house. When he came back, the first thing he did was to pour some tar upon my head, then rubbed it all over my face, took a torch with pitch on, and set it on fire; he put it out before it did me very great injury, but the pain which I endured was the most excruciating, nearly all my hair having been burnt off. On Monday, he puts irons on me again, weighing nearly fifty pounds. He threatened me again on the Sunday with another flogging; and on the Monday morning, before daybreak, I got away again, with my irons on, and was about three hours going a distance of two miles. I had gone a good distance, when I met with a coloured man, who got some wedges, and took my irons off. However, I was caught again, and put into prison in Charlotte, where Mr. Gooch came, and took me back to Chester. He asked me how I got my irons off. They having been got off by a slave, I would not answer his question, for fear of getting the man punished. Upon this he put the fingers of my hands into a vice, and squeezed all the nails off. He then had my feet put on an anvil, and ordered a man to beat my toes, till he smashed some of my nails off. The marks of this treatment still remain upon me, some of my nails never having grown perfect since.

5
Lewis Clarke

"HER INVENTION WAS WONDERFULLY QUICK"

As a slave child in Kentucky, Lewis Clarke was frequently whipped by his mistress. Here he describes the implements she used to punish him.

[My mistress's] instruments of torture were ordinarily the raw hide, or a bunch of hickory-sprouts seasoned in the fire and tied together. But if these were not at hand, nothing came amiss. She could relish a beating with a chair, the broom, tongs, shovel, shears, knife-handle, the heavy heel of her slipper, or a bunch of keys; her zeal was so active in these barbarous inflictions, that her invention was wonderfully quick, and some way of inflicting the requisite torture was soon found.

One instrument of torture is worthy of particular description. This was an oak club, a foot and a half in length, and an inch and a half square. With this delicate weapon she would beat us upon the hands and upon the feet until they were blistered. This instrument was carefully preserved for a period of four years. Every day, for that time, I was compelled to see that hated tool of cruelty lying in the chair by my side. The least degree of delinquency, either in not doing all the appointed work, or in look or behavior, was visited with a beating from this oak club. That club will always be a prominent object in the picture of horrors of my life of more than twenty years of bitter bondage. . . .

Mrs. Banton, as is common among slave-holding women, seemed to hate and abuse me all the more, because I had some of the blood of her father in my veins. There are no slaves that are so badly abused, as those that are related to some of the women, or the children of their own husband; it seems as though they never could hate these quite bad enough.

Source: *Interesting Memoirs and Documents Relating to American Slavery, and the Glorious Struggle Now Making for Complete Emancipation* (London, 1846).

Chapter 9

"Let My People Go":

RESISTANCE

Four times during the first thirty-one years of the nineteenth century, American slaves organized insurrections against slavery. In 1800, a twenty-four-year-old Virginia slave named Gabriel, a black-smith, led a march of perhaps fifty armed slaves on Richmond. The plot failed when a storm washed out the road to Richmond, giving the Virginia militia time to arrest the rebels. White authorities executed Gabriel and twenty-five other conspirators.

In 1811 in Louisiana, between 180 and 500 slaves led by Charles Deslondes, a free mulatto from Haiti, marched on New Orleans, armed with axes and other weapons. Slave owners retaliated by killing eighty-two blacks and placing the heads of sixteen leaders on pikes.

In 1822, a former slave named Denmark Vesey devised a scheme to take over Charleston, South Carolina, on a summer Sunday when many whites would be vacationing outside the city. Vesey, who had been born either in Africa or the Caribbean in the late 1760s, had won a lottery, purchased his freedom, and opened a carpentry shop. The decision by Charleston authorities to close the city's independent Afri-can church led Vesey to organize his conspiracy. Before the revolt could take place, however, a slave betrayed Vesey's plans. The author-ities proceeded to arrest 131 blacks and hang thirty-seven.

The bloodiest slave revolt in American history took place in 1831 when Nat Turner, a Baptist preacher, led a force of between sixty and eighty slaves on a rampage through Southampton County in south-ern Virginia, leaving more than fifty whites dead. White authorities retaliated by killing about a hundred blacks. Twenty more slaves, including Turner, were later executed.

Recognizing that open revolt against slavery was futile, most slaves expressed their opposition in more subtle ways, including sabotage, stealing, malingering, murder, arson, and infanticide. These acts of resistance most commonly occurred when a master or overseer overstepped customary bounds. Through these acts, slaves established a right to proper treatment.

Fugitive from slavery who lives in the Dismal Swamp in Virginia, *Osman* by Porte Crayon [David Hunter Strother] in TRAVELS IN THE LAND OF CANAAN, Harper, 1854.

1
Frederick Douglass

"COWARDICE DEPARTED, BOLD DEFIANCE TOOK ITS PLACE"

In this selection, Frederick Douglass describes his battles with a "Negro-breaker."

If at any one time of my life more than another, I was made to drink the bitterest dregs of slavery, that time was during the first six months of my stay with Mr. [Edward] Covey. We were worked in all weathers. It was never too hot or too cold; it could never rain, blow, hail, or snow too hard for us to work in the field. Work, work, work was scarcely more the order of the day than of the night. The longest days were too short for him, and the shortest nights too long for him. I was somewhat unmanageable when I first went there, but a few months of this discipline tamed me. Mr. Covey succeeded in breaking me. I was broken in body, soul, and spirit. My natural elasticity was crushed, my intellect languished, the disposition to read departed, the cheerful spark that lingered about my eye died; the dark night of slavery closed in upon me; and behold a man transformed into a brute!

Sunday was my only leisure time. I spent this in a sort of beast-like stupor, between sleep and wake, under some large tree. At times I would rise up, a flash of energetic freedom would dart through my soul, accompanied with a faint gleam of hope that flickered for a moment, and then vanished. I sank down again, mourning over my wretched condition. I was sometimes prompted to take my life and that of Covey, but was prevented by a combination of hope and fear. . . .

You have seen how a man was made a slave; you shall see how a slave was made a man. On one of the hottest days of the month of August, 1833, Bill Smith, William Hughes, a slave named Eli,

---

Source: Frederick Douglass, *Narrative of the Life of Frederick Douglass, An American Slave* (Boston, 1845).

and myself were engaged in fanning wheat. . . . The work was simple, requiring strength rather than intellect; yet, to one entirely unused to such work, it came very hard. About three o'clock of that day, I broke down; my strength failed me; I was seized with a violent aching of the head, attended with extreme dizziness; I trembled in every limb. . . .

Mr. Covey was at the house, about one hundred yards from the treading-yard where we were fanning. On hearing the fan stop, he left immediately, and came to the spot where we were. He hastily enquired what the matter was. Bill answered that I was sick, and there was no one to bring wheat to the fan. I had by this time crawled away under the side of the post and rail-fence by which the yard was enclosed, hoping to find relief by getting out of the sun. He then asked where I was. He was told by one of the hands. He came to the spot, and after looking at me awhile, asked me what was the matter. I told him as well as I could, for I scarce had strength to speak. He then gave me a savage kick in the side, and told me to get up. I tried to do so, but fell back in the attempt. He gave me another kick, and again told me to rise. I again tried, and succeeded in gaining my feet: but, stopping to get the tub with which I was feeding the fan, I again staggered and fell. While down in this situation, Mr. Covey took up the hickory slat with which Hughes had been striking off the half-bushel measure, and with it gave me a heavy blow upon the head, making a large wound, and the blood ran freely; and with this, again told me to get up. I made no effort to comply, having now made up my mind to let him do his worst. In a short time after receiving this blow, my head grew better. Mr. Covey had now left me to my fate. At this moment I resolved to go to my master, enter a complaint, and ask his protection. In order to [do] this, I must that afternoon walk seven miles; and this, under the circumstances, was truly a severe undertaking. I was exceedingly feeble; made so as much by the kicks and blows which I received, as by the severe fit of sickness to which I had been subjected. I, however, watched my chance, while Covey was looking in an opposite direction, and started for St. Michael's. I succeeded in getting a considerable distance on my way to the woods, when Covey discovered me, and called after me to come back, threatening what he would do if I did not come. I disregarded both his calls and his threats, and made my way to the woods as fast as my feeble state would allow; and thinking I might be overhauled by him if I kept the road, I walked through the woods, keeping far enough from the road to avoid detection, and near enough to prevent losing my way. I had not gone far, before my little strength again failed me. I could go no farther. I fell down, and lay for a considerable time. The blood was yet oozing from the wound on my head. For a time I thought I should bleed to death, and think now that I should have done so, but the blood so matted my hair as to stop the wound. After lying there about three quarters of an hour, I nerved myself up again, and started on my way, through bogs and briers, barefooted and bareheaded, tearing my feet sometimes at nearly every step; and after a journey of about seven miles, occupying some five hours to perform it, I arrived at master's store. I then presented an appearance enough to affect any but a heart of iron. From the crown of my head to my feet, I was covered with blood. My hair was all clotted with dust and blood, my shirt was stiff with briers and thorns, and were also covered with blood. I supposed I looked like a man who had escaped a den of wild beasts, and barely escaped them. In this state I appeared before my master, humbly entreating him to interpose his authority for my protection. I told him all the circumstances as well as I could, and it seemed, as I spoke, at times to affect him. He would then walk the floor, and seek to justify Covey by saying he expected I deserved it. He asked me what I wanted. I told him to let me get a new home; that as sure as I lived with Mr. Covey again, I should live with but to die with him; that Covey would surely kill me—he was in a fair way for it. Master Thomas ridiculed the idea that there was any danger of Mr. Covey's killing me, and said that he knew Mr. Covey; that he was a good man, and that he could not think of taking me from him; that should he do so, he would lose the whole year's wages; that I belonged to Mr. Covey for one year, and that I must go back to him, come what might; and that I must not trouble him with any more stories, or that he would get hold of me. After threatening me thus, he gave me a very large dose of salts, telling me that I might remain in St. Michael's that night, (it being quite late,) but that I must be off back to Mr. Covey's early in the morning; and that if I did not, he would get hold of me, which meant that he would whip me. I remained all night, and according to his orders, I started off to Covey's in the morning (Saturday morning) wearied in body and broken in spirit. I got no supper that night, or breakfast that morning. I reached Covey's about nine o'clock; and just as I was getting over the fence that divided Mrs. Kemp's fields from ours, out ran Covey with his cowskin, to give me another whipping. Before he could reach me, I succeeded in getting to the cornfield; and as the corn was very high, it afforded me the means of hiding. He seemed very angry, and searched for me a long time. My behaviour was altogether unaccountable. He finally gave up the chase, thinking, I suppose, that I must come home for something to eat; he would give himself no further trouble in looking for me. I spent that day mostly in the woods, having the alternative before me,—to go home and be whipped to death, or stay in the woods and be starved to death. That night, I fell in with Sandy Jenkins, a slave with whom I was somewhat acquainted. Sandy had a free wife, who lived about four miles from Mr. Covey's; and it being Saturday, he was on his way home to see her. I told him my circumstances, and he very kindly invited me to go home with him. I went home with him, and talked this whole matter over, and got his advice as to what course it was best for me to pursue. I found Sandy an old adviser. He told me, with great solemnity, I must go back to Covey; but that before I went, I must go with him into another part of the woods, where there was a certain root, which, if I would take some of it with me, carrying it always on my right side, would render it impossible for Mr. Covey, or any other white man, to whip me. He said he had carried it for years; and since he had done so, he had never received a blow, and never expected to, while he carried it. I at first rejected the idea, that the simple carrying of a root in my pocket would have any such effect as he had said, and was not disposed to take it; but Sandy impressed the necessity with such earnestness, telling me it could do no harm, if it did not good. To please him, I at length took the root, and, according to his direction, carried it upon my right side. This was Sunday morning. I immediately started for home; and upon entering the yard gate, out came Mr. Covey on his way to meeting. He spoke to me very kindly, bade me drive the pigs from a lot near by, and passed toward the church. Now this singular conduct of Mr. Covey really made me begin to think that there was something in the root which Sandy had given me; and had it been any other day than Sunday, I could have attributed the conduct to no other cause that the influence of that root; and as it was, I was half inclined to think the root to be something more than I at first had taken it to be. All went well till Monday morning. On this morning, the virtue of the root was fully tested. Long before daylight, I was called to go and rub, curry, and feed the horses. I obeyed, and was glad to obey. But whilst thus engaged, whilst in the act of throwing down some blades from the loft, Mr. Covey entered the stable with a long rope; and just as I was half way out of the loft, he caught hold of my legs, and was about tying me. As soon as I found what he was up to, I gave a sudden spring, and as I did so, he holding to my legs, I was brought sprawling on the stable floor. Mr. Covey seemed now to think he had me, and could do what he pleased; but at this moment—from whence came the spirit I don't know—I resolved to fight; and suiting my action to the resolution, I seized Covey hard by the throat; and as I did so, I rose. He held on to me, and I to him. My resistance was so entirely unexpected, that Covey seemed taken all aback. He trembled like a leaf. This gave me assurance, and I held him uneasy, causing the blood to run where I touched him with the ends of my fingers. Mr. Covey soon called out to Hughes for help. Hughes came, and, while Covey held me, attempted to tie my right hand. While he was in the act of doing so, I watched my chance, and gave him a heavy kick close under the ribs. This kick fairly sickened Hughes, so that he left me in the hands of Mr. Covey. This kick had the effect of not only weakening Hughes, but Covey also. While he saw Hughes bending over with pain, his courage quailed. He asked me if I meant to persist in my resistance. I told him I did, come what might; that he had used me like a brute for six months, and that I was determined to be used so no longer. With that, he strove to drag me to a stick that was lying just out of the stable door. He meant to knock me down. But just as he was leaning over to get the stick, I seized him with both hands by his collar, and brought him by a sudden snatch to the ground. By this time, Bill came. Covey called upon him for assistance, Bill wanted to know what he could do. Covey said, "Take hold of him, take hold of him!" Bill said his master hired him out to work, and not to help to whip me; so he left Covey and myself to fight our own battle out. We were at it for nearly two hours. Covey sat length let me go, puffing and blowing at a great rate, saying that if I had not resisted, he would not have whipped me half so much. The truth was, that he had not whipped me at all. I considered him as getting entirely the worst end of the bargain; for he had drawn no blood from me, but I had from him The whole six months afterwards, that I spent with Mr. Covey, he never laid the weight of his finger upon me in anger. He would occasionally say, he didn't want to get hold of me again. "No," thought I, "you need not; for you will come off worse than you did before."

This battle with Mr. Covey was the turning-point in my career as a slave. It rekindled the few expiring embers of freedom, and revived within me a sense of my own manhood. It recalled the departed self-confidence, and inspired me again with a determination to be free. The gratification afforded by the triumph was a full compensation for whatever else might follow, even death itself. He only can understand the deep satisfaction which I experienced, who had himself repelled by force the bloody arm of slavery. I felt as I never felt before. It was a glorious resurrection from the tomb of slavery to the heaven of freedom. My long-crushed spirit rose, cowardice departed, bold defiance took its place; and now I resolved that, however long I might remain a slave in form, the day had passed forever when I could be a slave in fact. I did not hesitate to let it be known of me, that the white man who expected to succeed in whipping, must also succeed in killing me.

From this time I was never again what might be called fairly whipped, though I remained a slave four years afterwards. I had several fights, but was never whipped.

It was for a long time a matter of surprise to me why Mr. Covey did not immediately have me taken by the constable to the whipping-post, and there regularly whipped for the crime of raising my hand against a white man in defence of myself. And the only explanation I can now think of does not entirely satisfy me; but such as it is, I will give it. Mr. Covey enjoyed the most unbounded reputation for being a first-rate overseer and Negro-breaker. It was of considerable importance to him. That reputation was at stake; and had he sent me—a boy of sixteen years old—to the whipping-post, his reputation would have been lost; so, to save his reputation, he suffered me to go unpunished.

2
Nat Turner

"THE LAST SHOULD BE FIRST"

In response to questions from a white lawyer named Thomas R. Gray, Nat Turner explains why he led his revolt against slavery.

Sir—You have asked me to give a history of the motives which induced me to undertake the late insurrection, as you call it—To do so I must go back to the days of my infancy. . . . In my childhood a circumstance occurred which made an indelible impression on my mind, and laid the groundwork of that enthusiasm, which has terminated so fatally to many, both white and black, and for which I am about to atone at the gallows. . . . Being at play with other children, when three or four years old, I was telling them something, which my mother overhearing, said it had happened before I was born . . . others being called on were greatly astonished . . . and caused them to say in my hearing, I surely would be a prophet. . . .

Source: *The Confessions of Nat Turner, the Leader of the Late Insurrection in Southampton, Va.* (Baltimore, 1831).

For two years [I] prayed continually, whenever my duty would permit—and then again I had [a] . . . revelation, which fully confirmed me in the impression that I was ordained for some great purpose, in the hands of the Almighty. . . .

About this time [around 1825] I had a vision—and I saw white spirits and black spirits engaged in battle, and the sun was darkened—the thunder rolled in the Heavens, and blood flowed in streams. . . .

And on the 12th of May, 1828, I heard a loud noise in the heavens, and the Spirit instantly appeared to me and said the Serpent was loosened, and Christ had laid down the yoke he had borne for the sins of men, and that I should take it on and fight against the Serpent, for the time was fast approaching when the first should be last and the last should be first.

[Question] Do you not find yourself mistaken now?

[Answer] Was not Christ crucified? And by signs in the heavens that it would be made known to me when I should commence the great work—and until the first sign appeared, I should conceal it from the knowledge of men—And on the appearance of the sign (the eclipse of the sun last February), I should arise and prepare myself, and slay my enemies with their own weapons. And immediately on the sign appearing in the heavens, the seal was removed from my lips, and I communicated the great work laid out before me to do to four in whom I had the greatest confidence (Henry, Hark, Nelson, and Sam)—It was intended by us to have begun the work of death on the 4th of July last—Many were the plans formed and rejected by us, and it affected my mind to such a degree, that I fell sick, and the time passed without our coming to any determination how to commence—Still forming new schemes and rejecting them, when the sign appeared again, which determined me not to wait longer.

Since the commencement of 1830, I had been living with Mr. Joseph Travis, who was to me a kind master, and placed the greatest confidence in me: in fact, I had no cause to complain of his treatment of me. On Saturday evening, the 20th of August, it was agreed between Henry, Hark, and myself, to prepare a dinner the next day for the men we expected, and then to concert a plan, as we had not yet determined on any. Hark, on the following morning, brought a pig, and Henry brandy, and being joined by Sam, Nelson, Will and Jack, they prepared in the woods a dinner, where, about three o'clock, I joined them. . . .

I saluted them on coming up, and asked Will how came he

there, he answered, his life was worth no more than others, and his liberty as dear to him. I asked him if he thought to obtain it? He said he would, or lose his life. This was enough to put him in full confidence. Jack, I knew, was only a tool in the hands of Hark, it was quickly agreed we should commence at home (Mr. J. Travis') on that night, and until we had armed and equipped ourselves, and gathered sufficient force, neither age nor sex was to be spared (which was invariably adhered to). We remained at the feast, until about two hours in the night, when we went to the house and found Austin; they all went to the cider press and drank, except myself. On returning to the house Hark went to the door with an axe, for the purpose of breaking it open, as we knew we were strong enough to murder the family, if they were awakened by the noise; but reflecting that it might create an alarm in the neighborhood, we determined to enter the house secretly, and murder them whilst sleeping. Hark got a ladder and set it against the chimney, on which I ascended, and hoisting a window, entered and came down stairs, unbarred the door, and removed the guns from their places. It was then observed that I must spill the first blood. On which, armed with a hatchet, and accompanied by Will, I entered my master's chamber, it being dark, I could not give a death blow, the hatchet glanced from his head, he sprang from the bed and called his wife, it was his last word, Will laid him dead, with a blow of his axe, and Mrs. Travis shared the same fate, as she lay in bed. The murder of this family, five in number, was the work of a moment, not one of them awoke; there was a little infant sleeping in a cradle, that was forgotten, until we had left the house and gone some distance, when Henry and Will returned and killed it; we got here, four guns that would shoot and several old muskets, with a pound or two of powder. We remained some time at the barn, where we paraded; I formed them in a line as soldiers, and . . . marched them off to Mr. Salthul Francis', about six hundred yards distant. Sam and Will went to the door and knocked. Mr. Francis asked who was there, Sam replied it was him, and he had a letter for him, on which he got up and came to the door; they immediately seized him, and dragging him out a little from the door, he was dispatched by repeated blows on the head; there was no other white person in the family. We started from there for Mrs. Reese's, maintaining the most perfect silence on our march, where finding the door un-locked, we entered, and murdered Mrs. Reese in her bed, while sleeping; her son awoke, but it was only to sleep the sleep of death, he had only time to say who is that, and he was no more. From Mrs. Reese's we went to Mrs. Turner's, a mile distant, which we reached about sunrise, on Monday morning. Henry, Austin, and Sam, went to the still, where, finding Mr. Peebles, Austin shot him, and the rest of us went to the house; as we approached, the family discovered us, and shut the door. Vain hope! Will, with one stroke of his axe opened it, and we entered and found Mrs. Turner and Mrs. Newsome in the middle of a room, almost frightened to death. Will immediately killed Mrs. Turner, with one blow of his axe. I took Mrs. Newsome by the hand, and with the sword I had when I was apprehended, I struck her several blows over the head, but not being able to kill her, as the sword was dull. Will turning around and discovering it, dispatched her also. A general destruction of property and search for money and ammunition, always succeeded the murders. By this time my company amounted to fifteen, and nine men mounted, who started for Mrs. Whitehead's. . . . As we approached the house we discovered Mr. Richard Whitehead standing in the cotton patch, near the lane fence; we called him over into the lane, and Will, the executioner, was near at hand, with his fatal axe, to send him to an untimely grave. . . . As I came around to the door I saw Will pulling Mrs. Whitehead out of the house, and at the step he nearly severed her head from her body, with his broad axe. Miss Margaret, when I discovered her, had concealed herself in the corner . . . on my approach she fled, but was soon overtaken, and after repeated blows with a sword, I killed her by a blow on the head, with a fence rail. . . .

    . . . 'Twas my object to carry terror and devastation wherever we went. . . . I sometimes got in sight in time to see the work of death completed, viewed the mangled bodies as they lay, in silent satisfaction, and immediately started in quest of other victims— Having murdered Mrs. Waller and ten children, we started for Mr. William Williams'—having killed him and two little boys that were there; while engaged in this, Mrs. Williams fled and got some distance from the house, but she was pursued, overtaken, and compelled to get up behind one of the company, who brought her back, and after showing her the mangled body of her lifeless husband, she was told to get down and lay by his side, where she was shot dead. . . .

    Our number amounted now to fifty or sixty, all mounted and armed with guns, axes, swords, and clubs. . . . We were met by a party of white men, who had pursued our blood-stained track. . . . The white men, eighteen in number, approached us in about one hundred yards, when one of them fired. . . . I then ordered my men to fire and rush them; the few remaining stood their ground until we approached within fifty yards, when they fired and retreated. . . . As I saw them re-loading their guns, and more coming up than I saw at first, and several of my bravest men being wounded, the others became panick struck and squandered over the field; the white men pursued and fired on us several times. . . .

All deserted me but two, (Jacob and Nat,) we concealed ourselves in the woods until near night, when I sent them in search of Henry, Sam, Nelson, and Hark, and directed them to rally all they could, at the place where we had our dinner the Sunday before, where they would find me, and I accordingly returned there as soon as it was dark and remained until Wednesday evening, when discovering white men riding around the place as though they were looking for someone, and none of my men joining me, I concluded Jacob and Nat had been taken, and compelled to betray me. On this I gave up all hope for the present; and on Thursday night after having supplied myself with provisions from Mr. Travis' I scratched a hole under a pile of fence rails in a field, where I concealed myself for six weeks, never leaving my hiding place but for a few minutes in the dead of night to get water which was very near. . . . I know not how long I might have led this life, if accident had not betrayed me, a dog in the neighborhood passing by my hiding place one night while I was out, was attracted by some meat I had in my cave, and crawled in and stole it, and was coming out just as I returned. A few nights after, two Negroes having started to go hunting with the same dog, and passed that way, the dog came again to the place, and having just gone out to walk about, discovered me and barked, on which thinking myself discovered, I spoke to them to beg concealment. On making myself known they fled from me. Knowing then they would betray me, I immediately left my hiding place, and was pursued almost incessantly until I was taken a fortnight afterwards by Mr. Benjamin Phipps, in a little hole I had dug out with my sword, for the purpose of concealment, under the top of a fallen tree.

Chapter 10

"Follow the Drinkin' Gourd":

FLIGHT

The images are indelibly etched in the American mind: fugitive slaves traveling furtively under cover of darkness, pursued by heavily armed slave catchers and vicious bloodhounds, assisted by benevolent abolitionists who hide them in haystacks and secret rooms and lead them to freedom. Few myths exert a more powerful hold on the American imagination than the underground railroad. But as the historian Larry Gara first demonstrated a generation ago, the underground railroad was more myth than reality.

Most runaways fled only a short distance. Slaves might hide in nearby swamps to escape punishment or sale. Many slaves ran away to visit spouses or children. Groups of slaves might run away temporarily to protest overwork or cruel punishment. Those fugitives who were trying to escape slavery did not necessarily flee northward. Many headed toward Florida or to the Great Dismal Swamp in Virginia and North Carolina, where they established "maroon" colonies. Others hid in southern cities.

The number of slaves who escaped from slavery is unknown; it appears that the number was about a thousand a year. And, for the most part, these fugitives could not depend on an organized system of underground railroad stations to ferry them to freedom. While some abolitionists like Levi Coffin, William Still, and Harriet Tubman actively assisted fugitives, most runaways had to rely on their own wits. They had to borrow or forge passes, devise disguises, locate hiding places, or stow away on boats or trains. As one Illinois abolitionist later pointed out: "I do not know of any fugitive ever being transported by anyone, they always had to pilot their own canoe, with the little help that they received."

1
Margaret Ward

"SHE WOULD NOT BE WHIPPED, SHE WOULD RATHER DIE"

Margaret Ward and her infant son Samuel Ringgold Ward, slaves from Maryland, follow the North Star to freedom.

At sixteen she went to live with her young mistress, who was married to a planter in that fertile country known as the "Eastern Shore." At eighteen Margaret was a large woman, tall and well formed, her complexion black as jet, her countenance always pleasant, though she seldom laughed. She talked but little, even to those of her own race. At twenty years of age she became the wife of a worthy young man to whom she had given her best affections. Not long after, her young master became very angry with her for what he called stubbornness and resistance to his will, and threatened to chastise her by whipping—a degradation that she had always felt that she could not submit to, and yet to obey her master in the thing he demanded would be still worse. She therefore told him that she would not be whipped, she would rather die, and gave him warning that any attempt to execute his threat would surely result in the death of one of them. He knew her too well to risk the experiment, and decided to punish her in another way. He sold her husband, and she saw him bound in chains and driven off with a large drove of men and women for the New Orleans market. He then put her in the hands of a brutal overseer, with directions to work her to the extent of her ability on a tobacco plantation, which command was enforced up to the day of the birth of her child. At the end of one week she was driven again to the field and compelled to perform a full task, having at no time any abatement of her work on account of her situation, with exception of one week. It was the

Source: Eber Pettit, *Sketches in the History of the Underground Railroad* (Fredonia, N.Y., 1879).

153

custom on the plantation to establish nurseries, presided over by old, broken down slaves, where mothers might leave their infants, but this privilege was denied to Margaret. She was obliged to leave her child under the shade of a bush in the field, returning to it but twice during the long day. On returning to the child one evening she found it apparently senseless, exhausted with crying, and a large serpent lying across it. Although she felt that it would be better for both herself and child if it were dead, yet a mother's heart impelled her to make an effort to save it, and by caressing him and careful handling she resuscitated it.

As soon as she heard its feeble, wailing cry, she made a vow to deliver her boy from the cruel power of slavery or die in the attempt, and falling prostrate, she prayed for strength to perform her vow, and for grace and patience to sustain her in her suffering, toil, and hunger; then pressing her child to her bosom, she fled with all the speed of which she was capable toward the North Star. Having gone a mile or two, she heard something pursuing her; on looking round she saw Watch, the old house dog. Watch was a large mastiff, somewhat old, and with him Margaret had ever been a favorite, and since she had been driven to the field, Watch often visited her at her cabin in the evening. She feared it would not be safe to allow Watch to go with her, but she could not induce him to go back, so she resumed her flight, accompanied by her faithful escort. At break of day she hid herself on the border of a plantation and soon fell asleep.

Toward evening she was aroused by the noise made by the slaves returning to their quarters, and seeing an old woman lingering behind all the others, she called her, told her troubles, and asked for food. The old woman returned about midnight with a pretty good supply of food, which Margaret divided with Watch, and then started on, taking the North Star for her guide. The second day after she left, the Overseer employed a hunter with his dogs to find her. He started with an old slut and three whelps, thinking, no doubt, that as the game was only a woman and her infant child, it would be a good time to train his pups.

Margaret had been missed at roll call the morning after her flight, but the Overseer supposed she was hiding near the place for a day or two, and that hunger would soon drive her up; therefore, when the hunter started, he led the old dog, expecting to find her in an hour or two, but not overtaking her the first day, on the next morning, he let his hounds loose, intending to follow on horseback, guided by their voices. About noon, the old dog struck the track at the place where Margaret had made her little camp the day before, and she bounded off with fresh vigor, leaving the man and the younger dogs beyond sight and hearing. The young dogs soon lost the track where Margaret forded the streams, and the old dog was miles away, leaving the hunter without a guide to direct him.

Margaret had been lying in the woods on the bank of a river, intending to start again as soon as it was dark, when she was startled by the whining and nervous motions of old Watch, and listening, she heard the hoarse ringing bay of a blood-hound. Although she had expected that she would be hunted with dogs, and recalled over and over again the shocking accounts related by Overseers to the slaves, of fugitives overtaken and torn in pieces by the savage Spanish blood-hounds, she had not, until now, realized the horrors of her situation. She expected to have to witness the destruction of her child by the savage brute, and then be torn in pieces herself. Meanwhile, old Watch lay with his nose between his feet, facing the coming foe. The hound, rendered more fierce by the freshness of the track, came rushing headlong with nose to the ground, scenting her prey, and seemed not to see old Watch, until, leaping to pass over him, she found her wind-pipe suddenly collapsed in the massive jaws of the old mastiff. The struggle was not very noisy, for Watch would not even growl, and the hound could not, for it was terribly energetic. The hound made rapid and persuasive gestures with her paws and tail, but it was of no use, the jaws of old Watch relaxed not until all signs of life in his enemy had ceased. Margaret came back from the river, and would have embraced her faithful friend, but fearing that a stronger pack was following, she hastily threw the dead hound into the river and pursued her journey.

Within a few hours after her providential escape by the aid of her faithful friend, old Watch, from the fangs of the slave hunter's hound, she fell into the hands of friends, who kept her secreted until she could be sent into a free State; while there, she learned about the pursuit by the hunter, and that he never knew what became of his best hound. After the chase was abandoned, she, through a regular line, similar to our Underground Railroad, was sent to Philadelphia and then to New York, where she became a celebrated nurse, and always befriended the poor of all colors and all nationalities.

2
Frederick Douglass

"A NEW WORLD BURST UPON
MY AGITATED VISION"

*Frederick Douglass uses a black sailor's papers to escape
from slavery.*

I have never approved of the very public manner, in which
some of our western friends have conducted what they call the
"Under-ground Railroad," but which, I think, by their open decla-
rations, has been made, most emphatically, the "Upper-ground
Railroad." Its stations are far better known to the slaveholders than
to the slaves. I honor those good men and women for their noble
daring, in willingly subjecting themselves to persecution, by openly
avowing their participation in the escape of slaves; nevertheless,
the good resulting from such avowals, is of a very questionable
character. It may kindle an enthusiasm, very pleasant to inhale; but
that is of no practical benefit to themselves, nor to the slaves escaping. Nothing is more evident, than that such disclosures are a positive evil to the slaves remaining, and seeking to escape. In pub-
lishing such accounts, the anti-slavery man addresses the slaveholder, not the slave; he stimulates the former to greater watchful-
ness, and adds to the facilities for capturing the slave. . . .

My condition in the year [1838] of my escape, was, comparatively, a free and easy one, so far, at least, as the wants of the physical man were concerned; but the reader will bear in mind, that my
troubles from the beginning, have been less physical than mental.
. . . The practice, from week to week, of openly robbing me of all
my earnings, kept the nature and character of slavery constantly
before me. I could be robbed by indirection, but this was too open
and barefaced to be endured. I could see no reason why I should,
at the end of each week, pour the reward of my honest toil into the
purse of any man. . . .

Held to a strict account, and kept under a close watch—the
old suspicion of my running away not having been entirely removed—escape from slavery, even in Baltimore, was very difficult.

Source: Frederick Douglass, *My Bondage and My Freedom* (New York, 1855); Frederick Holland, *Frederick Douglass* (New York, 1895).

The railroad from Baltimore to Philadelphia was under regulations so stringent, that even free colored travelers were almost excluded. They must have free papers; they must be measured and carefully examined, before they were allowed to enter the cars; they only went in the day time, even when so examined. The steamboats were under regulations equally stringent. All the great turnpikes, leading northward, were beset with kidnappers, a class of men who watched the newspapers for advertisements for runaway slaves, making their living by the accursed reward of slave hunting.

My discontent grew upon me, and I was on the lookout for means of escape. With money, I could easily have managed the matter, and, therefore, I hit upon the plan of soliciting the privilege of hiring my time. It is quite common, in Baltimore, to allow slaves this privilege, and it is the practice, also in New Orleans. A slave who is considered trustworthy, can, by paying his master a definite sum regularly, at the end of each week dispose of his time as he likes. . . .

The laws of Maryland required every free Negro to carry papers describing him accurately and to pay liberally for this protection. Slaves often escaped by borrowing papers from a friend, to whom the precious documents would be returned by mail. Whenever a coloured man came with free papers to the railroad station to buy a ticket, he was always examined carefully enough to insure the detection of a runaway, unless the resemblance was very close. Our hero was not acquainted with any free Negro who looked much like him; but he found out that passengers who paid on the cars were not scrutinized so minutely as those who bought tickets, and also that sailors were treated with peculiar indulgence by the conductors. . . .

Among his friends was a sailor who was of much darker hue than he was himself, but who owned a protection, setting forth his occupation, and bearing the sacred figure of the American eagle. This was borrowed; sailor's clothes were purchased, and on Monday morning, the fugitive jumped on the train just as it started. His baggage had been put aboard by a friendly hackman. He was greatly troubled, for, as he wrote to his master, ten years later, I was making a leap in the dark. The probabilities, so far as I could by reason determine them, were stoutly against the undertaking. The preliminaries and precautions I had adopted previously, all worked badly. I was like one going to war without weapons—ten chances of defeat to one of victory. One in whom I had confided, and one who had promised me assistance, appalled by the fear at the trial hour, deserted me. However, gloomy as was the prospect, thanks be to the Most High, who is ever the God of the oppressed, at the moment which was to determine my whole earthly career, His grace was sufficient; my mind was made up.

His anxiety increased in consequence of the harshness with which the conductor questioned other passengers in the Negro car. The sailor, however, was addressed kindly and told, after a mere glance at the protection, that it was all right. Thus far he was safe; but there were several people on the train who would have known him at once in any other clothes. A German blacksmith looked at him intently, and apparently recognized him, but said nothing. On the ferry boat, by which they crossed the Susquehanna, he found an old acquaintance employed, and was asked some dangerous questions. On they went, however, until they stopped to let the train from Philadelphia pass. At the window sat a man under whom the runaway had been at work but a few days before. He might easily have recognized him, and would certainly have him arrested; but fortunately he was looking another way. The passengers went on from Wilmington by steamer to Philadelphia, where one of them took the train for New York and arrived early on Tuesday. In less than twenty-four hours the slave had made himself a free man. It was but a few months since he had become twenty-one.

The flight was a bold and perilous one; but here I am, in the great city of New York, safe and sound, without loss of blood or bone. In less than a week after leaving Baltimore, I was walking amid the hurrying throng, and gazing upon the dazzling wonders of Broadway. The dreams of my childhood and the purposes of my manhood were now fulfilled. A free state around me, and a free earth under my feet! What a moment was this to me! A whole year was pressed into a single day. A new World burst upon my agitated vision.

3
Harriet Tubman

"THE MOST REMARKABLE WOMAN OF THIS AGE"

Harriet Tubman, the famous fugitive slave from Maryland, risks her life sneaking into slave territory to free slaves. Slaveholders posted a $40,000 reward for the capture of the "Black Moses."

Source: *Commonwealth* (July 17, 1863); *Freeman's Record* (March 1865).

One of the teachers lately commissioned by the New-England Freedmen's Aid Society is probably the most remarkable woman of this age. That is to say, she has performed more wonderful deeds by the native power of her own spirit against adverse circumstances than any other. She is well known to many by the various names which her eventful life has given her; Harriet Garrison, Gen. Tubman, &c.; but among the slaves she is universally known by her well earned title of Moses,—Moses the deliverer. She is a rare instance, in the midst of high civilization and intellectual culture, of a being of great native powers, working powerfully, and to beneficient ends, entirely untaught by schools or books.

Her maiden name was Araminta Ross. She is the granddaughter of a native African, and has not a drop of white blood in her veins. She was born in 1820 or 1821, on the Eastern Shore of Maryland. . . .

She seldom lived with her owner, but was usually "hired out" to different persons. She once "hired her time," and employed it in the rudest farming labors, ploughing, carting, driving the oxen, &c., to so good advantage that she was able in one year to buy a pair of steers worth forty dollars.

When quite young she lived with a very pious mistress; but the slaveholder's religion did not prevent her from whipping the young girl for every slight or fancied fault. Araminta found that this was usually a morning exercise; so she prepared for it by putting on all the thick clothes she could procure to protect her skin. She made sufficient outcry, however, to convince her mistress that her blows had full effect; and in the afternoon she would take off her wrappings, and dress as well as she could. When invited into family prayers, she preferred to stay on the landing, and pray for herself; "and I prayed to God," she says "to make me strong and able to fight and that's what I've allers prayed for ever since. . . . "

In her youth she received a severe blow on her head from a heavy weight thrown by her master at another slave, but which accidentally hit her. The blow produced a disease of the brain which was severe for a long time, and still makes her very lethargic. . . . She was married about 1844 to a free colored man named John Tubman, but never had any children. Owing to changes in her owner's family, it was determined to sell her and some other slaves; but her health was so much injured, that a purchaser was not easily found. At length she became convinced that she would soon be carried away, and she decided to escape. Her brothers did not agree with her plans, and she walked off alone, following the guidance of the brooks, which she had observed to run North. . . .

She remained two years in Philadelphia working hard and carefully hoarding her money. Then she hired a room, furnished it as well as she could, bought a nice suit of men's clothes, and went back to Maryland for her husband. But the faithless man had taken to himself another wife. Harriet did not dare venture into her presence, but sent word to her husband where she was. He declined joining her. At first her grief and anger were excessive . . . but finally she thought . . . "if he could do without her, she could without him," and so "he dropped out of her heart," and she determined to give her life to brave deeds. Thus all personal aims died out of her heart; and with her simple brave motto, "I can't die but once," she began the work which has made her Moses,—the deliverer of her people. Seven or eight times she has returned to the neighborhood of her former home, always at the risk of death in the most terrible forms, and each time has brought away a company of fugitive slaves, and led them safely to the free States, or to Canada. Every time she went, the dangers increased. In 1857, she brought away her old parents, and, as they were too feeble to walk, she was obliged to hire a wagon, which added greatly to the perils of the journey. In 1860 she went for the last time, and among her troop was an infant whom they were obliged to keep stupefied with laudanum to prevent its outcries. . . .

She always came in the winter when the nights are long and dark, and people who have homes stay in them. She was never seen on the plantation herself; but appointed a rendezvous for her company eight or ten miles distant, so that if they were discovered at the first start she was not compromised. She started on Saturday night; the slaves at that time being allowed to go away from home to visit their friends—so that they would not be missed until Monday morning. Even then they were supposed to have loitered on the way, and it would often be late on Monday afternoon before the flight would be certainly known. If by any further delay the advertisement was not sent out before Tuesday morning, she felt secure of keeping ahead of it; but if it were, it required all her ingenuity to escape. She resorted to various devices, she had confidential friends all along the road. She would hire a man to follow the one who put up the notices, and take them down as soon as his back was turned. She crossed creeks on railroad bridges by night, she hid her company in the woods while she herself not being advertised went into the towns in search of information. . . .

The expedition was governed by the strictest rules. If any man gave out, he must be shot. "Would you really do that?" she was asked. "Yes," she replied, "if he was weak enough to give out, he'd be weak enough to betray us all, and all who had helped us; and do you think I'd let so many die just for one coward man." "Did you ever have to shoot any one?" she was asked. "One time," she said, "a man gave out on the second night; his feet were sore and swollen, he couldn't go any further; he'd rather go back and die, if he must." They tried all arguments in vain, bathed his feet, tried to strengthen him, but it was of no use, he would go back. Then she said, "I told the boys to get their guns ready, and shoot him. They'd have done it in a minute; but when he heard that, he jumped right up and went on as well as any body. . . . "

When going on these journeys she often lay alone in the forests all night. Her whole soul was filled with awe of the mysterious Unseen Presence, which thrilled her with such depths of emotion, that all other care and fear vanished. Then she seemed to speak with her Maker "as a man talketh with his friend;" her childlike petitions had direct answers, and beautiful visions lifted her up above all doubt and anxiety into serene trust and faith. No man can be a hero without this faith in some form; the sense that he walks not in his own strength, but leaning on an almighty arm. Call it fate, destiny, what you will, Moses of old, Moses of to-day, believed it to be Almighty God.

4
Henry "Box" Brown

"HE . . . HIT UPON A NEW INVENTION ALTOGETHER"

Henry "Box" Brown escapes slavery by having himself nailed into a small box and shipped from Richmond to Philadelphia.

He was decidedly an unhappy piece of property in the city of Richmond, Va. In the condition of a slave he felt that it would be impossible for him to remain. Full well did he know, however, that it was no holiday task to escape the vigilance of Virginia slave-hunters, or the wrath of an enraged master for committing the unpardonable sin of attempting to escape to a land of liberty. So Brown counted well the cost before venturing upon his hazardous undertaking. Ordinary modes of travel he concluded might prove

Source: William Still, *Underground Railroad Records* (Philadelphia, 1872).

disastrous to his hopes; he, therefore, hit upon a new invention altogether, which was to have himself boxed up and forwarded to Philadelphia direct by express. The size of the box and how it was to be made to fit him most comfortably, was of his own ordering. Two feet eight inches deep, two feet wide, and three feet long were the exact dimensions of the box, lined with maize. His resources in regard to food and water consisted of the following: One bladder of water and a few small biscuits. His mechanical implement to meet the death-struggle for fresh air, all told, was one large gimlet. Satisfied that it would be far better to peril his life for freedom in this way than to remain under the galling yoke of Slavery, he entered his box, which was safely nailed up and hooped with five hickory hoops, and then was addressed by his next friend, James A. Smith, a shoe dealer, to Wm. H. Johnson, Arch Street, Philadelphia, marked, "This side up with care." In this condition he was sent to Adams' Express office in a dray, and thence by overland express to Philadelphia. It was twenty-six hours from the time he left Richmond until his arrival in the city of Brotherly Love. The notice, "This side up, etc.," did not avail with the different expressmen, who hesitated not to handle the box in the usual rough manner common to this class of men. For a while they actually had the box upside down, and had him on his head for miles. A few days before he was expected, certain intimation was conveyed to a member of the Vigilance Committee that a box might be expected by

Henry Box Brown in William Still, THE UNDERGROUND RAILROAD, RECORDS, 1872, p. 140.

the three o'clock morning train from the South, which might contain a man.

All was quiet. The door had been safely locked. The proceedings commenced. Mr. [J. M.] McKim rapped quietly on the lid of the box and called out, "All right!" Instantly came the answer from within, "All right, sir!"

The witnesses will never forget that moment. Saw and hatchet quickly had the five hickory hoops cut and the lid off, and the marvelous resurrection of Brown ensued. Rising up in the box, he reached out his hand, saying, "How do you do, gentlemen?" The little assemblage hardly knew what to think or do at the moment. He was about as wet as if he had come up out of the Delaware. Very soon he remarked that, before leaving Richmond he had selected for his arrival hymn (if he lived) the Psalm beginning with these words: "I awaited patiently for the Lord, and He heard my prayer." And most touchingly did he sing the psalm, much to his own relief, as well as to the delight of his small audience.

5
Margaret Garner

"SHE WOULD KILL HERSELF . . . BEFORE SHE WOULD RETURN TO BONDAGE"

Margaret Garner, a fugitive slave from Kentucky, killed one of her children rather than permit her to be returned to slavery. She drowned in a shipwreck as she was being brought back to slavery. Her story formed the basis of Toni Morrison's novel Beloved.

Perhaps no case that came under my notice, while engaged in aiding fugitive slaves, attracted more attention and aroused deeper interest and sympathy than the case of Margaret Garner, the slave mother who killed her child rather than see it taken back to slavery. This happened in the latter part of January, 1856. The Ohio River was frozen over at the time, and the opportunity thus offered for

Source: Levi Coffin, *Reminiscences* (Cincinnati, 1876).

escaping to a free State was embraced by a number of slaves living in Kentucky, several miles back from the river. A party of seventeen, belonging to different masters in the same neighborhood, made arrangements to escape together. There was snow on the ground and the roads were smooth, so the plan of going to the river on a sled naturally suggested itself. The time fixed for their flight was Sabbath night, and having managed to get a large sled and two good horses, belonging to one of their masters, the party of seventeen crowded into the sled and started on their hazardous journey in the latter part of the night. They drove the horses at full speed, and at daylight reached the River below Covington, opposite Wester Row. They left the sled and horses here, and as quickly as possible crossed the river on foot. It was now broad daylight, and people were beginning to pass about the streets and the fugitives divided their company that they might not attract so much notice.

An old slave named Simon and his wife Mary, together with their son Robert and his wife Margaret Garner and four children, made their way to the house of a colored man named Kite, who had formerly lived in their neighborhood and had been purchased from slavery by his father, Joe Kite. They had to make several inquiries in order to find Kite's house, which was below Mill Creek, in the lower part of the city. This afterward led to their discovery; they had been seen by a number of persons on their way to Kite's, and were easily traced by pursuers. The other nine fugitives were more fortunate. They made their way up town and found friends who conducted them to safe hiding-places, where they remained until night. They were put on the Underground Railroad, and went safely through to Canada. . . .

In a few minutes . . . [Kite's] house was surrounded by pursuers—the masters of the fugitives, with officers and a posse of men. The door and windows were barred, and those inside refused to give admittance. The fugitives were determined to fight, and to die, rather than to be taken back to slavery. Margaret, the mother of the four children, declared that she would kill herself and her children before she would return to bondage. The slave men were armed and fought bravely. The window was first battered down with a stick of wood, and one of the deputy marshals attempted to enter, but a pistol shot from within made a flesh wound on his arm and caused him to abandon the attempt. The pursuers then battered down the door with some timber and rushed in. The husband of Margaret fired several shots, and wounded one of the officers, but was soon overpowered and dragged out of the house. At this moment, Margaret Garner, seeing that their hopes of freedom were in vain, seized a butcher knife that lay on the table, and with one stroke cut the throat of her little daughter, whom she probably loved the best. She then attempted to take the life of the other children and to kill herself, but she was overpowered and hampered before she could complete her desperate work. The whole party was then arrested and lodged in jail.

The trial lasted two weeks, drawing crowds to the courtroom every day. . . . The counsel for the defense brought witnesses to prove that the fugitives had been permitted to visit the city at various times previously. It was claimed that Margaret Garner had been brought here by her owners a number of years before, to act as nurse girl, and according to the law which liberated slaves who were brought into free States by the consent of their masters, she had been free from that time, and her children, all of whom had been born since then—following the condition of the mother—were likewise free.

The Commissioner decided that a voluntary return to slavery, after a visit to a free State, re-attached the conditions of slavery, and that the fugitives were legally slaves at the time of their escape. . . .

But in spite of touching appeals, of eloquent pleadings, the Commissioner remanded the fugitives back to slavery. He said that it was not a question of feeling to be decided by the chance current of his sympathies; the law of Kentucky and the United States made it a question of property.

Chapter 11

"The Walls Come Tumblin' Down":

EMANCIPATION

The slave population did not respond to the Civil War with a single voice. While southern planters stressed their bondsmen's loyalty and fidelity, in Adams County, Mississippi, slave insurrectionaries plotted to burn down the city of Natchez. Other slaves served as informants to the Union Army, assisted Union soldiers who escaped from Confederate prisons, or defected to Union lines or hid out in nearby woods or swamps. Wartime resistance to slavery also took the form of work stoppages, arson, sabotage, and isolated cases of murder. Enlistment in the Union Army represented the most dramatic form of resistance. In August 1862, the first slave regiment was formed, the 1st South Carolina Volunteers, and by the war's end, 186,000 blacks— three-quarters of them former slaves—served in the Union Army.

News of emancipation evoked a variety of responses, ranging from exuberance and exhilaration to incredulity and caution to apprehension and fear. In Choctaw County, Mississippi, former slaves whipped a planter named Nat Best to retaliate for his cruelties. In Richmond, Virginia, some fifteen hundred ex-slaves gathered in the Free African Church to sing hymns. A parade in Charleston attracted ten thousand spectators and featured a black-draped coffin bearing the words "Slavery is Dead." But many freedmen felt a deep uncertainty about their status and rights.

Ex-slaves expressed their newly-won freedom in diverse ways. At first, many left farms or plantations for towns or cities "where freedom was free-er." Thousands sought to reunite families broken by sale and legalize marriage ties; others adopted new surnames and learned to read and write. Many black women withdrew from field labor to care for their families. Across the South, ex-slaves left white-dominated churches and formed independent black congregations;

founded schools; set up mutual aid societies; and held freedmen's conventions to air grievances, discuss pressing issues, and press for equal civil and political rights.

Reconstruction was a time of testing, when freedmen probed the boundaries and possibilities of freedom. Every aspect of southern life was subject to redefinition, from appropriate forms of racial etiquette to the systems of labor that would replace slavery.

1
Thomas Long

"WE WHIPPED DOWN ALL DAT"

Thomas Long, a former slave and a private in the 1st South Carolina Volunteers, assesses the meaning of black military service during the Civil War.

We can remember, when we fust enlisted, it was hardly safe for we to pass by de camps to Beaufort and back, lest we went in a mob and carried side arms. But we whipped down all dat—not by going into de white camps for whip um; we didn't tote our bayonets for whip um; but we lived it down by our naturally manhood; and now de white sojers take us by de hand and say Broder Sojer. Dats what dis regiment did for de Epiopian race.

If we hadn't become sojers, all might have gone back as it was before; our freedom might have slipped through de two houses of Congress and President Linkum's four years might have passed by and notin' been done for us. But now tings can neber go back, because we have showed our energy and our courage and our naturally manhood.

Source: Thomas Wentworth Higginson, *Army Life in a Black Regiment* (Boston, 1870).

2
Jackson Cherry

"WE OUGHT TO BE CONSIDERED AS MEN"

Corporal Jackson Cherry, Company I, 35th Regiment, United States Colored Troops, appeals for equal opportunity for freedmen.

We have been faithful in the field up to the present time, and think that we ought to be considered as men, and allowed a fair chance in the race of life. It has been said that a black man can not make his own living, but give us opportunities and we will show the whites that we will not come to them for any thing, if they do not come to us. We think the colored people have been the making of them, and can make something of ourselves in time. The colored people know how to work, and the whites have been dependent upon them. They can work again, and will work. A white man may talk very well, but put him to work, and what will he say? He will say that hard work is not easy. He will say that it is hard for a man who has owned so many able-bodied Negroes to have the Yankees come and take them all away.

Source: *South Carolina Leader*, December 16, 1865.

3
Jourdon Anderson

"I THOUGHT THE YANKEES WOULD HAVE HUNG YOU LONG BEFORE THIS"

Jourdon Anderson, an ex-Tennessee slave, declines his former master's invitation to return as a laborer on his plantation.

Source: *Cincinnati Commercial*, reprinted in *New York Tribune*, August 22, 1865.

Dayton, Ohio, August 7, 1865

To My Old Master, Colonel P. H. Anderson,
Big Spring, Tennessee

Sir: I got your letter and was glad to find you had not forgotten Jourdon, and that you wanted me to come back and live with you again, promising to do better for me than anybody else can. I have often felt uneasy about you. I thought the Yankees would have hung you long before this for harboring Rebs they found at your house. I suppose they never heard about your going to Col. Martin's to kill the Union soldier that was left by his company in their stable. Although you shot at me twice before I left you, I did not want to hear of your being hurt, and am glad you are still living. It would do me good to go back to the dear old home again and see Miss Mary and Miss Martha and Allen, Esther, Green, and Lee. Give my love to them all, and tell them I hope we will meet in the better world, if not in this. I would have gone back to see you all when I was working in the Nashville hospital, but one of the neighbors told me Henry intended to shoot me if he ever got a chance.

I want to know particularly what the good chance is you propose to give me. I am doing tolerably well here; I get $25 a month, with victuals and clothing; have a comfortable home for Mandy (the folks here call her Mrs. Anderson), and the children, Milly, Jane and Grundy, go to school and are learning well; the teacher says Grundy has a head for a preacher. They go to Sunday School, and Mandy and me attend church regularly. We are kindly treated; sometimes we overhear others saying, "The colored people were slaves" down in Tennessee. The children feel hurt when they hear such remarks, but I tell them it was no disgrace in Tennessee to belong to Col. Anderson. Many darkies would have been proud, as I used to was, to call you master. Now, if you will write and say what wages you will give me, I will be better able to decide whether it would be to my advantage to move back again.

As to my freedom, which you say I can have, there is nothing to be gained on that score, as I got my free-papers in 1864 from the Provost-Marshal-General of the Department of Nashville. Mandy says she would be afraid to go back without some proof that you are sincerely disposed to treat us justly and kindly—and we have concluded to test your sincerity by asking you to send us our wages for the time we served you. This will make us forget and forgive old scores, and rely on your justice and friendship in the future. I served you faithfully for thirty-two years and Mandy twenty years. At $25 a month for me, and $2 a week for Mandy, our earnings would amount to $11,680. Add to this the interest for the time our wages has been kept back and deduct what you paid for our clothing and three doctor's visits to me, and pulling a tooth for Mandy, and the balance will show what we are in justice entitled to. Please send the money by Adams Express, in care of V. Winters, esq, Dayton, Ohio. If you fail to pay us for faithful labors in the past we can have little faith in your promises in the future. We trust the good Maker has opened your eyes to the wrongs which you and your fathers have done to me and my fathers, in making us toil for you for generations without recompense. Here I draw my wages every Saturday night, but in Tennessee there was never any pay day for the Negroes any more than for the horses and cows. Surely there will be a day of reckoning for those who defraud the laborer of his hire.

In answering this letter please state if there would be any safety for my Milly and Jane, who are now grown up and both good-looking girls. You know how it was with Matilda and Catherine. I would rather stay here and starve and die if it comes to that than have my girls brought to shame by the violence and wickedness of their young masters. You will also please state if there has been any schools opened for the colored children in your neighborhood, the great desire of my life now is to give my children an education, and have them form virtuous habits.

P.S.—Say howdy to George Carter, and thank him for taking the pistol from you when you were shooting at me.

From your old servant,
Jourdon Anderson

4
Rufus Saxton

"THE WORD 'COLOR' SHOULD BE LEFT OUT OF ALL LAWS"

Major General Rufus Saxton commanded the area that included Georgia's Sea Islands and later became the Freedmen's Bureau's assistant commissioner for Florida, Georgia, and South Carolina. This selection, from his testimony

Source: *Report of the Joint Committee on Reconstruction* (Washington, 1866).

*before Congress's Joint Committee on Reconstruction in
1866, offers his assessment of the freedmen's aspirations
and the former Confederates' attitudes toward them.*

[Question] What is [the freedmen's] disposition in regard to purchasing land, and what is the disposition of the landowners in reference to selling land to Negroes?

[Answer] The object which the freedman has most at heart is the
purchase of land. They all desire to get small homesteads and to
locate themselves upon them, and there is scarcely any sacrifice too
great for them to make to accomplish this object. I believe it is the
policy of the majority of the farm owners to prevent Negroes from
becoming landholders. They desire to keep the Negroes landless,
and as nearly in a condition of slavery as it is possible for them to
do. I think that the former slaveholders know really less about the
freedmen than any other class of people. The system of slavery has
been one of concealment on the part of the Negro of all his feelings
and impulses; and that feeling of concealment is so ingrained with
the very constitution of the Negro that he deceives his former master on almost every point. The freedman has no faith in his former
master, nor has his former owner any faith in the capacity of the
freedman. A mutual distrust exists between them. But the freedman is ready and willing to contract to work for any northern man.
One man from the North, a man of capital, who employed large
numbers of freedmen, and paid them regularly, told me, as others
have, that he desired no better laborers; that he considered them
fully as easy to manage as Irish laborers. That was my own experience in employing several thousands of them in cultivating the soil.
I have also had considerable experience in employing white labor,
having, as quartermaster, frequently had large numbers of laborers
under my control.

[Question] If the Negro is put in possession of all his rights as a
man, do you apprehend any danger of insurrection among them?

[Answer] I do not; and I think that is the only thing which will prevent difficulty. I think if the Negro is put in possession of all his
rights as a citizen and as a man, he will be peaceful, orderly, and
self-sustaining as any other man or class of men, and that he will
rapidly advance. . . .

[Question] It has been suggested that, if the Negro is allowed to
vote, he will be likely to vote on the side of his former master, and

be inveigled in the support of a policy hostile to the government of the United States; do you share in that apprehension?

[Answer] I have positive information from Negroes, from the most intelligent freedmen in those States, those who are leaders among them, that they are thoroughly loyal, and know their friends, and they will never be found voting on the side of oppression. . . . I think it vital to the safety and prosperity of the two races in the south that the Negro should immediately be put in possession of all his rights as a man; and that the word "color" should be left out of all laws, constitutions, and regulations for the people; I think it vital to the safety of the Union that this should be done.

5
Samuel Thomas

"TO KILL A NEGRO
THEY DO NOT DEEM MURDER"

Colonel Samuel Thomas, a Freedmen's Bureau official, describes the attitude of ex-Confederates toward the former slaves.

Wherever I go—the street, the shop, the house, or the steamboat—I hear the people talk in such a way as to indicate that they are yet unable to conceive of the Negro as possessing any rights at all. Men who are honorable in their dealings with their white neighbors will cheat a Negro without feeling a single twinge of their honor. To kill a Negro they do not deem murder; to debauch a Negro woman they do not think fornication; to take the property away from a Negro they do not consider robbery. The people boast that when they get freedmen affairs in their own hands, to use their own classic expression, "the niggers will catch hell."

The reason of all this is simple and manifest. The whites

Source: Colonel Samuel Thomas, Assistant Commissioner, Bureau of Refugees, Freedmen and Abandoned Lands in 39 Cong., 1 Sess., Senate Exec. Doc. 2 (1865).

esteem the blacks their property by natural right, and however much they may admit that the individual relations of masters and slaves have been destroyed by the war and the President's emancipation proclamation, they still have an ingrained feeling that the blacks at large belong to the whites at large, and whenever opportunity serves they treat the colored people just as their profit, caprice or passion may dictate.

6
Francis L. Cardozo

"LET THE LANDS OF THE SOUTH BE . . . DIVIDED"

Francis L. Cardozo, a black graduate of the University of Glasgow and a minister in New Haven, Connecticut, returned to his native South Carolina immediately after the Civil War to serve as a principal of a Negro school. In this selection, he calls upon the South Carolina Constitutional Convention to grant land to the freedmen.

One of the greatest of slavery bulwarks was the infernal plantation system, one man owning his thousand, another his twenty, another fifty thousands acres of land. This is the only way by which we will break up that system, and I maintain that our freedom will be of no effect if we allow it to continue. What is the main cause of the prosperity of the North. It is because every man has his own farm and is free and independent. Let the lands of the South be similarly divided. I would not say for one moment they should be confiscated, but if sold to maintain the war, now that slavery is destroyed, let the plantation system go with it. We will never have true freedom until we abolish the system of agriculture which existed in the Southern States. It is useless to have any schools while we maintain the stronghold of slavery as the agricultural system of the country.

Source: Proceedings of Constitution Convention of South Carolina (1868).

7
Elias Hill

"THEY HIT ME WITH THEIR FISTS"

Elias Hill, a black minister in York County, South Carolina, testified before a congressional committee in 1871 about the Ku Klux Klan's aims and methods of operation.

Elias Hill is a remarkable character. He is crippled in both legs and arms, which are shriveled by rheumatism; he cannot walk, cannot help himself, has to be fed and cared for personally by others; was in early life a slave, whose freedom was purchased, his father buying his mother and getting Elias along with her, as a burden of which his master was glad to be rid. Stricken at seven years old with disease, he never was afterward able to walk, and he presents the appearance of a dwarf with the limbs of a child, the body of a man, and a finely developed intellectual head. He learned his letters and to read by calling the school children into the cabin as they passed, and also learned to write. He became a Baptist preacher, and after the war engaged in teaching colored children, and conducted the business correspondence of many of his colored neighbors. He is a man of blameless character, of unusual intelligence, speaks good English, and we put the story of his wrongs in his own language:

"On the night of the 5th of last May, after I had heard a great deal of what they had done in that neighborhood, they [the Ku Klux Klan] came. It was between 12 and 1 o'clock at night when I was awakened and heard the dogs barking, and something walking, very much like horses. . . . At last they came to my brother's door, which is in the same yard, and broke open the door and attacked his wife, and I heard her screaming and mourning. . . . At last I heard them have her in the yard. She was crying and the Ku-Klux were whipping her to make her tell where I lived. . . . Some one then hit my door. It flew open. One ran in the house, and stopping about the middle of the house, which is a small cabin, he turned around, as it seemed to me as I lay there awake, and said, 'Who's here?' Then I knew they would take me, and I answered, 'I am here.'

Source: *Report of the Joint Select Committee to Inquire into the Condition of Affairs in the Late Insurrectionary States* (Washington, 1872).

176

He shouted for joy, as it seemed, 'Here he is! Here he is! We have found him!' and he threw the bedclothes off of me and caught me by one arm, while another man took me by the other and they carried me into the yard between the houses. . . . The first thing they asked me was, 'Who did the burning? Who burned our houses?'—gin-houses, dwelling-houses and such. Some had been burned in the neighborhood. I told them it was not me; I could not burn houses; it was unreasonable to ask me. Then they hit me with their fists, and said I did it, I ordered it. They went on asking me didn't I tell the black men to ravish all the white women. No, I answered them. They struck me again with their fists on my breast, and then they went on. . . .

They pointed pistols at me all around my head once or twice, as if they were going to shoot me, telling me they were going to kill me; wasn't I ready to die, and willing to die? Didn't I preach? That they came to kill me—all the time pointing pistols at me. . . . One said 'G-d d—n it, hush!' He had a horsewhip, and he told me to pull up my shirt, and he hit me. He told me at every lick, 'Hold up your shirt.' I made a moan every time he cut with the horsewhip. I reckon he struck me eight cuts right on the hip bone; it was almost the only place he could hit my body, my legs are so short—all my limbs drawn up and withered away with pain. . . . They all had disguises on. I then thought they would not kill me. One of them then took a strap, and buckled it around my neck and said, 'Let's take him to the river and drown him. . . .'

They said 'Look here! Will you put a card in the paper next week like June Moore and Sol Hill?' They had been prevailed on to put a card in the paper to renounce all republicanism and never vote. I said, 'If I had the money to pay the expense, I could.' They said I could borrow, and gave me another lick. They asked me, 'Will you quit preaching?' I told them I did not know. I said that to save my life. They said I must stop the republican paper that was coming to Clay Hill. It has been only a few weeks since it stopped. The republican paper was then coming to me from Charleston. It came to my name. They said I must stop it, quit preaching, and put a card in the newspaper renouncing republicanism, and they would not kill me; but if I did not they would come back the next week and kill me."

8
Henry Blake

"AFTER FREEDOM, WE WORKED ON SHARES"

Henry Blake was born into slavery in Little Rock, Arkansas, and was approximately eighty years old when he was interviewed by the Works Progress Administration.

After freedom, we worked on shares a while. Then, we rented. When we worked on shares, we couldn't make nothing—just overalls, and something to eat. Half went to the white man, and you would destroy your half, if you weren't careful. A man that didn't know how to count would always lose. He might lose anyhow. The white folks didn't give no itemized statements. No, you just had to owe so much. No matter how good account you kept, you had to go by their account, and—now, brother, I'm telling you the truth about this—it's been that way for a long time. You had to take the white man's words and notes on everything. Anything you wanted you could get, if you were a good hand. If you didn't make no money, that's all right; they would advance you more. But you better not try to leave and get caught. They'd keep you in debt. They were sharp. Christmas come, you could take up twenty dollars in somethin'-to-eat and much as you wanted in whiskey. You could buy a gallon of whiskey—anything that kept you a slave. Because he was always right and you were always wrong, if there was a difference. If there was an argument, he would get mad and there would be a shooting take place.

Source: George P. Rawick, *The American Slave: A Composite Autobiography* (Westport, Conn., 1972) Ark. Narr., Vol. 8, 175–179.

9
Frederick Douglass

"THE SERFS OF RUSSIA . . . WERE GIVEN THREE ACRES OF GROUND"

Frederick Douglass assesses the meaning of emancipation in 1880.

How stands the case with the recently emancipated millions of colored people in our own country? What is their condition to-day? What is their relation to the people who formerly held them as slaves? These are important questions, and they are such as trouble the minds of thoughtful men of all colors, at home and abroad. By law, by the constitution of the United States, slavery has no existence in our country. The legal form has been abolished. By the law and the constitution, the Negro is a man and a citizen, and has all the rights and liberties guaranteed to any other variety of the human family, residing in the United States. . . .

In pursuance of this idea, the Negro was made free, made a citizen, made eligible to hold office, to be a juryman, a legislator, and a magistrate. To this end, several amendments to the constitution were proposed, recommended, and adopted. . . . This is our condition on paper and parchment. If only from the national statute book we were left to learn the true condition of the colored race, the result would be altogether creditable to the American people. . . .

We have laid the heavy hand of the constitution upon the matchless meanness of caste, as well as upon the hell-black crime of slavery. . . . But to-day, in most of the Southern States, the fourteenth and fifteenth amendments are virtually nullified.

The rights which they were intended to guarantee are denied and held in contempt. The citizenship granted in the fourteenth amendment is practically a mockery, and the right to vote, provided for in the fifteenth amendment, is literally stamped out in face of government. The old master class is to-day triumphant, and the newly-enfranchised class in a condition but little above that in which they were found before the rebellion.

Source: *Life and Times of Frederick Douglass* (Boston, 1892).

Do you ask me how, after all that has been done, this state of things has been made possible? I will tell you. Our reconstruction measures were radically defective. They left the former slave completely in the power of the old master, the loyal citizen in the hands of the disloyal rebel against the government. Wise, grand, and comprehensive in scope and desire as were the reconstruction measures, high and honorable as were the intentions of the statesmen by whom they were framed and adopted, time and experience, which try all things, have demonstrated that they did not successfully meet the case.

In the hurry and confusion of the hour, and the eager desire to have the Union restored, there was more care for the sublime superstructure of the republic than for the solid foundation upon which it could alone be upheld. . . . The old master class was not deprived of the power of life and death, which was the soul of the relation of master and slave. They could not, of course, sell their former slaves, but they retained the power to starve them to death, and wherever this power is held there is the power of slavery. He who can say to his fellow-man, "You shall serve me or starve," is a master and his subject is a slave. . . . Though no longer a slave, he is in a thralldom grievous and intolerable, compelled to work for whatever his employer is pleased to pay him, swindled out of his hard earnings by money orders redeemed in stores, compelled to pay the price of an acre of ground for its use during a single year, to pay four times more than a fair price for a pound of bacon and to be kept upon the narrowest margin between life and starvation. . . .

When the serfs of Russia were emancipated, they were given three acres of ground upon which they could live and make a living. But not so when our slaves were emancipated. They were sent away empty-handed, without money, without friends and without a foot of land upon which to stand. . . .

Greatness does not come on flowery beds of ease to any people. We must fight to win the prize. No people to whom liberty is given, can hold it as firmly and wear it as grandly as those who wrench liberty from the iron hand of the tyrant. The hardships and dangers involved in the struggle give strength and toughness to the character, and enable it to stand firm in storm as well as in sunshine.

BIBLIOGRAPHICAL ESSAY

Although slavery is now one of the most intensively-studied parts of United States history, for a long period it was largely ignored. The Progressive school of interpretation, which dominated the American history profession during the first half of the twentieth century, considered slavery to be less important than conflicts between classes, sections, and industrial and agrarian interests. Except for the works of a handful of African-American historians like Carter Woodson, Benjamin Quarles, and W. E. B. Du Bois and southern historians like Ulrich B. Phillips, slavery was widely regarded as an extraneous aspect of American history.

This prolonged period of scholarly neglect came to an end in the mid-1950s. Since the publication of Kenneth Stampp's *The Peculiar Institution* in 1956, no topic has produced a greater outpouring of important scholarly works or provoked more controversy than the study of slavery. In part, the explosion of scholarly interest reflected the increasing public concern with civil rights and race relations. It also reflected a recognition that slavery played a critical role in the settlement and economic development of the New World and the major political conflicts and alignments of the pre–Civil War period.

The study of slavery has contributed to a radical reshaping of the discipline of history, leading scholars to tap new sources of data and to employ new methods of analysis. Historical demographers have drawn upon census records to reconstruct slave birth and mortality rates and family and kinship patterns. Historical archaeologists have studied slave quarters in order to reconstruct patterns of everyday life. Medical historians have scrutinized records of height, weight, and disease. Cultural historians have analyzed African-American folklore and religious beliefs and customs. The result has been to reconstruct life under slavery in all of its complexity. Recent scholarship has decisively demonstrated that slaves were active agents who sustained ties with their African heritage and succeeded in creating a rich and vital culture.

The most comprehensive guides to the literature on slavery are Joseph C. Miller, *Slavery and Slaving in World History: A Bibliography, 1900–1996* (1999) and John David Smith, *Black Slavery in the Americas: An Interdisciplinary Bibliography, 1865–1980* (1982). Updated bibliographies appear annually in *Slavery & Abolition: A Journal of Comparative Studies*, which also publishes important articles and debates on slavery and antislavery.

General reference works that include succinct essays on important topics are Seymour Drescher and Stanley Engerman, eds., *A Historical Guide to World Slavery* (1998); Paul Finkelman and Joseph C. Miller, eds., *Macmillan Encyclopedia of World Slavery* (1998); Randall M. Miller and John David Smith, eds., *Dictionary of Afro-American Slavery* (updated ed., 1997); and Junius P. Rodriguez, ed., *The Historical Encyclopedia of World Slavery* (1997).

On the historiography of slavery in the United States, see Charles B. Dew, "The Slavery Experience," in John B. Boles and Evelyn Thomas Nolen, eds., *Interpreting Southern History* (1987); Peter J. Parish, *Slavery: History and Historians* (1989); John David Smith, *Slavery, Race, and American History: Historical Conflict, Trends, and Method, 1866–1953* (1999); and Mark M. Smith, *Debating Slavery: Economy and Society in the Antebellum American South* (1998).

An institution that began in prehistoric times, slavery was practiced on virtually every continent. Orlando Patterson, *Slavery and Social Death* (1982) contrasts the forms that slavery took in diverse societies around the world. For Asian slavery, see Anthony Reid, ed., *Slavery, Bondage, and Dependency in Southeast Asia* (1983) and James L. Watson, ed., *Asian and African Systems of Slavery* (1980). On Middle Eastern slavery, see Bernard Lewis, *Race and Slavery in the Middle East* (1990). An incisive overview of the origins, nature, and abolition of Islamic and New World slavery is David Brion Davis, *Slavery and Human Progress* (1984).

On African slavery and the African slave trade, see Patrick Manning, *Slavery and African Life* (1990); Paul E. Lovejoy, *Transformations in Slavery: A History of Slavery in Africa* (1983); Joseph C. Miller, *Way of Death: Merchant Capitalism and the Angolan Slave Trade, 1730–1830* (1988); and John Thornton, *Africa and Africans in the Making of the Atlantic World, 1400–1680* (2nd ed., 1998), a study which also examines the critical role of Africans in the development of New World economies and cultures.

Contradicting the conclusions of a much earlier authority on slavery, Ulrich B. Phillips, Stampp argued that nineteenth-century slavery was a profitable institution; that slaves suffered severely from disease and physical maltreatment; that they were inadequately fed, clothed, and housed; and that they expressed their discontent by breaking tools and running away as well as through more violent forms of resistance.

Stanley Elkins's *Slavery: A Problem in American Institutional Life* (1959), which came out three years after *The Peculiar Institution*, defined the issues that dominated subsequent scholarship. Drawing upon the work of two prominent Latin American historians, Gilberto Freyre and Frank Tannenbaum, Elkins argued that American slavery was much harsher and more exploitative than Latin American slavery. Indeed, he likened southern slave plantations to Nazi concentration camps and argued that slavery was so brutal and inhumane that it stripped slaves of their African heritage and transformed them into docile, submissive figures.

Much subsequent scholarship on American slavery can be viewed as a rebuttal of Elkins's arguments. Instead of portraying slaves as passive objects of oppression, later scholars focused their attention on the intricate ways that slaves resisted and accommodated to slavery; the nature of the culture and community that African Americans created within bondage; and the similarities and differences between southern slavery and bondage elsewhere. If any single theme can be said to unify the remarkable outpouring of scholarship on slavery, it is African Americans' extraordinary success in creating and sustaining vital kinship and cultural and religious traditions under conditions of extreme oppression. Among the important general studies that have emphasized slaves' capacity to resist slavery and establish separate communities are John B. Boles, *Black Southerners* (1983); John W. Blassingame, *The Slave Community* (1978); Eugene D. Genovese, *Roll, Jordan, Roll* (1974); Charles Joyner, *Down by the Riverside* (1984); Peter Kolchin, *American Slavery* (1993); and Leslie Howard Owens, *This Species of Property* (1976).

The modern study of slave culture traces its roots back to Melville J. Herskovit's *Myth of the Negro Past* (1941), which argued that many aspects of African-American culture—including art, family patterns, folklore, language, and music—represented cultural survivals from West Africa. More recent studies have substituted the notion of syncretism—the selective blending of African and European cultures—for Herskovit's concept of cultural survival. Valuable studies of slaves' culture include Daniel J. Crowley, ed., *African Folklore in the New World* (1977); Dena J. Epstein, *Sinful Tunes and Spirituals* (1977); Joseph E. Holloway, *Africanisms in American Culture* (1990); Lawrence Levine, *Black Culture and Black*

Consciousness (1977); Albert J. Raboteau, *Slave Religion* (1978); Mechal Sobel, *Trabelin' On: The Slave Journey to an Afro-Baptist Faith* (1979); Sterling Stuckey, *Slave Culture* (1987); Michael Vlach, *The Afro-American Tradition in Decorative Arts* (1978); and Thomas L. Webber, *Deep Like the Rivers: Education in the Slave Quarter Community* (1978).

Since Elkins's study appeared, a number of historians have penetrated America's national boundaries to compare southern slavery with other systems of slavery and forced labor. Important works that locate southern slavery in a comparative perspective include Carl N. Degler, *Neither Black Nor White: Slavery and Race Relations in Brazil and the United States* (1986); Richard S. Dunn, *Sugar and Slaves* (1972); George M. Frederickson, *White Supremacy: A Comparative Study in American and South African History* (1981); Herbert S. Klein, *Slavery in the Americas* (1967); and Peter Kolchin, *Unfree Labor: American Slavery and Russian Serfdom* (1987).

Not all of the scholars who have studied slavery are historians. Many economists interested in the impact of slavery on economic growth conducted intensive research on the institution. The modern debate over the profitability of slavery and its impact on the southern economy began with an article by Alfred H. Conrad and John R. Meyer entitled "The Economics of Slavery in the Antebellum South," which appeared in the *Journal of Political Economy* in 1958. Among the scholars inspired by Conrad and Meyer's approach were Robert William Fogel and Stanley L. Engerman, who used sophisticated econometric and statistical techniques in their highly controversial reinterpretation of the slave economy, *Time on the Cross* (1974). Relying on a wide array of quantitative data, this book argued that slavery was a highly profitable institution; that slave labor was highly efficient; that masters promoted stable nuclear families; and that slaves were healthy, well fed, rarely whipped, and seldom sold away from their spouses. The volume produced criticism that challenged the book's evidence, methods, and interpretations, including Herbert B. Gutman, *Slavery and the Numbers Game* (1975) and Paul A. David et al., *Reckoning with Slavery* (1976). Fogel responded to his critics and modified his views in 1989 in a volume entitled *Without Consent or Contract*, which synthesizes much recent quantitative research on slavery.

Until remarkably recently, there was a tendency to treat slavery as a static, unchanging institution. A number of recent volumes chronicle the historical evolution of American slavery. Valuable studies of colonial slavery include Ira Berlin, *Many Thousands Gone: The First Two Centuries of Slavery in North America* (1998); Timothy H. Breen and Stephen Innes, *"Myne Owne Ground": Race and Freedom on Virginia's Eastern Shore* (1980); Allan Kulikoff, *Tobacco and Slaves: Southern Culture in the Chesapeake* (1986); Daniel C. Littlefield, *Rice and Slaves: Ethnicity and the Slave Trade in Colonial South Carolina* (1981); Edmund S. Morgan, *American Slavery, American Freedom* (1975); Philip D. Morgan, *Slave Counterpoint: Black Culture in the Eighteenth-Century Chesapeake and Low Country* (1998); Robert Olwell, *Masters, Slaves, and Subjects: The Culture of Power in the South Carolina Low Country, 1740–1790* (1998); Mechal Sobel, *The World They Made Together: Black and White Values in Eighteenth-Century Virginia* (1987); Lorena S. Walsh, *From Calabar to Carter's Grove: The History of a Virginia Slave Community* (1997); and Donald R. Wright, *African Americans in the Colonial Era* (1990).

For slavery during the revolutionary era, see Ira Berlin and Ronald Hoffman, eds., *Slavery and Freedom in the Age of the American Revolution* (1983); Paul Finkelman, *Slavery and the Founders: Race and Liberty in the Age of Jefferson* (1996); Sylvia R. Frey, *Water from the Rock: Black Resistance in a Revolutionary Age* (1991); and Shane White, *Somewhat More Independent: The End of Slavery in New York City* (1991).

A large number of important recent studies have explored slavery's aftermath. Among the important recent works that focus on the African-American experience during the Civil War and Reconstruction are Ira Berlin, ed., *Freedom: A Documentary History of Emancipation, 1861–1867* (1982–); Barbara Jean Fields, *Slavery and Freedom on the Middle Ground. Maryland* (1985), Eric Foner, *Reconstruction* (1988); Joseph T. Glatthaar, *Forged in Battle: The Civil War Alliance Between Black Soldiers and White Officers* (1990); Leon Litwack *"Been in the Storm So Long"* (1979); and Jay R. Mandle, *Not Slave, Not Free* (1992).

No aspect of slavery has gone unexamined. For the origins and implications of racism, see George M. Fredrickson, *The Black Image in the White Mind* (1971) and Winthrop Jordan, *White Over Black* (1968). On the nature of antislavery movements and comparative emancipations, see Ira Berlin et al. *Slaves No More* (1992); David Brion Davis, *The Problem of Slavery in Western Culture* (1967) and *The Problem of Slavery in the Age of Revolution* (1975); Eric Foner, *Nothing But Freedom* (1983); Thomas C. Holt, *The Problem of Freedom: Race, Labor and Politics in Jamaica and Britain, 1832–1938* (1992); and Robert Brent Toplin, *The Abolition of Slavery in Brazil* (1975).

Many specialized studies are worthy of note. The law of slavery is analyzed in Paul Finkelman, ed., *Slavery and the Law* (1996); A. Leon Higginbotham, Jr., *In the Matter of Color* (1978); Mark

Tushnet, *The American Law of Slavery* (1981); and Alan Watson, *Slave Law in the Americas* (1989). On slave resistance in the Americas, see Eugene D. Genovese, *From Rebellion to Revolution: Afro-American Slave Revolts* (1979).

Women's lives under slavery are skillfully explored in Elizabeth Fox-Genovese, *Within the Plantation Household: Black and White Women of the Old South* (1988); Jacqueline Jones, *Labor of Love, Labor of Sorrow* (1985); Melton A. McLaurin, *Celia: A Slave* (1991); and Deborah Gray White, *Ar'n't I a Woman?* (1985). On slave families, see Herbert G. Gutman, *The Black Family in Slavery and Freedom* (1976) and Brenda Stevenson, *Life in Black and White: Family and Community in the Slave South* (1996). For slave children, see Wilma King, *Stolen Childhood: Slave Youth in Nineteenth-Century America* (1995). Medical histories of slavery include Kenneth F. Kiple and Virginia Himmelsteib King, *Another Dimension to the Black Diaspora: Diet, Disease, and Racism* (1981) and Todd L. Savitt, *Medicine and Slavery* (1978).

For urban slavery, see Claudia D. Goldin, *Urban Slavery in the American South* (1976) and Richard C. Wade, *Slavery in the Cities* (1967). On free blacks, see Ira Berlin, *Slaves Without Masters* (1974); and Michael P. Johnson and James L. Roark, *Black Masters* (1984) and *No Chariot Let Down: Charleston's Free People of Color* (1984).

A BIBLIOGRAPHY OF RECENT WORKS IN ENGLISH

SLAVERY AND ANTISLAVERY

COMPREHENSIVE GUIDES

BIBLIOGRAPHIES

Boles, John B. *Interpreting Southern History*. Baton Rouge: Louisiana State University Press, 1987.

Brignano, Russell C. *Black Americans in Autobiography: An Annotated Bibliography of Autobiographies and Autobiographical Books Written since the Civil War*. Rev. and expanded ed. Durham, N.C.: Duke University Press, 1984.

Hogg, Peter C. *The African Slave Trade and Its Suppression: A Classified and Annotated Bibliography of Books, Pamphlets and Periodical Articles*. Cass Library of African studies. General studies; no. 137. London: F. Cass, 1973.

Kujoory, Parvin. *Black Slavery in America: An Annotated Mediagraphy*. Lanham, Md.: Scarecrow Press, 1995.

Microfilming Corporation of America. *Slavery, A Bibliography and Union List of the Microform Collection*. Sanford, N.C.: Microfilming Corp. of America, 1980–.

Miller, Joseph Calder. *Slavery: A Worldwide Bibliography, 1900–1982*. White Plains, N.Y.: Kraus International, 1985.

————. *Slavery and Slaving in World History: A Bibliography, 1900–1996*. Armonk, N.Y.: M.E. Sharpe, 1999.

Olson, James Stuart. *Slave Life in America: A Historiography and Selected Bibliography*. Lanham, Md.: University Press of America, 1983.

Smith, John David, comp. *Black Slavery in the Americas: An Interdisciplinary Bibliography, 1865–1980*. Westport, Conn.: Greenwood Press, 1982.

Williams, Ethel L. and Clifton F. Brown, comps. *The Howard University Bibliography of African and Afro-American Religious Studies*. Wilmington, Del.: Scholarly Resources, 1977.

DICTIONARIES

Miller, Randall M. and John David Smith, eds. *Dictionary of Afro-American Slavery*. Updated ed. Westport, Conn.: Praeger, 1997.

ENCYCLOPEDIAS

Drescher, Seymour and Stanley Engerman, eds. *A Historical Guide to World Slavery*. New York: Oxford University Press, 1998.

Finkelman, Paul and Joseph C. Miller, eds. *Macmillan Encyclopedia of World Slavery*. New York: Macmillan, 1998.

Rodriguez, Junius P., ed. *The Historical Encyclopedia of World Slavery*. Santa Barbara: ABC Clio, 1997.

HISTORIOGRAPHY

Bragg, Gail. *An Historiography of American Slave Women*. CompuBibs; #6. Brooklyn, N.Y.: CompuBibs, 1984.
Dew, Charles B. "The Slavery Experience," in John B. Boles and Evelyn Thomas Nolen, eds., *Interpreting Southern History*. Baton Rouge: Louisiana State University Press, 1987.
Finkelman, Paul, ed. *Slavery and Historiography*. New York: Garland, 1989.
Olson, James Stuart. *Slave Life in America: A Historiography and Selected Bibliography*. Lanham, Md.: University Press of America, 1983.
Parish, Peter J. *Slavery: History and Historians*. New York: Harper & Row, 1989.
Smith, John David. *Slavery, Race, and American History: Historical Conflict, Trends, and Method, 1866–1953*. Armonk, N.Y.: M.E. Sharpe, 1999.
Smith, Mark M. *Debating Slavery: Economy and Society in the Antebellum American South*. New York: Cambridge University Press, 1998.

JOURNALS

Slavery & Abolition (1980–).

FILMS

Tomas Gutierrez Alea, "The Last Supper"
Charles Burnett, "Nightjohn"
Julie Dash, "Daughters of the Dust"
Jonathan Demme, "Beloved"
Carlos Diegues, "Quilombo"
Haile Gerima, "Sankofa"
Sergio Giral, "The Other Francisco," "Cimarron," "Maluala"
Steven Spielberg, "Amistad"

GENERAL WORKS

Blackburn, Robin. *The Making of New World Slavery: From the Baroque to the Modern, 1492–1800*. London: Verso, 1997.
——. *The Overthrow of Colonial Slavery, 1776–1848*. London: Verso, 1988.
Davis, David Brion. *The Problem of Slavery in the Age of Revolution*. New York: Oxford University Press, 1975.
——. *The Problem of Slavery in Western Culture*. New York: Oxford University Press, 1988.
——. *Slavery and Human Progress*. New York: Oxford University Press, 1984.
Duff, John B. and Larry A. Greene, eds. *Slavery: Its Origin and Legacy*. New York: Crowell, 1975.
Johnson, Charles Richard and Patricia Smith. *Africans in America: America's Journey Through Slavery*. New York: Harcourt Brace, 1998.
Keegan, Susanne. *History of Slavery*. London: Grange Books, 1996.
Meltzer, Milton. *Slavery: A World History*. New York: Da Capo, 1993.
Patterson, Orlando. *Freedom in the Making of Western Culture*. New York: Basic Books, 1991.
——. *Slavery and Social Death: A Comparative Study*. Cambridge, Mass.: Harvard University Press, 1982.
Phillips, William D. *Slavery from Roman Times to the Early Transatlantic Trade*. Minneapolis: University of Minnesota Press, 1985.
Sawyer, Roger. *Children Enslaved*. London; New York: Routledge, 1988.
——. *Slavery in the Twentieth Century*. London; New York: Routledge & Kegan Paul, 1986.
Walvin, James. *Slavery and the Slave Trade: A Short Illustrated History*. Jackson: University Press of Mississippi, 1983.
White, Shane and Graham White. *Stylin': African American Expressive Culture from Its Beginnings to the Zoot Suit*. Ithaca, N.Y.: Cornell University Press, 1998.

COLLECTIONS OF ESSAYS

Archer, Leonie J. *Slavery and Other Forms of Unfree Labor*. New York: Routledge, 1988.

Bieber, Judy. *Plantation Societies in the Era of European Expansion*. Aldershot: Variorum, 1997.

Bush, M. L. *Serfdom and Slavery: Studies in Legal Bondage*. London: Longman, 1996.

Craton, Michael. *Roots and Branches: Current Directions in Slave Studies*. Toronto; New York: Pergamon Press, 1979.

Curtin, Philip D. *The Rise and Fall in the Plantation Complex*. 2nd ed. Cambridge: Cambridge University Press, 1998.

Davis, David Brion. *From Homicide to Slavery*. New York: Oxford University Press, 1986.

Drescher, Seymour. *From Slavery to Freedom: Comparative Studies in the Rise and Fall of Atlantic Slavery*. New York: New York University Press, 1999.

Engerman, Stanley. *The Terms of Labor: Slavery, Serfdom, and Free Labor*. Stanford: Stanford University Press, 1999.

Fox-Genovese, Elizabeth. *Fruits of Merchant Capital: Slavery and Bourgeois Property in the Rise and Expansion of Capitalism*. Oxford; New York: Oxford University Press, 1983.

Fredrickson, George M. *The Arrogance of Race: Historical Perspectives on Slavery, Racism, and Social Inequality*. Middletown, Conn.: Wesleyan University Press, 1988.

Frey, Sylvia R. and Betty Wood. *From Slavery to Emancipation in the Atlantic World*. Portland: Frank Cass, 1999.

Lovejoy, Paul E., ed. *Unfree Labour in the Development of the Atlantic World*. London: Frank Cass, 1994.

Palmer, Colin A. *The Worlds of Unfree Labour: From Indentured Servitude to Slavery*. Aldershot: Variorum, 1998.

GEOGRAPHICAL REGIONS

AFRICA

Cooper, Frederick. *From Slaves to Squatters: Plantation Labor and Agriculture in Zanzibar and Coastal Kenya, 1890–1925*. New Haven: Yale University Press, 1980.

———. *Plantation Slavery on the East Coast of Africa*. Portsmouth, N.H.: Heinemann, 1997.

Fisher, Allan and Humphrey J. Fisher. *Slavery and Muslim Society in Africa*. London: C. Hurst, 1999.

Fomin, E. S. D. *Slave Settlements in the Banyang Country, 1800–1950*. Limbe, Cameroon: University of Buea, 1998.

Harris, Joseph E., ed. *Global Dimensions of the African Diaspora*. 2nd ed. Washington, D.C.: Howard University Press, 1993.

Klein, Martin A. *Breaking the Chains: Slavery, Bondage, and Emancipation in Modern Africa and Asia*. Madison: University of Wisconsin Press, 1993.

———. *Slavery and Colonial Rule in French West Africa*. New York: Cambridge University Press, 1998.

Lovejoy, Paul E., ed. *Africans in Bondage: Studies in Slavery and the Slave Trade*. Madison: University of Wisconsin, 1986.

———, ed. *The Ideology of Slavery in Africa*. Beverly Hills: Sage Publications, 1981.

———. *Transformations in Slavery: A History of Slavery in Africa*. African studies series; 36. Cambridge [Cambridgeshire]; New York: Cambridge University Press, 1983.

Manning, Patrick. *Slavery and African Life: Occidental, Oriental, and African Slave Trades*. New York: Cambridge University Press, 1990.

Miers, Suzanne and Martin Klein. *Slavery and Colonial Rule in Africa*. London: Frank Cass, 1998.

Miers, Suzanne and Igor Kopytoff. *Slavery in Africa: Historical and Anthropological Perspectives*. Madison: University of Wisconsin Press, 1977.

Miers, Suzanne and Richard Roberts, eds. *The End of Slavery in Africa*. Madison: University of Wisconsin Press, 1988.

Morton, Fred. *Children of Ham: Freed Slaves and Fugitive Slaves on the Kenya Coast, 1873 to 1907*. African modernization and development series. Boulder: Westview Press, 1990.

Morton, Rodger Frederic. *Slaves, Fugitives, and Freedmen on the Kenya Coast, 1873–1907*. Thesis—Syracuse University, 1976.

Mowafi, Reda. *Slavery, Slave Trade, and Abolition Attempts in Egypt and the Sudan, 1820–1882*. Lund studies in international history; 14. Scandinavian university books. Stockholm: Esselte Studium, 1981.

Nwulia, Moses D. E. *Britain and Slavery in East Africa*. Washington: Three Continents Press, 1975.

Robertson, Claire C. *Women and Slavery in Africa*. Madison: University of Wisconsin Press, 1983.

Samarin, William J. *The Black Man's Burden: African Colonial Labor on the Congo and Ubangi Rivers, 1880–1900*. Boulder: Westview Press, 1989.

Savage, Elizabeth. *The Human Commodity: Perspectives on the Trans-Saharan Slave Trade*. London: F. Cass, 1992.

Searing, James F. *West African Slavery and Atlantic Commerce: The Senegal River Valley, 1700–1860*. Cambridge: Cambridge University Press, 1993.

Sundiata, I. K. *Biafra's Isle: Fernando Po between Slaving and NeoSlavery, 1827–1930*. Madison: University of Wisconsin Press, 1995.

Temperley, Howard. *White Dreams, Black Africa: The Antislavery Expedition to the River Niger, 1841–1842*. New Haven: Yale University Press, 1991.

Thornton, John. *Africa and Africans in the Making of the Atlantic World, 1400–1680*. 2nd ed. Cambridge: Cambridge University Press, 1998.

———. *The Kongolese Saint Anthony: Dona Beatriz Kimpa Vita and the Antonian Movement, 1684–1706*. Cambridge: Cambridge University Press, 1998.

———. *Warfare in Atlantic Africa, 1500–1800*. London: UCL Press, 1999.

Twaddle, Michael, ed. *The Wages of Slavery: From Chattel Slavery to Wage Labour in Africa, the Caribbean and England*. London; Portland, Ore.: Frank Cass, 1993.

Watson, James L. *Asian and African Systems of Slavery*. Oxford: Blackwell, 1980.

Willis, John Ralph, ed. *Slaves and Slavery in Muslim Africa*. London: Frank Cass, 1985.

Wright, Marcia. *Strategies of Slaves and Women: Life-Stories from East/Central Africa*. New York: L. Barber Press, 1993.

EGYPT

Elbashir, Ahmed E. *The United States, Slavery, and the Slave Trade in the Nile Valley*. Lanham, Md.: University Press of America, 1983.

Mowafi, Reda. *Slavery, Slave Trade and Abolition Attempts in Egypt and the Sudan, 1820–1882*. Lund studies in international history; 14. Scandinavian university books. Stockholm: Esselte Studium, 1981.

LIBERIA

Belcher, Max. *A Land and Life Remembered: Americo-Liberian Folk Architecture*. Athens: University of Georgia, 1988.

Howard, Lawrence C. *American Involvement in Africa South of the Sahara, 1800–1860*. New York: Garland, 1988.

McDaniel, Antonio. *Swing Low, Sweet Chariot: The Mortality Cost of Colonizing Liberia in the Nineteenth Century*. Chicago: University of Chicago, 1995.

MAURITIUS

Barker, Anthony J. *Slavery and Antislavery in Mauritius, 1810–33*. Basingstoke: Macmillan, 1996.

Nwulia, Moses D. E. *The History of Slavery in Mauritius and the Seychelles, 1810–1875*. Rutherford, N.J.: Fairleigh Dickinson University Press; London: Associated University Presses, 1981.

Teelock, Vijaya. *Bitter Sugar: Sugar and Slavery in Nineteenth-Century Mauritius*. Moka: Mahatma Gandhi Institute, 1998.

MOROCCO

Ennaji, Mohammed. *Serving the Master: Slavery and Society in Nineteenth-Century Morocco*. New York: St. Martin's Press, 1999.

NIGERIA

Acholonu, Catherine Obianuju. *The Igbo Roots of Olaudah Equiano*. Owerri: AFA, 1989.

Lovejoy, Paul E. *Slow Death for Slavery: The Course of Abolition in Northern Nigeria, 1897–1936*. African studies series; 76. Cambridge [England]; New York: Cambridge University Press, 1993.

O'Hear, Ann. *Power Relations in Nigeria: Ilorin Slaves and Their Successors*. Rochester: University of Rochester Press, 1997.

SOMALIA

Besteman, Catherine Lowe. *Unraveling Somalia: Race, Violence, and the Legacy of Slavery*. Philadelphia: University of Pennsylvania Press, 1999.

SOUTH AFRICA

Bank, Andrew. *The Decline of Urban Slavery at the Cape, 1806 to 1843*. Communications; no. 22/1991. Rondebosch, South Africa: Centre for African Studies, 1991.

Eldredge, Elizabeth A. *Slavery in South Africa: Captive Labor on the Dutch Frontier*. [African modernization and development.] Boulder: Westview Press, 1994.

Scully, Pamela. *Liberating the Family: Gender and British Slave Emancipation in the Rural Western Cape, South Africa, 1823–1853*. Portsmouth, N.H.: Heinemann, 1997.

Shell, Robert Carl-Heinz. *Children of Bondage: A Social History of the Slave Society at the Cape of Good Hope, 1652–1838*. Hanover, N.H.: University Press of New England, 1994.

Watson, R. L. (Richard Lyness). *The Slave Question: Liberty and Property in South Africa*. [Middletown, Conn.]: Wesleyan University Press; Hanover: University Press of New England, 1990.

Worden, Nigel. *The Chains that Bind Us: A History of Slavery at the Cape*. Kenwyn: Juta, 1996.

———. *Slavery in Dutch South Africa*. African studies series; 44. Cambridge [Cambridgeshire]; New York: Cambridge University Press, 1985.

THE AMERICAS (General Works)

Berlin, Ira, ed. *Cultivation and Culture: Labor and the Shaping of Slave Life in the Americas*. Carter G. Woodson Institute series in Black Studies. Charlottesville: University Press of Virginia, 1993.

———, ed. *The Slaves' Economy: Independent Production by Slaves in the Americas*. London; Portland, Ore.: Frank Cass, 1991.

Binder, Wolfgang, ed. *Slavery in the Americas*. Wurzburg: Konigshausen & Neumann, 1993.

Cohen, David W., ed. *Neither Slave Nor Free: The Freedmen of African Descent in the Slave Societies of the New World*. Baltimore: Johns Hopkins University Press, 1972.

Conniff, Michael L. *Africans in the Americas: A History of the Black Diaspora*. New York: St. Martin's Press, 1994.

Curtin, Philip D. *The Rise and Fall of the Plantation Complex*. 2nd ed. New York: Cambridge University Press, 1998.

Engerman, Stanley L. and Eugene D. Genovese, eds. *Race and Slavery in the Western Hemisphere: Quantitative Studies*. Princeton, N.J.: Princeton University Press, 1975.

Finkelman, Paul, ed. *Comparative Issues in Slavery*. New York: Garland Press, 1989.

Genovese, Eugene D. *From Rebellion to Revolution: Afro-American Slave Revolts in the Making of the Modern World*. Baton Rouge: Louisiana State University Press, 1979.

———, ed. *The Slave Economies*. New York: Wylie, 1973.

Hoetink, H. *Slavery and Race Relations in the Americas*. New York: Harper & Row, 1973.

Rubin, Vera, ed. *Comparative Perspectives on Slavery in New World Plantation Societies*. New York: New York Academy of Sciences, 1977.

Thompson, Vincent. *The Making of the African Diaspora in the Americas, 1441–1900.* Harlow, Essex, England: Longman, 1987.

CANADA

Bertley, Leo W. *Canada and Its People of African Descent.* Pierrefonds, Que.: Bilongo Publishers, 1977.
Govia, Francine and Helen Lewis. *Blacks in Canada: In Search of the Promise: A Bibliographical Guide.* Edmonton: Harambee Centres Canada, 1988.
Hill, Daniel G. *The Freedom-Seekers: Blacks in Early Canada.* Agincourt: Book Society of Canada, 1981.
Hornby, Jim. *Black Islanders: Prince Edward Island's Historical Black Community.* Island studies; no. 3. Charlottetown, P.E.I.: Institute of Island Studies, 1991.
Tulloch, Headley. *Black Canadians: A Long Line of Fighters.* Toronto: NC Press, 1975.
Winks, Robin. *The Blacks in Canada: A History.* Montreal: McGill-Queen's University Press, 1971.

LATIN AMERICA AND THE CARIBBEAN (General Works)

Cardoso, Gerald. *Negro Slavery in the Sugar Plantations of Veracruz and Pernambuco 1550–1680: A Comparative Study.* Thesis—University of Nebraska.
Davis, Darien. *Slavery and Beyond: The African Impact on Latin America and the Caribbean.* Wilmington, Del.: Scholarly Resources, 1995.
Klein, Herbert S. *African Slavery in Latin America and the Caribbean.* New York: Oxford University Press, 1986.
Knight, Franklin W. *The African Dimension in Latin American Societies.* New York: Macmillan, 1974.
Mellafe, R. Rolando. *Negro Slavery in Latin America.* Berkeley: University of California Press, 1975.

ANTIGUA

Gaspar, David Barry. *Bondmen & Rebels: A Study of Master-Slave Relations in Antigua, With Implications for Colonial British America.* The Johns Hopkins studies in Atlantic history and culture. Baltimore: Johns Hopkins University Press, 1985.
Smith, Samuel. *To Shoot Hard Labour: The Life and Times of Samuel Smith, An Antiguan Workingman, 1877–1982.* Scarborough, Ont., Canada: Edan's Publishers, 1986.

ARGENTINA

Johnson, Lyman L. *The Development of Slave and Free Labor Regimes in Late Colonial Buenos Aires, 1770–1815.* Storrs: Center for Latin American & Caribbean Studies, University of Connecticut, 1997.

BAHAMAS

Johnson, Howard. *The Bahamas in Slavery and Freedom.* Kingston, Jamaica: Ian Randle Publishers; London: James Currey Publishers, 1991.
Saunders, Gail. *Bahamian Loyalists and Their Slaves.* London: Macmillan Caribbean, 1983.
———. *Slavery in the Bahamas, 1648–1838.* [Nassau?]: D.G. Saunders, 1985.
Saunders, Hartley Cecil. *The Other Bahamas.* 1st ed. Nassau, Bahamas: Bodab Publishers, 1991.

BARBADOS

Beckles, Hilary. *Afro-Caribbean Women and Resistance to Slavery in Barbados.* Karnak history. Women studies. London: Karnak House, 1988.
———. *Black Rebellion in Barbados: The Struggle against Slavery, 1627–1838.* Bridgetown, Barbados: Carib Research & Publications, 1987.
Emancipation I: A Series of Lectures to Commemorate the 150th Anniversary of Emancipation. Barbados: The Department: The Foundation, 1986.
Handler, Jerome S. *Plantation Slavery in Barbados: An Archaeological and Historical Investigation.* Cambridge, Mass.: Harvard University Press, 1978.

————. *The Unappropriated People: Freedmen in the Slave Society of Barbados*. Baltimore: Johns Hopkins University Press [1974].

Levy, Claude. *Emancipation, Sugar, and Federalism: Barbados and the West Indies, 1833–1876*. Latin American monographs; 2d ser., 25. Gainesville: University Presses of Florida, 1980.

Puckrein, Gary A. *Little England: Plantation Society and Anglo-Barbadian Politics, 1627–1700*. New York: New York University Press, 1984.

BERMUDA

Packwood, Cyril Outerbridge. *Chained on the Rock: Slavery in Bermuda*. New York: E. Torres, 1975.

Smith, James Ernest. *Slavery in Bermuda*. 1st ed. New York: Vantage Press, 1976.

BRAZIL

Barickman, B. J. *A Bahian Counterpoint: Sugar, Tobacco, Cassava, and Slavery in the Reconcavo, 1780–1860*. Stanford: Stanford University Press, 1998.

Butler, Kim D. *Freedoms Given, Freedoms Won: Afro-Brazilians in Post-Abolition Sao Paulo and Salvador*. New Brunswick: Rutgers University Press, 1998.

Cardoso, Gerald. *Negro Slavery in the Sugar Plantations of Veracruz and Pernambuco, 1550–1680: A Comparative Study*. Washington, D.C.: University Press of America, 1983.

Conrad, Robert Edgar. *Brazilian Slavery: An Annotated Research Bibliography*. Boston: G.K. Hall, 1977.

————. *Children of God's Fire: A Documentary History of Black Slavery in Brazil*. University Park: Pennsylvania State University Press, 1994.

————. *The Destruction of Brazilian Slavery, 1850–1888*. 2nd ed. Malabar, Fla.: Krieger Pub. Co., 1993.

————. *World of Sorrow: The African Slave Trade to Brazil*. Baton Rouge: Louisiana State University Press, 1986.

Degler, Carl N. *Neither Black Nor White: Slavery and Race Relations in Brazil and the United States*. Madison: University of Wisconsin Press, 1986.

Eisenberg, Peter L. *The Sugar Industry in Pernambuco: Modernization Without Change, 1840–1910*. Berkeley: University of California Press [1974].

Hellwig, David J. *African-American Reflections on Brazil's Racial Paradise*. Philadelphia: Temple University Press, 1992.

————. *Brazil and the World System*. Critical reflections on Latin America series. 1st ed. Austin: University of Texas Press, 1991.

Karasch, Mary C. *Slave Life in Rio de Janeiro, 1808–1850*. Princeton, N.J.: Princeton University Press, 1987.

Kowarick, Lucio. *The Subjugation of Labour: The Constitution of Capitalism in Brazil*. Latin America studies; 36. Amsterdam, the Netherlands: CEDLA; Providence, R.I.: Distributed by Foris Publications USA, 1987.

Mattoso, Katia M. de Queiros. *To Be a Slave in Brazil, 1550–1888*. New Brunswick, N.J.: Rutgers University Press, 1986.

Nabuco, Joaquim. *Abolitionism: The Brazilian Antislavery Struggle*. Blacks in the New World. Urbana: University of Illinois Press, 1977.

Reis, Joao Jose. *Slave Rebellion in Brazil: The Muslim Uprising of 1835 in Bahia*. Johns Hopkins studies in Atlantic history and culture. Baltimore: Johns Hopkins University Press, 1993.

Russell-Wood, A. J. R. *The Black Man in Slavery and Freedom in Colonial Brazil*. New York: St. Martin's Press, 1982.

Schwartz, Stuart B. *Sugar Plantations in the Formation of Brazilian Society: Bahia, 1550–1835*. Cambridge Latin American studies; 52. Cambridge: Cambridge University Press, 1985.

Scott, Rebecca J. *Abolition of Slavery and the Aftermath of Emancipation in Brazil*. Durham, N.C.: Duke University Press, 1988.

Silva, Eduardo da. *Prince of the People: The Life and Times of a Brazilian Free Man of Colour*. London; New York: Verso, 1993.

Taylor, Kit Sims. *Sugar and the Underdevelopment of Northeastern Brazil, 1500–1970*. University of Florida monographs. Social sciences; no. 63. Gainesville: University Presses of Florida, 1978.

Toplin, Robert Brent. *The Abolition of Slavery in Brazil.* Studies in American Negro life. Atheneum; NL34. 1st Atheneum paperback ed., College ed. New York: Atheneum, 1975.

———. *Freedom and Prejudice: The Legacy of Slavery in the United States and Brazil.* Contributions in Afro-American and African studies; no. 56. Westport, Conn.: Greenwood Press, 1981.

CARIBBEAN (General and Comparative Works)

Association of Caribbean Historians. *Some Papers on Social, Political and Economic Adjustments to the Ending of Slavery in the Caribbean.* Presented at the seventh annual conference of Caribbean historians, April 2nd–8th, 1975, U. W. I., Mona, Jamaica. [s.l.: s.n., 1975?].

Beckles, Hilary. *Centering Woman: Gender Relations in Caribbean Slave Society.* Oxford: James Currey, 1999.

———. *Inside Slavery: Process and Legacy in the Caribbean Experience.* Mona: University of the West Indies, 1996.

Bolland, O. Nigel. *Struggles for Freedom: Essays on Slavery, Colonialism, and Culture in the Caribbean and Central America.* Belize: Angelus Press, 1997.

Burn, William Laurence. *Emancipation and Apprenticeship in the British West Indies.* Reprints in social and economic history. New York: Johnson Reprint Corp. [1970].

Burton, Richard D. E. *Afro-Creole: Power, Opposition, and Play in the Caribbean.* Ithaca, N.Y.: Cornell University Press, 1997.

Butler, Kathleen Mary. *The Economics of Emancipation: Jamaica & Barbados, 1823–1843.* Chapel Hill: University of North Carolina Press, 1995.

Cox, Edward L. *Free Coloreds in the Slave Societies of St. Kitts and Grenada, 1763–1833.* Knoxville: University of Tennessee Press, 1984.

Craton, Michael. *Empire, Enslavement, and Freedom in the Caribbean.* Kingston: Ian Randle Pub., 1997.

Fraginals, Manuel Moreno, ed. *Between Slavery and Free Labor: The Spanish-Speaking Caribbean in the Nineteenth Century.* Baltimore: Johns Hopkins University Press, 1985.

Gaspar, David Barry and David P. Geggus. *A Turbulent Time: The French Revolution and the Greater Caribbean.* Bloomington: Indiana University Press, 1997.

Goveia, Elsa V. *Slave Society in the British Leeward Islands at the End of the Eighteenth Century.* Caribbean series, 8. Yale University Press, 1965.

Green, William A. *British Slave Emancipation: The Sugar Colonies and the Great Experiment, 1830–1865.* Oxford [Eng.]: Clarendon Press, 1976.

Hall, N. A. T. *Slave Society in the Danish West Indies: St. Thomas, St. John, and St. Croix.* Johns Hopkins studies in Atlantic history and culture. Baltimore: Johns Hopkins University Press, 1992.

Hayward, Jack. *Out of Slavery: Abolition and After.* Legacies of West Indian Slavery. London, England; Totowa, N.J.: F. Cass, 1985.

Higman, B. W. *Slave Populations of the British Caribbean, 1807–1834.* Johns Hopkins studies in Atlantic history and culture. Baltimore: Johns Hopkins University Press, 1984.

Kale, Madhavi. *Fragments of Empire: Capital, Slavery, and Indian Indentured Labor Migration in the British Caribbean.* Philadelphia: University of Pennsylvania Press, 1998.

Kiple, Kenneth F. *The Caribbean Slave: A Biological History.* Studies in environment and history. Cambridge [Cambridgeshire]; New York: Cambridge University Press, 1984.

Klein, Herbert S. *African Slavery in Latin America and the Caribbean.* New York: Oxford University Press, 1986.

Martinez-Fernandez, Luis. *Fighting Slavery in the Caribbean.* Armonk, N.Y.: M.E. Sharpe, 1998.

McDonald, Roderick A. *West Indies Accounts: Essays on the History of the British Caribbean and the Atlantic Economy.* Barbados: The Press, University of the West Indies, 1996.

McLewin, Philip J. *Power and Economic Change: The Response to Emancipation in Jamaica and British Guiana, 1840–1865.* South American and Latin American economic history. New York: Garland, 1987.

Mintz, Sidney Wilfred. *The Birth of African-American Culture: An Anthropological Perspective*. Boston: Beacon Press, 1992.

——. *Caribbean Transformations*. Morningside ed. New York: Columbia University Press, 1989.

Mullin, Michael. *Africa in America: Slave Acculturation and Resistance in the American South and the British Caribbean, 1736–1831*. Blacks in the New World. Urbana: University of Illinois Press, 1992.

Munford, Clarence J. *The Black Ordeal of Slavery and Slave Trading in the French West Indies, 1625–1715*. Lewiston, N.Y.: E. Mellen Press, 1991.

Ome, Aiyegoro. *The Story of Emancipation*. 1st ed. Port of Spain, Trinidad: National Action Cultural Committee, 1989.

Paiewonsky, Isidor. *Eyewitness Accounts of Slavery in the Danish West Indies; Also Graphic Tales of Other Slave Happenings on Ships and Plantations*. New York: Fordham University Press, 1989.

Prince, Mary. *The History of Mary Prince, a West Indian Slave*. Ann Arbor: University of Michigan, 1993.

Richardson, David, ed. *Abolition and Its Aftermath: The Historical Context, 1790–1916*. Legacies of West Indian Slavery. London, England; Totowa, N.J.: F. Cass, 1985.

Stinchcombe, Arthur L. *Sugar Island Slavery in the Age of Enlightenment: The Political Economy of the Caribbean World*. Princeton, N.J.: Princeton University Press, 1995.

Titus, Noel. *The Church and Slavery in the English-Speaking Caribbean*. CGSRS; no. 2, 1983. [Barbados, W.I.]: Caribbean Group for Social and Religious Studies, 1983.

Twaddle, Michael. *The Wages of Slavery: From Chattel Slavery to Wage Labour in Africa, the Caribbean and England*. London; Portland, Ore.: Frank Cass, 1993.

CENTRAL AMERICAN (General Works)

Sherman, William L. *Forced Native Labor in Sixteenth-Century Central America*. Lincoln: University of Nebraska Press, 1979.

COLOMBIA

Chandler, David L. *Health and Slavery in Colonial Colombia*. Dissertations in European economic history; 1981. New York: Arno Press, 1981.

Sharp, William Frederick. *Slavery on the Spanish Frontier: The Colombian Chocó, 1680–1810*. Norman: University of Oklahoma Press, 1976.

CUBA

Casanovas, Joan. *Bread, or Bullets! Urban Labor and Spanish Colonialism in Cuba, 1850–1898*. Pittsburgh: University of Pittsburgh Press, 1998.

Corwin, Arthur F. *Spain and the Abolition of Slavery in Cuba, 1817–1886*. Latin American monographs, no. 9. Austin: Published for the Institute of Latin American Studies by the University of Texas Press [1967].

Hall, Gwendolyn Midlo. *Social Control in Slave Plantation Societies: A Comparison of St. Domingue and Cuba*. The Johns Hopkins University studies in historical and political science; ser. 89, 1. Baltimore: Johns Hopkins Press [1971].

Kiple, Kenneth F. *Blacks in Colonial Cuba, 1774–1899*. Latin American monographs; 2d ser., 17. Gainesville: University Presses of Florida, 1976.

Klein, Herbert S. *Slavery in the Americas: A Comparative Study of Virginia and Cuba*. Chicago: University of Chicago Press [1967].

Knight, Franklin W. *Slave Society in Cuba during the Nineteenth Century*. Madison: University of Wisconsin Press, 1970.

——. *Slavery and the Transformation of Society in Cuba, 1511–1760: From Settler Society to Slave Society*. Elsa Goveia memorial lecture; 1988. Mona, Jamaica: Dept. of History, University of the West Indies, 1988.

Paquette, Robert L. *Sugar Is Made with Blood: The Conspiracy of La Escalera and the Conflict between Empires over Slavery in Cuba*. Middletown, Conn.: Wesleyan University Press, 1988.

Scott, Rebecca J. (Rebecca Jarvis). *Slave Emancipation in Cuba: The Transition to Free Labor, 1860–1899*. Princeton, N.J.: Princeton University Press, 1985.

DANISH WEST INDIES

The Danish West Indian Slave Trade: Virgin Islands Perspectives. St. Croix, V.I.: Virgin Islands Humanities Council, 1994.

Hall, N. A. T. *Slave Society in the Danish West Indies: St. Thomas, St. John, and St. Croix*. Johns Hopkins studies in Atlantic history and culture. Baltimore: Johns Hopkins University Press, 1992.

Highfield, Arnold R. *Slavery in the Danish West Indies: A Bibliography*. St. Croix, V.I.: The Virgin Islands Humanities Council, 1994.

Olwig, Karen Fog. *Cultural Adaptation and Resistance on St. John: Three Centuries of Afro-Caribbean Life*. Gainesville: University of Florida Press, 1985.

Paiewonsky, Isidor. *Eyewitness Accounts of Slavery in the Danish West Indies; Also Graphic Tales of Other Slave Happenings on Ships and Plantations*. New York: Fordham University Press, 1989.

GUATEMALA

Sherman, William L. *Indian Slavery in Spanish Guatemala, 1524–1550*. Ann Arbor: University of Michigan Press, 1985.

GUYANA

Costa, Emilia Viotti da. *Crowns of Glory, Tears of Blood: The Demerara Slave Rebellion of 1823*. New York: Oxford University Press, 1994.

HAITI

Cooper, Anna J. *Slavery and the French Revolutionists*. Lewiston, N.Y.: E. Mellen, 1988.

Fick, Carolyn E. *The Making of Haiti: The Saint Domingue Revolution from Below*. Knoxville: University of Tennessee Press, 1990.

Stoddard, T. Lothrop. *The French Revolution in San Domingo*. Boston: Houghton, Mifflin, 1914.

JAMAICA

Armstrong, Douglas V. *The Old Village and the Great House: An Archaeological and Historical Examination of Drax Hall Plantation, St. Ann's Bay, Jamaica*. Blacks in the New World. Urbana: University of Illinois Press, 1990.

Bakan, Abigail B. (Abigail Bess). *Ideology and Class Conflict in Jamaica: The Politics of Rebellion*. Montreal; Buffalo: McGill-Queen's University Press, 1990.

Brathwaite, Edward. *The Folk Culture of the Slaves in Jamaica*. Rev. ed. London: New Beacon Books, 1981.

Brathwaite, Kamau. *The Development of Creole Society in Jamaica, 1770–1820*. Oxford: Clarendon Press, 1971.

Campbell, Mavis Christine. *The Dynamics of Change in a Slave Society: A Sociopolitical History of the Free Coloreds of Jamaica, 1800–1865*. Rutherford, N.J.: Fairleigh Dickinson University Press, 1976.

———. *The Maroons of Jamaica, 1655–1796: A History of Resistance, Collaboration and Betrayal*. Granby, Mass.: Bergin & Garvey, 1988.

Craton, Michael. *Searching for the Invisible Man: Slaves and Plantation Life in Jamaica*. Cambridge, Mass.: Harvard University Press, 1978.

Dunn, Richard S. *Moravian Missionaries at Work in a Jamaican Slave Community, 1754–1835*. James Ford Bell lectures, no. 32. [Minneapolis]: The Associates of the James Ford Bell Library, University of Minnesota, 1994.

Higman, B. W. *Slave Population and Economy in Jamaica, 1807–1834*. Cambridge; New York: Cambridge University Press, 1976.

Holt, Thomas C. (Thomas Cleveland). *The Problem of Freedom: Race, Labor, and Politics in Jamaica and Britain, 1832–1938*. Johns Hopkins studies in Atlantic history and culture. Baltimore: Johns Hopkins University Press, 1992.

McDonald, Roderick A. (Roderick Alexander). *The Economy and Material Culture of Slaves: Goods and Chattels on the Sugar Plantations of Jamaica and Louisiana*. Baton Rouge: Louisiana State University Press, 1993.

McLewin, Philip J. *Power and Economic Change: The Response to Emancipation in Jamaica and British Guiana, 1840–1865*. South American and Latin American economic history. New York: Garland, 1987.

Patterson, Orlando. *The Sociology of Slavery: An Analysis of the Origins, Development and Structure of Negro Slave Society in Jamaica.* Studies in society. London: MacGibbon & Kee, 1967.

Schuler, Monica. *"Alas, Alas, Kongo": A Social History of Indentured African Immigration into Jamaica, 1841–1865.* Johns Hopkins studies in Atlantic history and culture. Baltimore: Johns Hopkins University Press, 1980.

Scott, Karen A. (Karen Anne). *Causes of the Natural Decrease in the Jamaican Slave population, 1760–1850, and the Use of these Explanations in the Slavery Debates.* Thesis (A.B., Honors)—Harvard University, 1982.

Turner, Mary. *Slaves and Missionaries: The Disintegration of Jamaican Slave Society, 1787–1834.* Blacks in the New World. Urbana: University of Illinois Press, 1982.

Wilmot, Swithin R. *Adjustments to Emancipation in Jamaica.* Mona, Kingston, Jamaica: Social History Project, Department of History, Univ. of the West Indies, 1988.

MARTINIQUE

Tomich, Dale W. *Slavery in the Circuit of Sugar: Martinique and the World Economy, 1830–1848.* Johns Hopkins studies in Atlantic history and culture. Baltimore: Johns Hopkins University Press, 1990.

MAURITIUS

Barker, Anthony J. *Slavery and Anti-Slavery in Mauritius, 1810–33: The Conflict between Economic Expansion and Humanitarian Reform under British Rule.* Basingstoke; London: Macmillan, 1996.

PERU

Blanchard, Peter. *Slavery and Abolition in Early Republican Peru.* Latin American silhouettes. Wilmington, Del.: SR Books, 1992.

Bowser, Frederick P. *The African Slave in Colonial Peru, 1524–1650.* Stanford, Calif.: Stanford University Press, 1974.

Hunefeldt, Christine. *Paying the Price of Freedom: Family and Labor among Lima's Slaves, 1800–1854.* Berkeley: University of California Press, 1994.

PUERTO RICO

Scarano, Francisco A. (Francisco Antonio). *Sugar and Slavery in Puerto Rico: The Plantation Economy of Ponce, 1800–1850.* Madison: University of Wisconsin Press, 1984.

Sued Badillo, Jalil. *Puerto Rico Negro.* 1a ed. Rio Piedras, P.R.: Editorial Cultural, 1986.

SURINAME

Heilbron, Waldo. *Colonial Transformations and the Decomposition of Dutch Plantation Slavery in Surinam.* Caribbean culture studies; 3. London: Goldsmiths' College, University of London, 1993.

Lamur, H. E. *The Production of Sugar and the Reproduction of Slaves at Vossenburg (Suriname), 1705–1863.* Caribbean culture studies; 1. Amsterdam, The Netherlands: Amsterdam Centre for Caribbean Studies, 1987.

Price, Richard. *Alabi's World.* Johns Hopkins studies in Atlantic history and culture. Baltimore: Johns Hopkins University Press, 1990.

Shute, Gary Brana. *Resistance and Rebellion in Suriname: Old and New.* Studies in Third World societies; publication no. 43 (Nov. 1990). Williamsburg, Va.: Dept. of Anthropology, College of William and Mary, 1990.

Stedman, John Gabriel. *Narrative of a Five Years Expedition against the Revolted Negroes of Surinam.* Transcribed for the first time from the original 1790 manuscript. Baltimore: Johns Hopkins University Press, 1988.

———. *Stedman's Surinam: Life in Eighteenth-Century Slave Society.* Baltimore: Johns Hopkins University Press, 1992.

TRINIDAD

Campbell, Carl C. *Cedulants and Capitulants: The Politics of the Coloured Opposition in the Slave Society of Trinidad, 1783–1838.* University series; no. 1. 1st ed. Trinidad, W.I.: Paria Pub. Co., 1992.

De Verteuil, Anthony. *Seven Slaves and Slavery: Trinidad, 1777–1838*. [Port of Spain, Trinidad and Tobago?: s.n.], 1992 (Port of Spain, Trinidad, Republic of Trinidad and Tobago: Scrip-J Printers).

Huggins, A. B. *The Saga of the Companies*. Rev. enl. ed. [S.l.: s.n.], 1978 (Freeport, Trinidad, W.I.: HEM Printers).

John, A. Meredith. *The Plantation Slaves of Trinidad, 1783–1816: A Mathematical and Demographic Enquiry*. Cambridge [England]; New York: Cambridge University Press, 1988.

UNITED STATES

Abzug, Robert H., ed. *New Perspectives on Race and Slavery in America*. Lexington: University Press of Kentucky, 1986.

Barney, William L. *The Road to Secession*. New York: Praeger, 1972.

Berlin, Ira, ed. *Slavery and Freedom in the Age of the American Revolution*. Blacks in the New World. Urbana: Published for the United States Capitol Historical Society by the University of Illinois Press, 1986.

Blassingame, John W. *The Slave Community: Plantation Life in the Antebellum South*. Rev. and enl. ed. New York: Oxford University Press, 1978.

Boles, John B. *Black Southerners, 1619–1869*. Lexington: University Press of Kentucky, 1983.

Bradley, Patricia. *Slavery, Propaganda, and the American Revolution*. Jackson: University Press of Mississippi, 1998.

Castronovo, Russ. *Fathering the Nation: American Geneaologies of Slavery and Freedom*. Berkeley: University of California Press, 1995.

David, Paul A. *Reckoning with Slavery: A Critical Study in the Quantitative History of American Negro Slavery*. New York: Oxford University Press, 1976.

Elkins, Stanley M. *Slavery: A Problem in American Institutional and Intellectual Life*. 3d ed., rev. Chicago: University of Chicago Press, 1976.

Finkelman, Paul, ed. *Economics, Industrialization, Urbanization, and Slavery*. Articles on American Slavery; vol. 10. New York: Garland, 1989.

Fogel, Robert William. *Time on the Cross: The Economics of American Negro Slavery*. New York: Norton, 1989, c1974.

———. *Without Consent or Contract. Technical papers: The Rise and Fall of American Slavery*. New York: Norton, 1992, c1989.

Foner, Eric. *Slavery and Freedom in Nineteenth-Century America*. Oxford: Clarendon Press, 1994.

Freehling, William W. *The Reintegration of American History: Slavery and the Civil War*. New York: Oxford University Press, 1994.

Genovese, Eugene D. *A Consuming Fire: The Fall of the Confederacy in the Mind of the White Christian South*. Athens: University of Georgia Press, 1998.

———. *In Red and Black: Marxian Explorations in Southern and Afro-American History*. New York: Vintage, 1972.

———. *Political Economy of Slavery*. 2nd ed. Middletown, Conn.: Wesleyan University Press, 1989.

———. *Roll, Jordan, Roll: The World the Slaves Made*. New York: Vintage Books, 1976.

———. *The Southern Front: History and Politics in the Cultural War*. Columbia: University of Missouri, 1995.

———. *The World the Slaveholders Made*. New York: Pantheon, 1969.

Gilmore, Al-Tony. *Revisiting Blassingame's* The Slave Community. Westport, Conn.: Greenwood, 1978.

Goodheart, Lawrence B., ed. *Slavery in American Society*. 3rd ed. Lexington, Mass.: D.C. Heath, 1993.

Gordon-Reed, Annette. *Thomas Jefferson and Sally Hemings: An American Controversy*. Charlottesville: University Press of Virginia, 1997.

Greenberg, Kenneth S. *Honor and Slavery*. Princeton, N.J.: Princeton University Press, 1996.

Gutman, Herbert George. *Slavery and the Numbers Game: A Critique of* Time on the Cross. Blacks in the New World. An Illini book. Urbana: University of Illinois Press [1975].

Harris, J. William, ed. *Society and Culture in the Slave South*. Re-writing histories. London; New York: Routledge, 1992.

Hirschfeld, Fritz. *George Washington and Slavery: A Documentary Portrayal*. Columbia: University of Missouri, 1997.

Hodges, Graham Russell. *Slavery, Freedom and Culture among Early American Workers*. Armonk, N.Y.: M.E. Sharpe, 1998.

Hudson, Larry E., Jr. *Working toward Freedom: Slave Society and Domestic Economy in the American South*. Rochester, N.Y.: University of Rochester Press, 1994.

Huggins, Nathan Irvin. *Black Odyssey: The Afro-American Ordeal in Slavery*. New York: Vintage, 1990.

Jones, Jacqueline. *Labor of Love, Labor of Sorrow: Black Women, Work, and the Family from Slavery to the Present*. New York: Basic, 1985.

Kolchin, Peter. *American Slavery, 1619–1877*. New York: Hill and Wang, 1993.

Lane, Ann J. *The Debate over Slavery: Stanley Elkins and His Critics*. Urbana: University of Illinois, 1971.

Lee, Susan. *The Westward Movement of the Cotton Economy, 1840–1860: Perceived Interests and Economic Realities*. Dissertations in American economic history. New York: Arno Press, 1977.

Levine, Bruce C. *Half Slave and Half Free: The Roots of Civil War*. New York: Hill and Wang, 1991.

Miller, Elinor, comp. *Plantation, Town and County: Essays on the Local History of American Slave Society*. Urbana: University of Illinois, 1974.

Oakes, James. *Slavery and Freedom: An Interpretation of the Old South*. New York: Knopf, 1990.

Owens, Leslie Howard. *This Species of Property: Slave Life and Culture in the Old South*. Oxford; New York: Oxford University Press, 1976.

Ransom, Roger L. *Conflict and Compromise: The Political Economy of Slavery, Emancipation, and the American Civil War*. Cambridge: Cambridge University Press, 1989.

Remini, Robert Vincent. *The Legacy of Andrew Jackson*. Baton Rouge: Louisiana State University, 1988.

Roediger, David and Martin Blatt. *The Meaning of Slavery in the North*. New York: Garland Pub., 1998.

Rose, Willie Lee Nichols. *Slavery and Freedom*. Exp. ed. Oxford: Oxford University Press, 1982.

Smith, Mark M. *Mastered by the Clock: Time, Slavery, and Freedom in the American South*. Chapel Hill: University of North Carolina Press, 1997.

Wiencek, Henry. *The Hairstons: An American Family in Black and White*. New York: St. Martin's Press, 1999.

ALABAMA

Brown, Alan and David Taylor. *Gabr'l Blow Sof': Sumter County, Alabama Slave Narratives*. Livingston, Ala.: Livingston Press, 1997.

Fuller, Willie J. *Blacks in Alabama, 1528–1865*. Exchange bibliography—Council of Planning Librarians; 1033. Monticello, Ill.: Council of Planning Librarians, 1976.

Nall, James Rastus. *Free Born Slave: Diary of a Black Man in the South*. Birmingham, Ala.: Crane Hill Publishers, 1995.

APPALACHIA

Inscoe, John C. *Mountain Masters, Slavery, and the Sectional Crisis in Western North Carolina*. 1st ed. Knoxville: University of Tennessee Press, 1989.

CALIFORNIA

Lapp, Rudolph M. *Blacks in Gold Rush California*. Yale Western Americana series; 29. New Haven: Yale University Press, 1977.

CHESAPEAKE

Davis, David Brion. *Slavery in the Colonial Chesapeake*. The Foundations of America. Williamsburg, Va.: Colonial Williamsburg Foundation, 1986.

Kulikoff, Allan. *Tobacco and Slaves: The Development of Southern Cultures in the Chesapeake, 1680–1800*. Chapel Hill: Published for the Institute of Early American History and Culture, Williamsburg, Virginia by the University of North Carolina Press, 1986.

COLONIAL SLAVERY (General Interpretations)

Berlin, Ira. *Many Thousands Gone: The First Two Centuries of Slavery in North America*. Belknap Press of Harvard University Press, 1998.

Countryman, Edward. *How Did American Slavery Begin?* Bedford: Macmillan, 1999.

Gomez, Michael Angelo. *Exchanging Our Country Marks: The Transformation of African Identities in the Colonial and Antebellum South*. Chapel Hill: University of North Carolina Press, 1998.

Morgan, Philip D. *Slave Counterpoint: Black Culture in the Eighteenth-Century Chesapeake and Lowcountry*. Chapel Hill: University of North Carolina Press, 1998.

Reiss, Oscar. *Blacks in Colonial America*. Jefferson: McFarland & Co., 1997.

Walsh, Lorena S. *From Calabar to Carter's Grove: The History of a Virginia Slave Community*. Charlottesville: University Press of Virginia, 1997.

Wood, Betty. *The Origins of American Slavery: Freedom and Bondage in the English Colonies*. New York: Hill and Wang, 1997.

Wright, Donald R. *African Americans in the Colonial Era*. Arlington Heights: Harlan Davidson, 1984.

CONNECTICUT

Mead, Jeffrey B. *Chains Unbound: Slave Emancipation in the Town of Greenwich, Connecticut*. Baltimore: Gateway, 1995.

DELAWARE

Essah, Patience. *A House Divided: Slavery and Emancipation in Delaware, 1638–1865*. Charlottesville: University Press of Virginia, 1996.

Williams, William Henry. *Slavery and Freedom in Delaware, 1639–1865*. Wilmington: SR Books, 1996.

FLORIDA

Landers, Jane. *Black Society in Spanish Florida*. Urbana: University of Illinois Press, 1997.

GEORGIA

Bullard, Mary Ricketson. *Robert Stafford of Cumberland Island: Growth of a Planter*. Athens: University of Georgia Press, 1995.

Clifton, James M. *Life and Labor on Argyle Island: Letters and Documents of a Savannah River Rice Plantation, 1833–1867*. Savannah: Beehive Press, 1978.

Ehrenhard, John E. *Stafford Plantation, Cumberland Island National Seashore, Georgia: Archaeological Investigations of a Slave Cabin*. Tallahassee, Fla.: Southeast Archaeological Center, National Park Service, U.S. Dept. of the Interior, 1981.

Harris, J. William. *Plain Folk and Gentry in a Slave Society: White Liberty and Black Slavery in Augusta's Hinterlands*. Baton Rouge: Louisiana State University Press, 1998.

Kemble, Fanny. *Principles and Privilege: Two Women's Lives on a Georgia Plantation*. Ann Arbor paperbacks. Ann Arbor: University of Michigan Press, 1995.

Killion, Ronald G., comp. *Slavery Time When I Was Chillun Down on Marster's Plantation: Interviews with Georgia Slaves*. Savannah: Beehive Press [1973].

Lane, Mills, ed. *Neither More Nor Less Than Men: Slavery in Georgia: A Documentary History*. Library of Georgia. Savannah: Beehive Press, 1993.

Mohr, Clarence L. *On the Threshold of Freedom: Masters and Slaves in Civil War Georgia*. Athens: University of Georgia Press, 1986.

Reidy, Joseph P. (Joseph Patrick). *From Slavery to Agrarian Capitalism in the Cotton Plantation South: Central Georgia, 1800–1880*. The Fred W. Morrison series in Southern studies. Chapel Hill: University of North Carolina Press, 1992.

Slave Bills of Sale Project. Atlanta, Ga. (P.O. Box 115268, Atlanta 30310): African-American Family History Association [1986].

Smith, Julia Floyd. *Slavery and Rice Culture in Low Country Georgia, 1750–1860*. Knoxville: University of Tennessee Press, 1985.

Wood, Betty. *Slavery in Colonial Georgia, 1730–1775*. Athens: University of Georgia Press, 1984.

———. *Women's Work, Men's Work: The Informal Slave Economies of Lowcountry Georgia*. Athens: University of Georgia Press, 1995.

Young, Jeffrey Robert. *Domesticating Slavery: The Ideological Formation of the Master Class in Georgia and South Carolina, from Colonization to 1837*. Chapel Hill: University of North Carolina Press, 1999.

KANSAS

Sengupta, Gunja. *For God and Mammon: Evangelicals and Entrepreneurs, Masters and Slaves in Territorial Kansas*. Athens: University of Georgia Press, 1996.

KENTUCKY

Browne, Martha Griffith. *Autobiography of a Female Slave*. Jackson: University Press of Mississippi, 1998.

Pickard, Kate E. R. *The Kidnapped and the Ransomed: The Narrative of Peter and Vina Still after Forty Years of Slavery*. Lincoln: University of Nebraska Press, 1995.

LOUISIANA

Fox, Tryphena Blanche Holder. *A Northern Woman in the Plantation South: Letters of Tryphena Blanche Holder Fox, 1856–1876*. Women's diaries and letters of the nineteenth-century South. Columbia: University of South Carolina Press, 1993.

Hall, Gwendolyn Midlo. *Africans in Colonial Louisiana: The Development of Afro-Creole Culture in the Eighteenth Century*. Baton Rouge: Louisiana State University Press, 1992.

Ingersoll, Thomas N. *Mammon and Manon in Early New Orleans: The First Slave Society in the Deep South, 1718–1819*. Knoxville: University of Tennessee Press, 1999.

Kilbourne, Richard Holcombe. *Debt, Investment, Slaves: Credit Relations in East Feliciana Parish, Louisiana, 1825–1885*. Tuscaloosa: University of Alabama Press, 1995.

McDonald, Roderick A. (Roderick Alexander). *The Economy and Material Culture of Slaves: Goods and Chattels on the Sugar Plantations of Jamaica and Louisiana*. Baton Rouge: Louisiana State University Press, 1993.

Whitten, David O. *Andrew Durnford: A Black Sugar Planter in the Antebellum South*. New Brunswick: Transaction, 1995.

Xavier University of Louisiana. *Guide to the Heartman Manuscripts on Slavery*. Boston, Mass.: G.K. Hall, 1982.

MARYLAND

Clayton, Ralph. *Slavery, Slaveholding, and the Free Black Population of Antebellum Baltimore*. Bowie: Heritage, 1993.

Fields, Barbara Jeanne. *Slavery and Freedom on the Middle Ground: Maryland during the Nineteenth Century*. Yale historical publications. Miscellany; 123. New Haven: Yale University Press, 1985.

Preston, Dickson J. *Young Frederick Douglass: The Maryland Years*. Baltimore: Johns Hopkins University Press, 1980.

Whitman, T. Stephen. *The Price of Freedom: Slavery and Manumission in Baltimore and Early National Maryland*. Lexington: University Press of Kentucky, 1997.

MISSISSIPPI

Alford, Terry. *Prince among Slaves*. New York: Oxford University Press [1986].

Hermann, Janet Sharp. *The Pursuit of a Dream*. New York: Oxford University Press, 1981.

Jordan, Winthrop D. *Tumult and Silence at Second Creek: An Inquiry into a Civil War Slave Conspiracy*. Baton Rouge: Louisiana State University Press, 1993.

Moore, John Hebron. *The Emergence of the Cotton Kingdom in the Old Southwest: Mississippi, 1770–1860*. Baton Rouge: Louisiana State University Press, 1988.

Sydnor, Charles S. (Charles Sackett). *Slavery in Mississippi*. Baton Rouge: Louisiana State University Press, 1966 [1933].

MISSOURI

Hurt, R. Douglas. *Agriculture and Slavery in Missouri's Little Dixie*. Columbia: University of Missouri Press, 1992.

Poole, Stafford. *Church and Slave in Perry County, Missouri, 1818–1865*. Studies in American religion; v. 22. Lewiston, N.Y.: E. Mellen Press, 1986.

NEW JERSEY

Hodges, Graham Russell. *Slavery and Freedom in the Rural North: African Americans in Monmouth County, New Jersey, 1665–1865*. Madison, Wis.: Madison House, 1997.

Pingeon, Frances D. *Blacks in the Revolutionary Era*. New Jersey's Revolutionary Experience; 14. Trenton: New Jersey Historical Commission, 1975.

NEW MEXICO

Murphy, Lawrence R. *Antislavery in the Southwest: William G. Kephart's Mission to New Mexico, 1850–53*. Southwestern studies; monograph no. 54. El Paso: Texas Western Press, 1978.

NEW YORK

Davis, Thomas J. *A Rumor of Revolt: The "Great Negro Plot" in Colonial New York*. New York: Free Press, 1985.

Foote, Thelma Wills. *Black Life in Colonial Manhattan, 1664–1786*. Thesis (Ph.D.)—Harvard University, 1991.

Ginsberg, Judah B. (Judah Bennett). *The Tangled Web: The New York Democratic Party and the Slavery Controversy, 1844–1860*. University Microfilms. Publication no. 74-19915. [Doctoral dissertation series]. Microfilm of Ph.D. Dissertation, University of Wisconsin, 1974.

Kobrin, David. *The Black Minority in Early New York*. Albany: New York State American Bicentennial Commission, 1975.

Moss, Richard Shannon. *Slavery on Long Island: A Study in Local Institutional and Early African-American Communal Life*. Studies in African American history and culture. New York: Garland, 1993.

Phelan, Helene C. *And Why Not Every Man? An Account of Slavery, the Underground Railroad, and the Road to Freedom in New York's Southern Tier*. Interlaken, N.Y.: Heart of the Lakes Pub., 1987.

Power, Michael. *Slavery and Freedom in Niagara*. Niagara-on-the-Lake, Ont.: Niagara Historical Society, 1993.

White, Shane. *Somewhat More Independent: The End of Slavery in New York City, 1770–1810*. Athens: University of Georgia Press, 1991.

Wilson, Sherrill D. *New York City's African Slave Owners: A Social and Material Culture History*. Studies in African American history and culture. New York: Garland Pub. Co., 1994.

NORTH CAROLINA

Bassett, John Spencer. *Slavery and Servitude in the Colony of North Carolina*. [New York: Johnson Reprint Corp., 1973.]

Cecil-Fronsman, Bill. *Common Whites: Class and Culture in Antebellum North Carolina*. Lexington: University Press of Kentucky, 1992.

Hilty, Hiram H. *By Land and by Sea: Quakers Confront Slavery and Its Aftermath in North Carolina*. Greensboro, N.C.: North Carolina Friends Historical Society, 1993.

Inscoe, John C. *Mountain Masters, Slavery, and the Sectional Crisis in Western North Carolina*. Knoxville: University of Tennessee Press, 1989.

Kay, Marvin L. Michael. *An African Diaspora: Slavery in North Carolina, 1748–1775*. Chapel Hill: University of North Carolina Press, 1995.

Kay, Marvin L. Michael and Lorin Lee Cary. *Slavery in North Caorlina, 1748–1775*. Chapel Hill: University of North Carolina Press, 1995.

McKiever, Charles Fitzgerald. *Slavery and the Emigration of North Carolina Friends*. Murfreesboro, N.C.: Johnson Pub. Co. [1970].

Sensbach, Jon F. *A Separate Canaan: The Making of an Afro-Moravian World in North Carolina, 1763–1840*. Chapel Hill: University of North Carolina, 1998.

Stealing a Little Freedom: Advertisements for Slave Runaways in North Carolina, 1791–1840. Garland reference library of the humanities; vol. 1812. New York: Garland, 1994.

PENNSYLVANIA

Brouwer, Merle Gerald. *The Negro as a Slave and as a Free Black in Colonial Pennsylvania*. Thesis (Ph.D.)—Wayne State University, 1973.

Nash, Gary B. *Freedom by Degrees: Emancipation in Pennsylvania and Its Aftermath*. New York: Oxford University Press, 1991.

The Pennsylvania Abolition Society and the Pennsylvania Black: Two hundredth anniversary exhibition, April 17, 1974–July 17, 1974, at the Historical Society of Pennsylvania: from its collections, those of Charles L. Blockson, and others. — Philadelphia: Pennsylvania Abolition Society, 1974.

RHODE ISLAND

Fitts, Robert K. *Inventing New England's Slave Paradise: Master/Slave Relations in Eighteenth Century Narragansett, Rhode Island*. New York: Garland Pub., 1998.

SOUTH CAROLINA

Ball, Edward. *Slaves in the Family*. New York: Farrar, Straus and Giroux, 1998.

Clarke, Erskine. *Wrestlin' Jacob: A Portrait of Religion in the Old South*. Atlanta: John Knox Press, 1979.

Creel, Margaret Washington. *A Peculiar People: Slave Religion and Community-Culture among the Gullahs*. New York: New York University, 1988.

Dusinberre, William. *Them Dark Days: Slavery in the American Rice Swamps*. New York: Oxford University Press, 1996.

Ferguson, Leland G. *Uncommon Ground: Archaeology and Early African America, 1650–1800*. Washington, D.C.: Smithsonian Institution Press, 1992.

Hammond, James Henry. *Secret and Sacred: The Diaries of James Henry Hammond, A Southern Slaveholder*. New York: Oxford University Press, 1988.

Hurmence, Belinda. *Before Freedom, When I Just Can Remember: Twenty-Seven Oral Histories of Former South Carolina Slaves*. Winston-Salem, N.C.: J.F. Blair, 1989.

Jones, Norrece T. *Born a Child of Freedom, Yet a Slave: Mechanisms of Control and Strategies of Resistance in Antebellum South Carolina*. Middletown, Conn.: Wesleyan University Press; Scranton, Pa.: Distributed by Harper & Row, 1989.

———. *Control Mechanisms in South Carolina Slave Society, 1800–1865*. Thesis (Ph.D.)—Northwestern University, 1981.

Joyner, Charles W. *Down by the Riverside: A South Carolina Slave Community*. Blacks in the New World. Urbana: University of Illinois Press, 1984.

Klein, Rachel N. *Unification of a Slave State: The Rise of the Planter Class in the South Carolina Backcountry, 1760–1808*. Chapel Hill: University of North Carolina Press; Williamsburg, Va.: Published for the Institute of Early American History and Culture, 1990.

Koger, Larry. *Black Slave Owners: Free Black Slave Masters in South Carolina, 1790–1860*. Jefferson, N.C.: McFarland, 1985.

Littlefield, Daniel C. *Rice and Slaves: Ethnicity and the Slave Trade in Colonial South Carolina*. Baton Rouge: Louisiana State University Press, 1981.

Lofton, John. *Denmark Vesey's Revolt: The Slave Plot that Lit a Fuse to Fort Sumter*. Kent, Ohio: Kent State University Press, 1983.

McCurry, Stephanie. *Masters of Small Worlds: Yeoman Households, Gender Relations, and the Political Culture of the Antebellum South Carolina Low Country*. New York: Oxford University Press, 1995.

Olwell, Robert. *Masters, Slaves, and Subjects: The Culture of Power in the South Carolina Low Country, 1740–1790*. Ithaca, N.Y.: Cornell University Press, 1998.

Pearson, Edward A. *Designs Against Charleston: The Trial Record of the Denmark Vesey Slave Conspiracy of 1822*. Chapel Hill: University of North Carolina, 1999.

Saville, Julie. *The Work of Reconstruction: From Slave to Wage Laborer in South Carolina, 1860–1870*. Cambridge: Cambridge University Press, 1994.

Singleton, Theresa, ed. *The Archaeology of Slavery and Plantation Life*. Studies in historical archaeology. Orlando: Academic Press, 1985.

Walker, Karen Jo. *Kingsley and His Slaves: Anthropological Interpretation and Evaluation*. Volumes in historical archaeology; 5. Columbia: South Carolina Institute of Archaeology and Anthropology, the University of South Carolina, 1988.

Wood, Peter H. *Black Majority: Negroes in Colonial South Carolina from 1670 through the Stono Rebellion*. New York: Norton, 1975.

Young, Jeffrey Robert. *Domesticating Slavery: The Ideological Formation of the Master Class in Georgia and South Carolina, from Colonization to 1837.* Chapel Hill: University of North Carolina Press, 1999.

TENNESSEE

Cimprich, John. *Slavery's End in Tennessee, 1861–1865.* University, Ala.: University of Alabama Press, 1985.

Howington, Arthur F. *What Sayeth the Law: The Treatment of Slaves and Free Blacks in the State and Local Courts of Tennessee.* American legal and constitutional history. New York: Garland Pub., 1986.

Thomas, James P. *From Tennessee Slave to St. Louis Entrepreneur: The Autobiography of James Thomas.* Columbia: University of Missouri Press, 1984.

TEXAS

Baker, T. Lindsay and Julie P. Baker. *Till Freedom Cried Out: Memories of Texas Slave Life.* College Station: Texas A&M University Press, 1997.

Campbell, Randolph. *An Empire for Slavery: The Peculiar Institution in Texas, 1821–1865.* Baton Rouge: Louisiana State University Press, 1989.

Tyler, Ronnie C. *The Slave Narratives of Texas.* Austin: Encino Press, 1974.

VIRGINIA

Boskin, Joseph. *Into Slavery: Racial Decisions in the Virginia Colony.* The America's alternatives series. Philadelphia: Lippincott, 1976.

Brossard, Carlos Antonio. *Indians, Economic Development and African Literacy in Colonial Virginia before 1660: A Study in Afro-American Literacy before Absolute Bondage.* Thesis (Ed.D.)—Harvard Graduate School of Education, 1976.

Carson, Jane. *Plantation Housekeeping in Colonial Virginia, 1974.* Williamsburg, Va.: Colonial Williamsburg Foundation; Guilford, Conn.: OPUS Publications, 1989.

Cope, Robert S. *Carry Me Back: Slavery and Servitude in Seventeenth-Century Virginia.* [1st ed.] Pikeville, Ky.: Pikeville College Press of the Appalachian Studies Center, 1973.

Craven, Wesley Frank. *White, Red, and Black: The Seventeenth-Century Virginian.* Richard lectures for 1970–71. Charlottesville: University Press of Virginia [1971].

Davis, David Brion. *Slavery in the Colonial Chesapeake.* The Foundations of America. Williamsburg, Va.: Colonial Williamsburg Foundation, 1986.

Dew, Charles B. *Bond of Iron: Master and Slave at Buffalo Forge.* New York: W.W. Norton, 1994.

Freehling, Alison Goodyear. *Drift toward Dissolution: The Virginia Slavery Debate of 1831–1832.* Baton Rouge: Louisiana State University Press, 1982.

Hopkins, Margaret Lail. *Index to the Tithables of Loudoun County, Virginia, and to Slaveholders and Slaves: 1758–1786.* Baltimore, Md.: Genealogical Pub. Co., 1991.

Hucles, Michael. *"Don't Grieve After Me": The Black Experience in Virginia, 1619–1986.* Hampton, Va.: Hampton University, 1986.

Latimer, Frances Bibbins. *Instruments of Freedom: Deeds and Wills of Emancipation, Northampton County, Virginia, 1782 to 1864.* Bowie, Md.: Heritage Books, 1994.

McColley, Robert. *Slavery and Jeffersonian Virginia.* 2d ed. Urbana: University of Illinois Press [1973].

Minchinton, Walter E. *Virginia Slave-Trade Statistics, 1698–1775.* Richmond: Virginia State Library, 1984.

Morgan, Edmund Sears. *American Slavery, American Freedom: The Ordeal of Colonial Virginia.* New York: Norton, 1975.

Morgan, Lynda J. *Emancipation in Virginia's Tobacco Belt, 1850–1870.* Athens: University of Georgia Press, 1992.

Mullin, Gerald W. *Flight and Rebellion: Slave Resistance in Eighteenth-Century Virginia.* New York: Oxford University Press, 1972.

Siegel, Frederick F. *The Roots of Southern Distinctiveness: Tobacco and Society in Danville, Virginia, 1780–1865.* Chapel Hill: University of North Carolina, 1987.

Silvers, Damon Abraham. *Industry, Immigration, and Slavery: The Working People of Richmond, Virginia, 1845–1865.* Thesis (A.B., Honors)—Harvard University, 1986.

Takagi, Midori. *"Rearing Wolves to Our Own Destruction": Slavery in Richmond, Virginia, 1782–1865*. Charlottesville: University Press of Virginia, 1999.

Tate, Thad W. *The Negro in Eighteenth-Century Williamsburg*. Williamsburg, Va.: Colonial Williamsburg Foundation; [Charlottesville, Va.]: Distributed by the University Press of Virginia, 1965.

Tyler-McGraw, Marie. *In Bondage and Freedom: Antebellum Black Life in Richmond, Virginia*. Richmond, Va.: Valentine Museum; [Chapel Hill, N.C.]: Distributed by the University of North Carolina Press, 1988.

ASIA

Harris, Joseph E. *The African Presence in Asia: Consequences of the East African Slave Trade*. Evanston, Ill.: Northwestern University Press, 1971.

Klein, Martin A. *Breaking the Chains: Slavery, Bondage, and Emancipation in Modern Africa and Asia*. Madison: University of Wisconsin Press, 1993.

Reid, Anthony, ed. *Slavery, Bondage, and Dependency in Southeast Asia*. St. Lucia; New York: University of Queensland Press, 1983.

Scarr, Deryck. *Slaving and Slavery in the Indian Ocean*. Basingstoke: Macmillan, 1998.

Watson, James L., ed. *Asian and African Systems of Slavery*. Oxford: Blackwell, 1980.

BABYLONIA

Dandamaev, M. A. *Slavery in Babylonia: From Nabopolassar to Alexander the Great (626–331 B.C.)*. Rev ed. Translated by Victoria A. Powell; edited by Marvin A. Powell; David B. Weisberg, co-editor. DeKalb: Northern Illinois University Press, 1984.

INDIA

Bissoondoyal, U., ed. *Slavery in South West Indian Ocean*. Moka, Mauritius: Mahatma Gandhi Institute, 1989.

Manickam, Sundararaj. *Slavery in the Tamil Country: A Historical Over view*. Madras: Christian Literature Society, 1982.

Patnaik, Utsa, ed. *Chains of Servitude: Bondage and Slavery in India*. Madras: Sangam Books; Hyderabad, India: Distributed by Orient Longman, 1985.

Pinto, Jeanette. *Slavery in Portuguese India, 1510–1842*. Bombay: Himalaya Pub. House, 1992.

Ramachandran Nair, Adoor K. K. *Slavery in Kerala*. Delhi: Mittal Publications. Distributed by Mittal Publishers' Distributors, 1986.

Saradamoni, K. (Kunjulekshmi). *Emergence of a Slave Caste: Pulayas of Kerala*. New Delhi: People's Pub. House, 1980.

KOREA

Kim, Ellen J. *The Enduring Institution: A Case Study of Slavery in Traditional Korea*. Thesis (A.B., Honors in East Asian Languages and Civilizations)—Harvard University, 1991.

Salem, Ellen. *Slavery in Medieval Korea*. Thesis (Ph.D.)—Columbia University, 1978.

MALAYA

Sullivan, Patrick (Patrick J.). *Social Relations of Dependence in a Malay State: Nineteenth Century Perak*. Monograph / The Malaysian Branch of the Royal Asiatic Society, no. 10. Kuala Lumpur: Printed for the Council of the M.B.R.A.S. by Art Printing Works, 1982.

MIDDLE EAST and NEAR EAST

Ayalon, David. *Islam and the Abode of War: Military Slaves and Islamic Adversaries*. Collected studies series; CS456. Aldershot, Great Britain; Brookfield, Vt.: Variorum, 1994.

Chirichigno, Gregory. *Debt-Slavery in Israel and the Ancient Near East*. Journal for the Study of the Old Testament. Supplement series, 141. Sheffield: JSOT Press, 1993.

Gordon, Murray. *Slavery in the Arab World*. New York: New Amsterdam, 1989.

Lewis, Bernard. *Race and Slavery in the Middle East: An Historical Enquiry*. New York: Oxford University Press, 1990.

Marmon, Shaun E. *Slavery in the Islamic Middle East*. Princeton, N.J.: M. Wiener, 1999.

Pipes, Daniel. *Slave Soldiers and Islam: The Genesis of a Military System*. New Haven: Yale University Press, 1981.

Toledano, Ehud R. *Slavery and Abolition in the Ottoman Middle East*. Seattle: University of Washington Press, 1998.

OTTOMAN EMPIRE

Erdem, Hakan. *Slavery in the Ottoman Empire and Its Demise, 1800–1909*. Houdmills: Macmillan, 1996.

Toledano, Ehud R. *The Ottoman Slave Trade and Its Suppression, 1840–1890*. Princeton, N.J.: Princeton University Press, 1982.

PHILIPPINES

Scott, William Henry. *Slavery in the Spanish Philippines*. Manila, Philippines: De la Salle University Press, 1991.

EUROPE

Bloch, Marc Leopold Benjamin. *Slavery and Serfdom in the Middle Ages: Selected Essays*. Publications of the Center for Medieval and Renaissance Studies, UCLA; 8. Berkeley: University of California Press, 1975.

Bonnassie, Pierre. *From Slavery to Feudalism in South-western Europe*. Past and present publications. Cambridge [England]; New York: Cambridge University Press; Paris: Editions de la Maison des sciences de l'homme, 1991.

Dockes, Pierre. *Medieval Slavery and Liberation*. London: Methuen, 1982.

Jordan, William C. *From Servitude to Freedom: Manumission in the Senonais in the Thirteenth Century*. The Middle Ages. Philadelphia: University of Pennsylvania Press, 1986.

Karras, Ruth Mazo. *Slavery and Society in Medieval Scandinavia*. Yale historical publications; 135. New Haven: Yale University Press, 1988.

ANCIENT GREECE AND ROME

Bradley, K. R. *Slavery and Rebellion in the Roman World, 140 B.C.–70 B.C.* Bloomington: Indiana University Press; London: B.T. Batsford, 1989.

———. *Slavery and Society at Rome*. Key themes in ancient history. Cambridge; New York: Cambridge University Press, 1994.

———. *Slaves and Masters in the Roman Empire: A Study in Social Control*. New York: Oxford University Press, 1987.

Finley, M. I. (Moses I.). *Ancient Slavery and Modern Ideology*. Expanded ed. Princeton, N.J.: Markus Wiener, 1998.

———. *Classical Slavery*. London, England; Totowa, N.J.: F. Cass, 1987.

Garlan, Yvon. *Slavery in Ancient Greece*. Rev. and expanded ed. Ithaca, N.Y.: Cornell University Press, 1988.

Hopkins, Keith. *Conquerors and Slaves*. Sociological studies in Roman history; v. 1. Cambridge; New York: Cambridge University Press, 1978.

Hughes, Kenneth. *Slavery*. Greek and Roman topics; 3. London: Allen & Unwin [1975].

Hunt, Peter. *Slaves, Warfare, and Ideology in the Greek Historians*. Cambridge: Cambridge University Press, 1998.

Joshel, Sandra R. and Sheila Murnaghan. *Women and Slaves in Greco-Roman Culture*. London: Routledge, 1998.

Vogt, Joseph. *Ancient Slavery and the Ideal of Man*. Cambridge, Mass.: Harvard University Press, 1975.

Wiedemann, Thomas E. J. *Greek and Roman Slavery*. London: Croom Helm, 1981.

———. *Slavery. Greece & Rome*. New surveys in the classics; no. 19. Oxford: Published for the Classical Association at the Clarendon Press, 1987.

Wood, Ellen Meiksins. *Peasant-Citizen and Slave: The Foundations of Athenian Democracy*. Corrected pbk. ed. London; New York: Verso, 1989.

Yavetz, Zvi. *Slaves and Slavery in Ancient Rome*. New Brunswick, N.J.: Transaction Books, 1988.

BRITAIN

Barley, Tony. *Myths of the Slave Power: Confederate Slavery, Lancashire Workers, and the* Alabama. Liverpool: Coach House, 1992.

Bean, Richard Nelson. *The British Trans-Atlantic Slave Trade, 1650–1775*. New York: Arno, 1975.

Craton, Michael. *Sinews of Empire: A Short History of British Slavery*. [1st ed.] Garden City, N.Y.: Anchor Press, 1974.

———. *Testing the Chains: Resistance to Slavery in the British West Indies*. Ithaca, N.Y.: Cornell University Press, 1982.

Drescher, Seymour. *Capitalism and Antislavery: British Mobilization in Comparative Perspective*: The Second Anstey Memorial Lectures in the University of Kent at Canterbury, 1984. Houndmills, Basingstoke, Hampshire: Macmillan, 1986.

———. *Econocide: British Slavery in the Era of Abolition*. Pittsburgh: University of Pittsburgh, 1977.

Elder, Melinda. *The Slave Trade and the Economic Development of Eighteenth-Century Lancaster*. Krumlin: Ryburn, 1992.

Gerzina, Gretchen. *Black England: Life Before Emancipation*. London: J. Murray, 1995.

Hamshere, Cyril. *The British in the Caribbean*. London: Weidenfeld and Nicolson, 1972.

Hurwitz, Edith F. *Politics and the Public Conscience: Slave Emancipation and the Abolitionist Movement in Britain*. Historical problems: studies and documents, 23. London: Allen & Unwin; New York: Barnes & Noble Books, 1973.

Jakobsson, Stiv. *Am I Not a Man and a Brother? British Missions and the Abolition of the Slave Trade in West Africa and the West Indies, 1786–1838*. Lund: Gleerup, 1972.

Mathieson, William Law. *British Slave Emancipation, 1838–1849*. New York: Octagon Books, 1967.

Pelteret, David Anthony Edgell. *Slavery in Early Mediaeval England: From the Reign of Alfred until the Twelfth Century*. Studies in Anglo-Saxon history, 7. Woodbridge, Suffolk, UK; Rochester, N.Y.: Boydell Press, 1995.

Shyllon, F. O. *Black People in Britain, 1555–1833*. London; New York: Published for the Institute of Race Relations by Oxford University Press, 1977

———. *Black Slaves in Britain*. London; New York: Published for the Institute of Race Relations by Oxford University Press, 1974.

Walvin, James. *Black Ivory: A History of British Slavery*. London: HarperCollins, 1992.

———. *England, Slaves, and Freedom, 1776–1838*. Jackson: University Press of Mississippi, 1986.

———. *Slavery and British Society, 1776–1846*. Baton Rouge: Louisiana State University Press, 1982.

———. *Slaves and Slavery: The British Colonial Experience*. Manchester [England]; New York: Manchester University Press; New York: Distributed exclusively in the USA and Canada by St. Martin's Press, 1992.

Ward, J. R. *British West Indian Slavery, 1750–1934*. Oxford: Oxford University Press, 1988.

FRANCE

Cooper, Anna J. (Anna Julia). *Slavery and the French Revolutionists (1788–1805)*. Studies in French civilization; v. 1. Lewiston, N.Y.: E. Mellen Press, 1988.

Peabody, Sue. *There Are No Slaves in France: The Political Culture of Race and Slavery in the Ancien Regime*. New York: Oxford University Press, 1996.

RUSSIA

Hellie, Richard. *Slavery in Russia, 1450–1725*. Chicago: University of Chicago Press, 1985.

Kolchin, Peter. *Unfree Labor: American Slavery and Russian Serfdom*. Cambridge, Mass.: Harvard University Press, 1987.

SCANDINAVIA

Karras, Ruth Mazo. *Slavery and Society in Medieval Scandinavia*. New Haven: Yale University Press, 1988.

TOPICS

ABOLITION (General Interpretations)

Bender, Thomas. *The Antislavery Debate: Capitalism and Abolitionism as a Problem in Historical Interpretation*. Berkeley: University of California Press, 1992.

Blackburn, Robin. *The Overthrow of Colonial Slavery, 1776–1848*. London: Verso, 1988.

Cunliffe, Marcus. *Chattel Slavery and Wage Slavery: The Anglo-American Context, 1830–1860*. Mercer University Lamar memorial lectures; no. 22. Athens: University of Georgia Press, 1979.

Rice, C. Duncan. *The Rise and Fall of Black Slavery*. New York: Harper & Row, 1975.

AMERICAN ABOLITION

Abbott, Richard H. *Cotton and Capital: Boston Businessmen and Antislavery Reform, 1854–1868*. Amherst: University of Massachusetts Press, 1991.

Azevedo, Celia Maria Marinho de. *Abolitionism in the United States and Brazil: A Comparative Perspective*. New York: Garland, 1995.

Bilotta, James D. *Race and the Rise of the Republican Party, 1848–1865*. New York: P. Lang, 1992.

Blackett, R. J. M. *Building an Antislavery Wall: Black Americans in the Atlantic Abolitionist Movement, 1830–1860*. Baton Rouge: Louisiana State University Press, 1983.

Buckmaster, Henrietta. *Let My People Go: The Story of the Underground Railroad and the Growth of the Abolition Movement*. Columbia: University of South Carolina Press, 1992.

Clark, Christopher. *The Communitarian Moment: The Radical Challenge of the Northampton Association*. Ithaca, N.Y.: Cornell University Press, 1995.

Cook, Robert. *Baptism of Fire: The Republican Party of Iowa, 1838–1878*. Ames: Iowa State University Press, 1994.

DeBoer, Clara Merritt. *Be Jubilant My Feet: African American Abolitionists in the American Missionary Association, 1839–1861*. New York: Garland, 1994.

Dillon, Merton Lynn. *Slavery Attacked: Southern Slaves and Their Allies, 1619–1865*. Baton Rouge: Louisiana State University Press, 1990.

Dixon, Chris. *Perfecting the Family: Antislavery Marriages in Nineteenth-Century America*. Amherst: University of Massachusetts Press, 1997.

Fogel, Robert W. *Without Consent or Contract: The Rise and Fall of American Slavery*. New York: Norton, 1989.

Foner, Philip S. and Herbert Shapiro. *Northern Labor and Antislavery: A Documentary History*. Westport, Conn.: Greenwood, 1994.

Goodheart, Lawrence B. and Hugh Hawkins. *The Abolitionists: Means, Ends, and Motivations*. 3rd ed. Lexington: D.C. Heath and Co., 1995.

Gougeon, Len. *Virtue's Hero: Emerson, Antislavery, and Reform*. Athens: University of Georgia Press, 1990.

Grimstead, David. *American Mobbing, 1828–1861*. New York: Oxford University Press, 1998.

Guy, Anita Aidt. *Maryland's Persistent Pursuit to End Slavery, 1850–1864*. New York: Garland, 1997.

Harrold, Stanley. *The Abolitionists and the South, 1831–1861*. Lexington: University Press of Kentucky, 1995.

Horton, James Oliver and Lois E. Horton. *In Hope of Liberty: Culture, Community, and Protest Among Northern Free Blacks, 1700–1860*. New York: Oxford University Press, 1997.

Howard, Victor B. *The Evangelical War Against Slavery and Caste: The Life and Times of John G. Fee*. Selinsgrove, Pa.: Susquehanna University Press, 1996.

Jacobs, Donald M. *Courage and Conscience: Black and White Abolitionists in Boston*. Bloomington: Indiana University Press, 1993.

Jeffrey, Julie Roy. *The Great Silent Army of Abolitionism: Ordinary Women in the Antislavery Movement*. Chapel Hill: University of North Carolina Press, 1998.

Jennings, Lawrence C. *French Reaction to British Slave Emancipation*. Baton Rouge: Louisiana State University Press, 1988.

Marshall, Peter D. *Bristol and the Abolition of Slavery: The Politics of Emancipation*. Local history pamphlets; no. 37. Bristol: Bristol Branch of the Historical Association, The University, 1975.

McGlynn, Frank, ed. *Meaning of Freedom: Economics, Politics, and Culture after Slavery*. Pittsburgh: University of Pittsburgh, 1992.

McInerney, Daniel John. *The Fortunate Heirs of Freedom: Abolition and Republican Thought*. Lincoln: University of Nebraska Press, 1994.

McManus, Michael J. *Political Abolitionism in Wisconsin, 1840–1861*. Kent, Ohio: Kent State University Press, 1998.

Melish, Joanne Pope. *Disowning Slavery: Gradual Emancipation and "Race" in New England, 1780–1860*. Ithaca, N.Y.: Cornell University Press, 1998.

Nash, Gary B. *Race and Revolution*. Madison, Wis.: Madison House, 1990.

Perry, Lewis. *Radical Abolitionism: Anarchy and the Government of God in Antislavery Thought*. Knoxville: University of Tennessee Press, 1995.

Perry, Lewis and Michael Fellman. *Antislavery Reconsidered: New Perspectives on the Abolitionists*. Baton Rouge: Louisiana State University Press, 1979.

Ripley, C. Peter. *Witness for Freedom: African American Voices on Race, Slavery, and Emancipation*. Chapel Hill: University of North Carolina Press, 1993.

Rogers, William B. *"We Are All Together Now": Frederick Douglass, William Lloyd Garrison, and the Prophetic Tradition*. New York: Garland, 1995.

Sanchez-Eppler, Karen. *Touching Liberty: Abolition, Feminism, and the Politics of the Body*. Berkeley: University of California Press, 1993.

Sears, Richard D. *The Kentucky Abolitionists in the Midst of Slavery*. Lewiston, N.Y.: E. Mellen Press, 1993.

Stewart, James Brewer. *Holy Warriors: The Abolitionists and American Slavery*. Rev. ed. New York: Hill and Wang, 1996.

Strong, Douglas M. *Perfectionist Politics: Abolitionism and the Religious Tensions of American Democracy*. Syracuse, N.Y.: Syracuse University Press, 1998.

Volpe, Vernon L. *Forlorn Hope of Freedom: The Liberty Party in the Old Northwest, 1838–1848*. Kent, Ohio: Kent State University Press, 1990.

Vorenberg, Michael. *Final Freedom: The Civil War, the End of Slavery, and the Thirteenth Amendment*. Thesis (Ph.D.)—Harvard University, 1995.

Yee, Shirley J. *Black Women Abolitionists: A Study in Activism, 1828–1860*. Knoxville: University of Tennessee Press, 1992.

Yellin, Jean Fagan and John C. Van Horne. *The Abolitionist Sisterhood: Women's Political Culture in Antebellum America*. Ithaca, N.Y.: Cornell University Press, 1994.

Young, R. J. *Antebellum Black Activists: Race, Gender, and Self*. New York: Garland Pub., 1996.

BRAZILIAN ABOLITION

Azevedo, Celia Maria Marinho de. *Abolitionism in the United States and Brazil: A Comparative Perspective*. New York: Garland, 1995.

Conrad, Robert Edgar. *The Destruction of Brazilian Slavery, 1850–1888*. 2nd ed. Malabar: Krieger Pub. Co., 1993.

BRITISH ABOLITION

Anstey, Roger. *Liverpool, the African Slave Trade, and Abolition*. Liverpool: Historic Society of Lancashire and Cheshire, 1989.

Bolt, Christine and Seymour Drescher. *Anti-Slavery, Religion and Reform*. Folkestone: W. Dawson, 1980.

D'Anjou, Leo. *Social Movements and Cultural Change: The First Abolition Campaign Revisited*. New York: Aldine de Gruyter, 1996.

Drescher, Seymour. *Capitalism and Antislavery: British Mobilization in Comparative Perspective*. New York: Oxford University Press, 1987.

———. *Econocide: British Slavery in the Era of Abolition*. Pittsburgh: University of Pittsburgh Press, 1977.

Halversleben, Karen I. *Women's Participation in the British Antislavery Movement, 1824–1865*. Lewiston, N.Y.: E. Mellen Press, 1993.

Hurwitz, Edith F. *Politics and the Public Conscience: Slave Emancipation and the Abolitionist Movement in Britain*. London: Allen & Unwin, 1973.

Midgley, Clare. *Women Against Slavery: The British Campaigns, 1780–1870*. London: Routledge, 1992.
Oldfield, J. R. *Popular Politics and British Anti-Slavery: The Mobilisation of Public Opinion Against the Slave Trade, 1787–1807*. London: Frank Cass, 1998.
Temperley, Howard. *White Dreams, Black Africa: The Antislavery Expedition to the River Niger, 1941–1842*. New Haven: Yale University Press, 1991.
Turley, David. *The Culture of English Antislavery, 1780–1860*. London: Routledge, 1991.
Walvin, James. *Questioning Slavery*. London: Routledge, 1996.

CANADIAN ANTISLAVERY

Stouffer, Allen P. *The Light of Nature and the Law of God: Antislavery in Ontario, 1833–1877*. Baton Rouge: Louisiana State University Press, 1992.

DUTCH ANTISLAVERY

Oostindie, Gert. *Fifty Years Later: Antislavery, Capitalism, and Modernity in the Dutch Orbit*. Leiden: KITLV Press, 1995.

FRENCH ANTISLAVERY

Peabody, Sue. *There Are No Slaves in France: The Political Culture of Race and Slavery in the Ancien Regime*. New York: Oxford University Press, 1996.

SPANISH ANTISLAVERY

Schmidt-Nowara, Christopher. *Empire and Antislavery: Spain, Cuba, and Puerto Rico, 1833–1874*. Pittsburgh: University of Pittsburgh Press, 1998.

WEST INDIAN ABOLITION

Levy, Claude. *Emancipation, Sugar, and Federalism: Barbados and the West Indies, 1833–1876*. Gainesville: University Presses of Florida, 1980.

ANTHROPOLOGY AND ARCHAEOLOGY OF SLAVERY

African-American Archaeology: Newsletter of the African-American Archaeology Network. No. 1 (spring 1990). Washington, D.C.: Dept. of Anthropology, National Museum of Natural History, Smithsonian Institution [1990–].
Crist, Thomas A. J. *The Bone Chemical Analysis and Bioarchaeology of an Historic South Carolina African-American Cemetery*. Volumes in historical archaeology; 18. Columbia, S.C.: South Carolina Institute of Archaeology and Anthropology, University of South Carolina, 1991.
Delle, James A. *An Archaeology of Social Space: Analyzing Coffee Plantations in Jamaica's Blue Mountains*. New York: Plenum Press, 1998.
Ferguson, Leland G. *Uncommon Ground: Archaeology and Early African America, 1650–1800*. Washington, D.C.: Smithsonian Institution Press, 1992.
Meillassoux, Claude. *The Anthropology of Slavery: The Womb of Iron and Gold*. London: Athlone, 1991.
Otto, John Solomon. *Cannon's Point Plantation, 1794–1860: Living Conditions and Status Patterns in the Old South*. Studies in historical archaeology. Orlando: Academic Press, 1984.
Singleton, Theresa A. *The Archaeology of Slavery and Plantation Life*. Orlando: Academic Press, 1985.
Trinkley, Michael. *Archaeological Studies Associated with the Nineteenth-Century Owens-Thomas Carriage House, Savannah, Georgia*. Columbia: Chicora Foundation, 1993.

ARCHITECTURE

Vlach, John Michael. *Back of the Big House: The Architecture of Plantation Slavery*. The Fred W. Morrison series in Southern studies. Chapel Hill: University of North Carolina Press, 1993.

BIOGRAPHICAL STUDIES

Blight, David W. *Frederick Douglass' Civil War: Keeping Faith in Jubilee*. Baton Rouge: Louisiana State University Press, 1989.

Blue, Frederick J. *Charles Sumner and the Conscience of the North.* Arlington Heights: Harlan Davidson, 1994.

Brown, Ira V. *Mary Grew: Abolitionist and Feminist, 1813–1896.* Selinsgrove, Pa.: Susquehanna University Press, 1991.

Burke, Ronald K. *Samuel Ringgold Ward, Christian Abolitionist.* New York: Garland Pub., 1995.

Cheek, William F. *John Mercer Langston and the Fight for Black Freedom, 1829–65.* Urbana: University of Illinois Press, 1989.

Davis, Hugh. *Joshua Leavitt: Evangelical Abolitionist.* Baton Rouge: Louisiana State University Press, 1990.

Eisan, Frances K. *Saint or Demon? The Legendary Delia Webster Opposing Slavery.* New York: Pace University Press, 1998.

Goodheart, Lawrence B. *Abolitionist, Actuary, Atheist: Elizur Wright and the Reform Impulse.* Kent, Ohio: Kent State University Press, 1990.

Hamilton, Virginia. *Anthony Burns: The Defeat and Triumph of a Fugitive Slave.* New York: A.A. Knopf, 1988.

Hansen, Debra Gold. *Strained Sisterhood: Gender and Class in the Boston Female Anti-Slavery Society.* Amherst: University of Massachusetts Press, 1993.

Heller, Charles E. *Portrait of an Abolitionist: A Biography of George Luther Stearns, 1809–1867.* Westport, Conn.: Greenwood Press, 1996.

Hunter, Carol M. *To Set the Captives Free: Reverend Jermain Wesley Loguen and the Struggle for Freedom in Central New York, 1835–1872.* New York: Garland, 1993.

Lampe, Gregory P. *Frederick Douglass: Freedom's Voice, 1818–1945.* East Lansing: Michigan State University Press, 1998.

Lerner, Gerda. *The Grimké Sisters from South Carolina.* New York: Oxford University Press, 1998.

Mabee, Carleton. *Sojourner Truth—Slave, Prophet, Legend.* New York: New York University Press, 1993.

Mayer, Henry. *All on Fire: William Lloyd Garrison and the Abolition of Slavery.* New York: St. Martin's Press, 1998.

Painter, Nell Irvin. *Sojourner Truth: A Life, A Symbol.* New York: W.W. Norton, 1996.

Pasternak, Martin B. *Rise Now and Fly to Arms: The Life of Henry Highland Garnet.* New York: Garland, 1995.

Runyon, Randolph. *Delia Webster and the Underground Railroad.* Lexington: University Press of Kentucky, 1996.

Salitan, Lucille and Eve Lewis Perera. *Virtuous Lives: Four Quaker Sisters Remember Family Life, Abolitionism, and Women's Suffrage.* New York: Continuum, 1994.

Simon, Paul. *Freedom's Champion: Elijah Lovejoy.* Carbondale: Southern Illinois University Press, 1994.

Spevack, Edmund. *Charles Follen's Search for Nationality and Freedom.* Cambridge, Mass.: Harvard University Press, 1997.

Sterling, Dorothy. *Ahead of Her Time: Abby Kelley and the Politics of Anti-Slavery.* New York: W.W. Norton, 1991.

Stewart, James Brewer. *William Lloyd Garrison and the Challenge of Emancipation.* Arlington Heights: Harlan Davidson, 1992.

Thomas, Herman Edward. *James W. C. Pennington: African American Churchman and Abolitionist.* New York: Garland Press, 1995.

Von Frank, Albert J. *The Trials of Anthony Burns.* Cambridge, Mass.: Harvard University Press, 1998.

Walvin, James. *An African's Life: The Life and Times of Olaudah Equiano, 1745–1797.* Washington: Cassell, 1998.

Wilson, Ellen Gibson. *Thomas Clarkson: A Biography.* 2nd ed. York: William Sessions, 1996.

Yacovone, Donald. *Samuel Joseph May and the Dilemmas of the Liberal Persuasion, 1797–1871.* Philadelphia: Temple University Press, 1991.

BLACK SLAVE OWNERS

Johnson, Michael P. and James L. Roark. *No Chariot Let Down: Charleston's Free People of Color on the Eve of the Civil War.* Chapel Hill: University of North Carolina Press, 1984.

Koger, Larry. *Black Slave Owners: Free Black Slave Masters in South Carolina, 1790–1860.* Columbia: University of South Carolina, 1994.

Whitten, David O. *Andrew Durnford: A Black Sugar Planter in the Antebellum South*. New Brunswick: Transaction, 1995.

CIVIL WAR AND SLAVERY

Berlin, Ira, ed. *Black Military Experience*. Freedom, a documentary history of emancipation, 1861–1867. Cambridge: Cambridge University Press, 1982.
———. *The Destruction of Slavery*. Freedom, a documentary history of emancipation, 1861–1867. Cambridge: Cambridge University Press, 1985.
———. *Free at Last*. Freedom, a documentary history of emancipation, 1861–1867. Cambridge: Cambridge University Press, 1985.
———. *Slave No More: Three Essays on Emancipation and the Civil War*. Cambridge: Cambridge University Press, 1985.
———. *The Wartime Genesis of Free Labor: The Upper South*. Freedom, a documentary history of emancipation, 1861–1867; ser. 1, v. 2. Cambridge [England]; New York: Cambridge University Press, 1993.
Durden, Robert Franklin. *The Gray and the Black: The Confederate Debate on Emancipation*. Baton Rouge: Louisiana State University Press [1972].
Gerteis, Louis S. *From Contraband to Freedman: Federal Policy toward Southern Blacks, 1861–1865*. Westport, Conn.: Greenwood, 1977.
Glatthaar, Joseph. *Forged in Battle: The Civil War Alliance between Black Soldiers and White Officers*. New York: Free Press, 1990.

COLONIAL AND REVOLUTIONARY ERAS

Bruns, Roger, ed. *"Am I Not a Man and a Brother?": The Antislavery Crusade of Revolutionary America*. New York: Chelsea House, 1977.
Finkelman, Paul. *Slavery, Revolutionary America, and the New Nation*. New York: Garland, 1989.
Hodges, Graham Russell. *Slavery and Freedom in the Rural North: African Americans in Monmouth County, New Jersey, 1665–1865*. Madison, Wis.: Madison House, 1995.
Macleod, Duncan J. *Slavery, Race and the American Revolution*. New York: Cambridge University Press, 1974.
Silver, Timothy. *A New Face on the Countryside: Indians, Colonists, and Slaves in South Atlantic Forests, 1500–1800*. Cambridge: Cambridge University Press, 1990.
Voelz, Peter Michael. *Slave and Soldier: The Military Impact of Blacks in Colonial Americas*. New York: Garland, 1993.
Wright, Donald R. *African Americans in the Colonial Era*. Arlington Heights: Harlan Davidson, 1984.

CULTURE

Abrahams, Roger D. *Singing the Master: The Emergence of African American Culture in the Plantation South*. 1st ed. New York: Pantheon Books, 1992.
Campbell, Edward D. C., Jr. *Before Freedom Came: African-American Life in the Antebellum South*. To Accompany an Exhibition organized by the Museum of the Confederacy. 1st ed. Richmond: The Museum; Charlottesville: University Press of Virginia, 1991.
Ownby, Ted, ed. *Black and White Cultural Interaction in the Antebellum South*. Chancellor's symposium series. Jackson: University Press of Mississippi, 1993.
Palmie, Stephan, ed. *Slave Cultures and the Cultures of Slavery*. Knoxville: University of Tennessee, 1995.

ECONOMICS OF SLAVERY

Aitken, Hugh G. J., comp. *Did Slavery Pay? Readings in the Economics of Black Slavery in the United States*. New perspectives in history. Boston: Houghton Mifflin [1971].
America, Richard F. *The Wealth of Races: The Present Value of Benefits from Past Injustices*. Contributions in Afro-American and African studies; no. 132. New York: Greenwood Press, 1990.
Chaplin, Joyce E. *An Anxious Pursuit: Agricultural Innovation and Modernity in the Lower South, 1730–1815*. Chapel Hill: University of North Carolina, 1993.
Conrad, Alfred H. *Studies in Econometric History*. London: Chapman & Hall, 1965.

Dew, Charles B., ed. *Slavery in Ante-bellum Southern Industries*. Selections from the Duke University Library; Southern Historical Collection, University of North Carolina; Virginia Historical Society.

Fogel, Robert William. *Slave Sales and Appraisals, 1775–1865*. ICPSR; 7421.

Galenson, David W. *Traders, Planters, and Slaves: Market Behavior in Early English America*. Cambridge [Cambridgeshire]; New York: Cambridge University Press, 1986.

Parker, William Nelson. *Southern Farms Study, 1860*. ICPSR; 7419.

Shore, Laurence. *Southern Capitalists: The Ideological Leadership of an Elite, 1832–1885*. Chapel Hill: University of North Carolina, 1986.

Woodman, Harold D., ed. *Slavery and the Southern Economy: Sources and Readings*. The Forces in American economic growth series. New York: Harcourt, Brace & World [1966].

EDUCATION

Albanese, Anthony Gerald. *The Plantation School*. New York: Vantage, 1976.

Cornelius, Janet Duitsman. *"When I Can Read My Title Clear": Literacy, Slavery, and Religion in the Antebellum South*. Columbia: University of South Carolina, 1991.

Webber, Thomas L. *Deep Like the Rivers: Education in the Slave Quarter Community, 1831–1865*. New York: Norton, 1978.

FAMILY AND CHILDREN

Barrow, Christine. *Family in the Caribbean: Themes and Perspectives*. Kingston: I. Randle, 1996.

Clark, Elizabeth. *Matrimonial Bonds: Slavery, Contract and the Law of Divorce in Nineteenth-Century America*. Working papers/Legal History Program; 1–10. Madison: Institute for Legal Studies, University of Wisconsin—Madison Law School [1987].

Finkelman, Paul. *Women and the Family in a Slave Society*. Articles on American Slavery; vol. 9. New York: Garland Pub., 1989.

Gutman, Herbert. *The Black Family in Slavery and Freedom*. New York: Pantheon, 1976.

Hunefeldt, Christine. *Paying the Price of Freedom: Family and Labor among Lima's Slaves, 1800–1854*. Berkeley: University of California, 1994.

King, Wilma. *Stolen Childhood: Slave Youth in Nineteenth-Century America*. Bloomington: Indiana University Press, 1995.

Malone, Ann Patton. *Sweet Chariot: Slave Family and Household Structure in Nineteenth Century Louisiana*. Chapel Hill: University of North Carolina Press, 1992.

Stevenson, Brenda E. *Life in Black and White: Family and Community in the Slave South*. New York: Oxford University Press, 1996.

Tate, Thad. *Race and Family in the Colonial South: Essays*. Jackson: University Press of Mississippi, 1987.

FUGITIVE SLAVES

Franklin, John Hope and Loren Schweninger. *Runaway Slaves*. New York: Oxford University Press, 1999.

Windley, Lathan A. *Runaway Slave Advertisements: A Documentary History from the 1730s to 1790*. Westport, Conn.: Greenwood, 1983.

GENEALOGY

Streets, David H. *Slave Genealogy: A Research Guide with Case Studies*. Bowie, Md.: Heritage Books, 1986.

INTELLECTUAL AND CULTURAL HISTORY

Cusick, Richard. *Coloring Slavery: Enlightenment Attitudes toward Slavery and the Emancipation of Blacks during the French Revolution*. Thesis (A.B., Honors in History)—Harvard University, 1992.

Garnsey, Peter. *Ideas of Slavery from Aristotle to Augustine*. Cambridge: Cambridge University Press, 1996.

Lott, Tommy L. *Subjugation and Bondage: Critical Essays on Slavery and Social Philosophy*. Lanham, Md.: Rowman & Littlefield, 1998.

Panzer, Joel S. *The Popes and Slavery*. New York: Alba Houe, 1996.
Papenfuse, Eric Robert. *The Evils of Necessity: Robert Goodloe Harper and the Moral Dilemma of Slavery*. Philadelphia: American Philosophical Society, 1997.
Spiegel, Marjorie. *The Dreaded Comparison: Human and Animal Slavery*. New York: Mirror Books, 1996.
Stanley, Amy Dru. *From Bondage to Contract: Wage Labor, Marriage, and the Market in the Age of Slave Emancipation*. Cambridge: Cambridge University Press, 1998.
Stuckey, Sterling, ed. *The Ideological Origins of Black Nationalism*. Boston: Beacon, 1972.

JEWS AND THE SLAVE TRADE

Faber, Eli. *Jews, Slaves and the Slave Trade*. New York: New York University Press, 1998.
Friedman, Saul S. *Jews and the American Slave Trade*. New Brunswick: Transaction Pub., 1998.

LABOR

Dew, Charles B. *Bond of Iron: Master and Slave at Buffalo Forge*. New York: W.W. Norton, 1994.
Fogel, Robert William. *Slave Hires, 1775–1865*. ICPSR; 7422.
———. *Slave Sales and Appraisals, 1775–1865*. ICPSR; 7421.
Jernegan, Marcus Wilson. *Laboring and Dependent Classes in Colonial America, 1607–1783*. Westport, Conn.: Greenwood, 1980.
Lewis, Ronald L. *Coal, Iron, and Slaves: Industrial Slavery in Maryland and Virginia, 1715–1865*. Westport, Conn.: Greenwood, 1979.
Mintz, Sidney J. *Was the Plantation Slave a Proletarian?* Binghamton: State University of New York at Binghamton, 1977.
Scarborough, William Kauffman. *The Overseer: Plantation Management in the Old South*. Athens: University of Georgia, 1984.
Van Deburg, William L. *The Slave Drivers: Black Agricultural Labor Supervisors in the Antebellum South*. Contributions in Afro-American and African studies; no. 43. Westport, Conn.: Greenwood Press, 1979.

LANGUAGE

Bailey, Guy, ed. *The Emergence of Black English: Text and Commentary*. Creole language library, v. 8. Amsterdam; Philadelphia: J. Benjamins Pub. Co., 1991.

LAW AND SLAVERY

Brandon, Mark E. *Free in the New World: American Slavery and Constitutional Failure*. Princeton, N.J.: Princeton University Press, 1998.
Brandwein, Pamela. *Reconstructing Reconstruction: The Supreme Court and the Production of Historical Truth*. Durham, N.C.: Duke University Press, 1999.
Cardoza Symposium on Bondage, Freedom and the Constitution. New York: Cardoza Law Review, 1996.
Cover, Robert M. *Justice Accused: Antislavery and the Judicial Process*. New Haven: Yale University Press, 1975.
Fede, Andrew. *People Without Rights: An Interpretation of the Fundamentals of the Law of Slavery in the U.S. South*. Distinguished studies in American legal and constitutional history. New York: Garland Pub., 1992.
Fehrenbacher, Don Edward. *The Dred Scott Case: Its Significance in American Law and Politics*. New York: Oxford University Press, 1978.
———. *Slavery, Law, and Politics: The Dred Scott Case in Historical Perspective*. New York: Oxford University Press, 1981.
Finkelman, Paul. *Dred Scott v. Sandford: A Brief History with Documents*. Boston: Bedford Books, 1997.
———. *An Imperfect Union: Slavery, Federalism, and Comity*. Studies in legal history. Chapel Hill: University of North Carolina Press, 1981.
———. *The Law of Freedom and Bondage: A Casebook*. The New York University School of Law series in legal history. Ingram documents in American legal history. New York: Oceana Publications, 1986.
———. *Slavery in the Courtroom: An Annotated Bibliography of American Cases*.

Washington, D.C.: Library of Congress: For sale by the Supt. of Docs., U.S. G.P.O., 1985.

———. *Slavery and the Founders: Race and Liberty in the Age of Jefferson*. Armonk, N.Y.: M.E. Sharpe, 1995.

———. *Slavery and the Law*. Madison, Wis.: Madison House, 1997.

———. *Southern Slaves in Free State Courts: The Pamphlet Literature*. Slavery, Race, and the American legal system, 1700–1872; ser. 1. New York: Garland, 1988.

Flanigan, Daniel J. *The Criminal Law of Slavery and Freedom, 1800–1868*. American legal and constitutional history. Thesis (Ph.D.)—Rice University, 1973.

Hall, Kermit L. *The Law of American Slavery: Major Historical Interpretations*. United States constitutional and legal history; v. 9. New York: Garland Pub., 1987.

Hindus, Michael Stephen. *Slave Trials in Anderson and Spartanburg Counties, South Carolina, 1818–1861*. ICPSR, 8674.

Hoemann, George H. *What God Hath Wrought: The Embodiment of Freedom in the Thirteenth Amendment*. American legal and constitutional history: a Garland series of outstanding dissertations. New York: Garland Pub., 1987.

Howington, Arthur F. *What Sayeth the Law: The Treatment of Slaves and Free Blacks in the State and Local Courts of Tennessee*. American legal and constitutional history. New York: Garland Pub., 1986.

Hyman, Harold M. *The Reconstruction Justice of Salmon P. Chase: In Re Turner and Texas v. White*. Lawrence: University Press of Kansas, 1997.

Lively, Donald E. *The Constitution and Race*. New York: Praeger, 1992.

McLaurin, Melton Alonza. *Celia, a Slave*. Athens: University of Georgia Press, 1991.

Middleton, Stephen. *Ohio and the Antislavery Activities of Attorney Salmon Portland Chase, 1830–1849*. Distinguished studies in American legal and constitutional history. New York: Garland Pub., 1990.

Morris, Thomas D. *Southern Slavery and the Law, 1619–1860*. Chapel Hill: University of North Carolina Press, 1996.

Nieman, Donald G. *The Constitution, Law, and American Life: Critical Aspects of the Nineteenth-Century Experience*. Athens: University of Georgia Press, 1992.

Schafer, Judith Kelleher. *Slavery, the Civil Law, and the Supreme Court of Louisiana*. Baton Rouge: Louisiana State University Press, 1994.

Schwarz, Philip J. *Slave Laws in Virginia*. Athens: University of Georgia Press, 1996.

———. *Twice Condemned: Slaves and the Criminal Laws of Virginia, 1705–1865*. [Baton Rouge]: Louisiana State University Press, 1988.

Shaw, Robert B. *A Legal History of Slavery in the United States*. Potsdam, N.Y.: Northern Press, 1991.

Tushnet, Mark V. *The American Law of Slavery, 1810–1860: Considerations of Humanity and Interest*. Princeton, N.J.: Princeton University Press, 1981.

Wahl, Jenny Bourne. *The Bondsman's Burden: An Economic Analysis of the Common Law of Southern Slavery*. Cambridge: Cambridge University Press, 1998.

Watson, Alan. *Slave Law in the Americas*. Athens: University of Georgia Press, 1989.

West, Thomas G. *Vindicating the Founders: Race, Sex, Class, and Justice in the Origins of America*. Lanham, Md.: Rowman & Littlefield, 1997.

Wiecek, William M. *The Sources of Antislavery Constitutionalism in America, 1760–1848*. Ithaca, N.Y.: Cornell University Press, 1977.

Wiethoff, William E. *A Peculiar Humanism: The Judicial Advocacy of Slavery in High Courts of the Old South, 1820–1850*. Athens: University of Georgia Press, 1996.

Williams, Oscar R. *African Americans and Colonial Legislation in the Middle Colonies*. New York: Garland Pub., 1998.

MEDICINE AND DEMOGRAPHY

Bankole, Katherine Kemi. *Slavery and Medicine: Enslavement and Medical Practices in Antebellum Louisiana*. New York: Garland Pub., 1998.

Chandler, David L. *Health and Slavery in Colonial Colombia*. Dissertations in European economic history; 1981. New York: Arno Press, 1981.

Kiple, Kenneth F. *The African Exchange: Toward a Biological History of Black People*. Durham, N.C.: Duke University Press, 1987.

———. *Another Dimension to the Black Diaspora: Diet, Disease, and Racism*. Cambridge: Cambridge University Press, 1981.

———. *The Caribbean Slave: A Biological History*. Cambridge: Cambridge University Press, 1984.

McClelland, Peter D. *Demographic Dimensions of the New Republic: American Interregional Migration, Vital Statistics, and Manumission, 1800–1860*. Cambridge: Cambridge University, 1982.
Numbers, Ronald, ed. *Science and Medicine in the Old South*. Baton Rouge: Louisiana State University Press, 1989.
Postell, William Dosite. *The Health of Slaves on Southern Plantations*. Louisiana State University studies: Social science series; no. 1. Gloucester, Mass.: P. Smith, 1970.
Savitt, Todd Lee. *Medicine and Slavery: The Diseases and Health Care of Blacks in Antebellum Virginia*. Blacks in the New World. Urbana: University of Illinois Press, 1978.
———, ed. *Disease and Distinctiveness in the American South*. Knoxville: University of Tennessee, 1988.
Sheridan, Richard B. *Doctors and Slaves: A Medical and Demographic History of Slavery in the British West Indies, 1680–1834*. Cambridge [Cambridgeshire]; New York: Cambridge University Press, 1985.

NATIVE AMERICANS AND SLAVERY

Averkieva, Iuliia Pavlovna. *Slavery Among the Indians of North America*. Rev. Translation by G. R. Elliott. Victoria, B.C.: Victoria College, 1966.
Halliburton, R. *Red Over Black: Black Slavery among the Cherokee Indians*. Westport, Conn.: Greenwood, 1977.
Leland, Donald. *Aboriginal Slavery on the Northwest Coast of North America*. Berkeley: University of California Press, 1997.
Littlefield, Daniel F. *Africans and Seminoles: From Removal to Emancipation*. Contributions in Afro-American and African studies; no. 32. Westport, Conn.: Greenwood Press, 1977.
Magnaghi, Russell M. *Indian Slavery, Labor, Evangelization, and Captivity in the Americas: An Annotated Bibliography*. Lanham, Md.: Scarecrow Press, 1998.
Olexer, Barbara. *The Enslavement of the American Indian*. Monroe, N.Y.: Library Research Associates, 1982.
Perdue, Theda. *Slavery and the Evolution of Cherokee Society, 1540–1866*. Knoxville: University of Tennessee, 1979.

NORTH AFRICAN "WHITE SLAVERY"

Baepler, Paul. *White Slaves, African Masters: An Anthology of American Barbary Captivity Narratives*. Chicago: University of Chicago Press, 1999.

PHILOSOPHY AND SLAVERY

McGary, Howard. *Between Slavery and Freedom: Philosophy and American Slavery*. Blacks in the diaspora. Bloomington: Indiana University Press, 1992.
Thomas, Laurance. *Vessels of Evil: American Slavery and the Holocaust*. Philadelphia: Temple University Press, 1993.

POLITICS OF SLAVERY

Anbinder, Tyler. *Nativism and Slavery: The Northern Know Nothings and the Politics of the 1850s*. New York: Oxford University Press, 1992.
Ashworth, John. *Slavery, Capitalism and Politics in the Antebellum Republic*. Cambridge: Cambridge University Press, 1995.
Bilotta, James D. *Race and the Rise of the Republican Party, 1848–1865*. New York: P. Lang, 1992.
Cooper, William J. *The South and the Politics of Slavery, 1828–1856*. Baton Rouge: Louisiana State University Press, 1978.
Davis, David Brion. *Slave Power Conspiracy and the Paranoid Style*. Baton Rouge: Louisiana State University Press, 1986.
Freehling, William W. *The Reintegration of American History: Slavery and the Civil War*. New York: Oxford University Press, 1994.
Johannsen, Robert Walter. *Lincoln, the South, and Slavery: The Political Dimension*. Baton Rouge: Louisiana State University Press, 1991.
Lynd, Staughton. *Class Conflict, Slavery, and the United States Constitution*. Westport, Conn.: Greenwood, 1980.

Miller, William Lee. *Arguing About Slavery: The Great Battle in the United States Congress*. New York: A.A. Knopf, 1996.
Morrison, Michael A. *Slavery and the American West: The Eclipse of Manifest Destiny and the Coming of the Civil War*. Chapel Hill: University of North Carolina Press, 1997.
Robinson, Donald L. *Slavery in the Structure of American Politics, 1765–1820*. New York: Norton, 1979.

PRO-SLAVERY ARGUMENT

Ambrose, Douglas. *Henry Hughes and Proslavery Thought in the Old South*. Baton Rouge: Louisiana State University Press, 1997.
Faust, Drew Gilpin. *A Sacred Circle: The Dilemma of the Intellectual in the Old South, 1840–1860*. Baltimore: Johns Hopkins University Press, 1977.
Greenberg, Kenneth S. *Honor and Slavery*. Princeton, N.J.: Princeton University Press, 1996.

PSYCHOLOGICAL ASPECTS OF SLAVERY

Black, Daniel P. *Dismantling Black Manhood: An Historical and Literary Analysis of the Legacy of Slavery*. New York: Garland, 1997.
Hartman, Saidiya V. *Scenes of Subjection: Terror, Slavery, and Self-Making in Nineteenth-Century America*. New York: Oxford University Press, 1997.
Patterson, Orlando. *Rituals of Blood: Consequences of Slavery in Two American Centuries*. Washington: Civitas, 1998.

RACE

Freimarck, Vincent, ed. *Race and the American Romantics*. New York: Schocken Books, 1971.
Jordan, Winthrop D. *The White Man's Burden: Historical Origins of Racism in the United States*. New York: Oxford University Press, 1974.
———. *White Over Black: American Attitudes toward the Negro, 1550–1812*. Chapel Hill: University of North Carolina, 1968.
Miller, John Chester. *The Wolf by the Ears: Thomas Jefferson and Slavery*. New York: Free Press, 1977.
Peterson, Thomas Virgin. *Ham and Japheth: The Mythic World of Whites in the Antebellum South*. Metuchen, N.J.: Scarecrow, 1978.
Roediger, David R. *The Wages of Whiteness: Race and the Making of the American Working Class*. London: Verso, 1991.
Smedley, Audrey. *Race in North America: Origin and Evolution of a Worldview*. 2nd ed. Boulder: Westview, 1999.
Tise, Larry E. *Proslavery: A History of the Defense of Slavery in America, 1701–1840*. Athens: University of Georgia, 1987.

RELIGION

Alho, Olli. *The Religion of the Slaves*. Helsinki: Suomalainen Tiedeakatemia, 1976.
Bailey, David T. *Shadow on the Church: Southwestern Evangelical Religion and the Issue of Slavery, 1783–1860*. Ithaca, N.Y.: Cornell University Press, 1985.
Boles, John B. *The Irony of Southern Religion*. Rockwell lecture series; vol. 5. New York: P. Lang, 1994.
———. *Masters and Slaves in the House of the Lord: Race and Religion in the American South, 1740–1870*. Lexington: University Press of Kentucky, 1988.
Bolt, Christine, ed. *Anti-Slavery, Religion and Reform: Essays in Memory of Roger Anstey*. Hamden, Conn.: Archon, 1980.
Burke, Ronald K. *Samuel Ringgold Ward, Christian Abolitionist*. Studies in African American history and culture. New York: Garland Pub., 1995.
Chesebrough, David B. *Clergy Dissent in the Old South, 1830–1865*. Carbondale: Southern Illinois University Press, 1996.
Clarke, Erskine. *Wrestlin' Jacob: A Portrait of Religion in the Old South*. Atlanta: John Knox Press, 1979.
Combes, I. A. H. *The Metaphor of Slavery in the Writings of the Early Church*. Sheffield: Sheffield Academic Press, 1998.
Cornelius, Janet Duitsman. *Slave Missions and the Black Church in the Antebellum South*. Columbia: University of South Carolina Press, 1999.

DeBoer, Clara Merritt. *Be Jubilant My Feet: African American Abolitionists in the American Missionary Association, 1839–1861.* Studies in African American history and culture. New York: Garland Pub., 1994.

Diouf, Sylviane. *Servants of Allah: African Muslims Enslaved in the Americas.* New York: New York University Press, 1998.

Earl, Riggins Renal. *Dark Symbols, Obscure Signs: God, Self, and Community in the Slave Mind.* The Bishop Henry McNeal Turner studies in North American Black religion; v. 7. Maryknoll, N.Y.: Orbis Books, 1993.

Essig, James D. *The Bonds of Wickedness: American Evangelicals against Slavery, 1770–1808.* Philadelphia: Temple University Press, 1982.

Farmer, James Oscar. *The Metaphysical Confederacy: James Henley Thornwell and the Synthesis of Southern Values.* Macon, Ga.: Mercer University Press, 1986.

Finkelman, Paul, ed. *Religion and Slavery.* Articles on American Slavery; vol. 16. New York: Garland Pub., 1989.

Genovese, Eugene D. *"Slavery Ordained of God": The Southern Slaveholders' View of Biblical History and Modern Politics.* 24th annual Robert Fortenbaugh memorial lecture. Gettysburg: Gettysburg College, 1985.

Goatley, David Emmanuel. *Were You There? Godforsakenness in Slave Religion.* Maryknoll, N.Y.: Orbis, 1996.

Gravely, William B. *Gilbert Haven, Methodist Abolitionist.* Nashville: Abingdon Press, 1973.

Hilty, Hiram H. *By Land and by Sea: Quakers Confront Slavery and Its Aftermath in North Carolina.* Greensboro: North Carolina Friends Historical Society, 1993.

———. *Toward Freedom for All: North Carolina Quakers and Slavery.* Richmond, Ind.: Friends United Press, 1984.

Hopkins, Dwight N., ed. *Cut Loose Your Stammering Tongue: Black Theology in the Slave Narratives.* Maryknoll, N.Y.: Orbis Books, 1991.

Howard, Victor B. *Conscience and Slavery: The Evangelistic Calvinist Domestic Missions, 1837–1861.* Kent, Ohio: Kent State University Press, 1990.

———. *Religion and the Radical Republican Movement, 1860–1870.* Lexington: University Press of Kentucky, 1990.

Hunter, Carol M. *To Set the Captives Free: Reverend Jermain Wesley Loguen and the Struggle for Freedom in Central New York, 1835–1872.* Studies in African American history and culture. New York: Garland, 1993.

Lesick, Lawrence Thomas. *The Lane Rebels: Evangelicalism and Antislavery in Antebellum America.* Studies in evangelicalism; no. 2. Metuchen, N.J.: Scarecrow Press, 1980.

Mathews, Donald G. *Slavery and Methodism: A Chapter in American Morality, 1780–1845.* Westport, Conn.: Greenwood Press, 1978.

Maxwell, John Francis. *Slavery and the Catholic Church: The History of Catholic Teaching Concerning the Moral Legitimacy of the Institution of Slavery.* Chichester: Rose [for] the Anti-Slavery Society for the Protection of Human Rights, 1975.

McKivigan, John R. *The War Against Proslavery Religion: Abolitionism and the Northern Churches, 1830–1865.* Ithaca, N.Y.: Cornell University Press, 1984.

McKivigan, John R. and Mitchell Snay. *Religion and the Antebellum Debate Over Slavery.* Athens: University of Georgia Press, 1998.

Poole, Stafford. *Church and Slave in Perry County, Missouri, 1818–1865.* Studies in American religion; v. 22. Lewiston, N.Y.: E. Mellen Press, 1986.

Raboteau, Albert J. *Slave Religion: The "Invisible Institution" in the Antebellum South.* New York: Oxford University Press, 1978.

Scherer, Lester B. *Slavery and the Churches in Early America, 1619–1866.* Grand Rapids: Eerdmans, 1975.

Smith, Warren Thomas. *John Wesley and Slavery.* Nashville: Abingdon Press, 1986.

Sobel, Mechal. *Trabelin' On: The Slave Journey to an Afro-Baptist Faith.* Princeton, N.J.: Princeton University Press, 1988.

Stange, Douglas C. *Patterns of Antislavery among American Unitarians, 1831–1860.* Thesis (Ph.D.)—Harvard University, 1974.

Titus, Noel. *The Church and Slavery in the English-Speaking Caribbean.* CGSRS; no. 2, 1983. [Barbados, W.I.]: Caribbean Group for Social and Religious Studies, 1983.

————. *The Development of Methodism in Barbados, 1823–1883*. Bern; New York: P. Lang, 1994.

Turley, David. *The Culture of English Antislavery, 1780–1860*. London; New York: Routledge, 1991.

Turner, Mary. *Slaves and Missionaries: The Disintegration of Jamaican Slave Society, 1787–1834*. Blacks in the New World. Urbana: University of Illinois Press, 1982.

Washington, Joseph R. *Anti-Blackness in English Religion, 1500–1800*. Texts and studies in religion; 19. New York: E. Mellen Press, 1984.

————. *Race and Religion in Early Nineteenth Century America, 1800–1850: Constitution, Conscience, and Calvinist Compromise*. Studies in American religion; v. 39. Lewiston, N.Y.: E. Mellen Press, 1988.

————. *Race and Religion in Mid-Nineteenth Century America, 1850–1877: Protestant Parochial Philanthropists*. Studies in American religion; v. 40. Lewiston, N.Y.: E. Mellen Press, 1988.

Zanca, Kenneth J., ed. *American Catholics and Slavery, 1789–1866: An Anthology of Primary Documents*. Lanham, Md.: University Press of America, 1994.

RESISTANCE

Abraham, Arthur. *The Amistad Revolt: An Historical Legacy of Sierra Leone and the United States*. Freetown, Sierra Leone: United States Information Service [1987].

Aptheker, Herbert. *Negro Slave Revolts in the United States, 1526–1860*. New York: International Publishers, 1939.

Best, Felton O. *Black Resistance Movements in the United States and Africa, 1800–1993: Oppression and Retaliation*. African studies; v. 38. Lewiston, N.Y.: E. Mellen Press, 1995.

Bracey, John H., comp. *American Slavery: The Question of Resistance*. A Wadsworth series: explorations in the Black experience. Belmont, Calif.: Wadsworth Pub. Co. [1971].

Egerton, Douglas R. *Gabriel's Rebellion: The Virginia Slave Conspiracies of 1800 and 1802*. Chapel Hill: University of North Carolina Press, 1993.

Frey, Sylvia R. *Water from the Rock: Black Resistance in a Revolutionary Age*. Princeton, N.J.: Princeton University Press, 1991.

Genovese, Eugene D. *From Rebellion to Revolution: Afro-American Slave Revolts in the Making of the Modern World*. The Walter Lynwood Fleming lectures in southern history. Louisiana State University. Baton Rouge: Louisiana State University Press, 1979.

Halasz, Nicholas. *The Rattling Chains: Slave Unrest and Revolt in the Antebellum South*. New York: D. McKay Co. [1966].

Hinks, Peter P. *To Awaken My Afflicted Brethren: David Walker and the Problem of Antebellum Slave Resistance*. University Park: Pennsylvania State University Press, 1997.

Jones, Howard. *Mutiny on the* Amistad*: The Saga of a Slave Revolt and Its Impact on American Abolition, Law, and Diplomacy*. New York: Oxford University Press, 1987.

Mullin, Michael. *Africa in America: Slave Acculturation and Resistance in the American South and the British Caribbean, 1736–1831*. Blacks in the New World. Urbana: University of Illinois Press, 1992.

Oates, Stephen B. *The Fires of Jubilee: Nat Turner's Fierce Rebellion*. New York: HarperPerennial, 1990.

Okihio, Gary Y. *In Resistance: Studies in African, Caribbean, and Afro-American History*. Amherst: University of Massachusetts Press, 1986.

Rossbach, Jeffery S. *Ambivalent Conspirators: John Brown, the Secret Six, and a Theory of Slave Violence*. Philadelphia: University of Pennsylvania Press, 1982.

Sidbury, James. *Ploughshares into Swords: Race, Rebellion and Identity in Gabriel's Virginia, 1730–1810*. Cambridge: Cambridge University Press, 1997.

SLAVE OWNERS AND THE PLANTER CLASS

Allmendinger, David F. *Ruffin: Family and Reform in the Old South*. New York: Oxford University Press, 1990.

Brugger, Robert J. *Beverley Tucker: Heart over Head in the Old South*. Johns Hopkins

University studies in historical and political science; 96th ser., no. 2. Baltimore: Johns Hopkins University Press, 1978.

Faust, Drew Gilpin. *James Henry Hammond and the Old South: A Design for Mastery*. Southern biography series. Baton Rouge: Louisiana State University Press, 1982.

————. *Southern Stories: Slaveholders in Peace and War*. Columbia: University of Missouri, 1992.

Franklin, John Hope. *A Southern Odyssey: Travelers in the Antebellum North*. Baton Rouge: Louisiana State University Press, 1976.

Gay, Dorothy Ann. *The Tangled Skein of Romanticism and Violence in the Old South: The Southern Response to Abolitionism and Feminism, 1830–1861*. Thesis (Ph.D.)— University of North Carolina at Chapel Hill, 1975.

Genovese, Eugene D. *The Slaveholders' Dilemma: Freedom and Progress in Southern Conservative Thought, 1820–1860*. Columbia: University of South Carolina, 1992.

Greenberg, Kenneth S. *Masters and Statesmen: The Political Culture of American Slavery*. New studies in American intellectual and cultural history. Baltimore: Johns Hopkins University Press, 1985.

Hughes, Henry. *Selected Writings of Henry Hughes, Antebellum Southerner, Slavocrat, Sociologist*. Jackson: University Press of Mississippi, 1985.

Mathew, William M. *Edmund Ruffin and the Crisis of Slavery in the Old South: The Failure of Agricultural Reform*. Athens: University of Georgia, 1988.

Newton, James E. and Ronald L. Lewis, eds. *The Other Slaves: Mechanics, Artisans, and Craftsmen*. Boston: G.K. Hall, 1978.

Oakes, James. *The Ruling Race: A History of American Slaveholders*. New York: Knopf, 1982.

Roark, James L. *Masters without Slaves: Southern Planters in the Civil War and Reconstruction*. New York: Norton, 1977.

Rosengarten, Theodore. *Tombee: Portrait of a Cotton Planter*. New York: Morrow, 1986.

SLAVE TRADE

Ali, Abbas Ibrahim Muhammad. *The British, the Slave Trade, and Slavery in the Sudan, 1820–1881*. [Khartoum]: Khartoum University Press, 1972.

Alpers, Edward A. *The East African Slave Trade*. Historical Association of Tanzania. Paper; no. 3. Nairobi: Published for the Historical Association of Tanzania by the East African Pub. House, 1967.

————. *Ivory and Slaves: Changing Pattern of International Trade in East Central Africa to the Later Nineteenth Century*. Berkeley: University of California Press, 1975.

Anstey, Roger. *The Atlantic Slave Trade and British Abolition, 1760–1810*. Atlantic Highlands, N.J.: Humanities Press, 1975.

————. *Liverpool, the African Slave Trade, and Abolition: Essays to Illustrate Current Knowledge and Research*. Historic Society of Lancashire and Cheshire. Occasional series, 2d. Enl. ed. [Liverpool]: Historic Society of Lancashire and Cheshire, 1989.

Beachey, R. W. *The Slave Trade of Eastern Africa*. New York: Barnes & Noble Books, 1976.

Bean, Richard Nelson. *The British Trans-Atlantic Slave Trade, 1650–1775*. Dissertations in American economic history. New York: Arno Press, 1975.

Bethell, Leslie. *The Abolition of the Brazilian Slave Trade: Britain, Brazil and the Slave Trade Question, 1807–1869*. Cambridge Latin American studies, 6. Cambridge [Eng.]: University Press, 1970.

Birmingham, David. *Trade and Conflict in Angola: The Mbundu and Their Neighbours under the Influence of the Portuguese, 1483–1790*. Oxford studies in African affairs. Oxford: Clarendon Press, 1966.

Bristol, Africa and the Eighteenth-Century Slave Trade to America. Gloucester: Bristol Record Society, 1986–.

Burnside, Madeleine. *Spirits of the Passage: The Transatlantic Slave Trade in the Seventeenth Century*. New York: Simon & Schuster, 1997.

Clarence-Smith, William Gervase, ed. *The Economics of the Indian Ocean Slave Trade in the Nineteenth Century*. London, England; Totowa, N.J.: Frank Cass, 1989.

Clarke, John Henrik. *Christopher Columbus and the Afrikan Holocaust: Slavery and the Rise of European Capitalism.* Brooklyn, N.Y.: A & B Brooks, 1992.

Clarke, Richard F. (Richard Frederick). *Cardinal Lavigerie and the African Slave Trade.* New York: Negro Universities Press [1969].

Collister, Peter. *The Sullivans and the Slave Trade.* London: R. Collings, 1980.

Conrad, Robert Edgar. *World of Sorrow: The African Slave Trade to Brazil.* Baton Rouge: Louisiana State University Press, 1986.

Cottman, Michael H. *The Wreck of the* Henrietta Marie. New York: Harmony Books, 1999.

Craton, Michael. *Sinews of Empire: A Short History of British Slavery.* Garden City, N.Y.: Anchor Press, 1974.

Curtin, Philip D. *The Atlantic Slave Trade: A Census.* Madison: University of Wisconsin Press, 1969.

———. *Economic Change in Precolonial Africa: Senegambia in the Era of the Slave Trade.* [Madison]: University of Wisconsin Press [1975].

Davidson, Basil. *Black Mother: The Years of the African Slave Trade.* Boston: Little, Brown, 1961.

Dow, George Francis. *Slave Ships and Slaving.* Westport, Conn.: Negro Universities Press, 1970.

Duignan, Peter. *The United States and Africa: A History.* Cambridge [Cambridgeshire]; New York: Cambridge University Press; [Stanford, Calif.]: Hoover Institution, 1984.

Elder, Melinda. *The Slave Trade and the Economic Development of Eighteenth-Century Lancaster.* Krumlin, Halifax [England]: Ryburn Pub., 1992.

Eltis, David. *Economic Growth and the Ending of the Transatlantic Slave Trade.* New York: Oxford University Press, 1987.

———, ed. *The Abolition of the Atlantic Slave Trade: Origins and Effects in Europe, Africa, and the Americas.* Madison: University of Wisconsin Press, 1981.

Eltis, David and David Richardson. *Routes to Slavery: Direction, Ethnicity, and Mortality in the Transatlantic Slave Trade.* London: Frank Cass, 1997.

Emmer, P. C. *The Dutch in the Atlantic Economy, 1580–1880: Trade, Slavery, and Emancipation.* Aldershot: Ashgate, 1998.

Fage, J. D. *States and Subjects in Sub-Saharan African History.* Raymond Dart lectures; lecture 10. Johannesburg: Witwatersand University Press for Institute for the Study of Man in Africa and Museum of Man and Science, 1974.

Findlay, Ronald. *The "Triangular Trade" and the Atlantic Economy of the Eighteenth Century: A Simple General-Equilibrium Model.* Essays in international finance, no. 177 (Mar. 1990). Princeton, N.J.: International Finance Section, Dept. of Economics, Princeton University Press, 1990.

Great Britain. Foreign Office. *Guide to the Microfilm Edition of the Slave Trade, 1858–1892.* British Foreign Office: collection 541, confidential print series. Wilmington, Del.: Michael Glazier [1977?].

Hair, P. E. H. (Paul Edward Hedley). *The Atlantic Slave Trade and Black Africa.* Liverpool historical essays; 1. Liverpool: Liverpool University Press, 1989.

Harris, Joseph E. *The African Presence in Asia: Consequences of the East African Slave Trade.* Evanston, Ill.: Northwestern University Press, 1971.

Hogg, Peter C. *The African Slave Trade and Its Suppression: A Classified and Annotated Bibliography of Books, Pamphlets and Periodical Articles.* Cass Library of African studies. General studies; no. 137. London: F. Cass, 1973.

Howard, Thomas. *Black Voyage: Eyewitness Accounts of the Atlantic Slave Trade.* Boston: Little, Brown [1971].

Howell, Raymond. *The Royal Navy and the Slave Trade.* London: Croom Helm, 1987.

Hutchinson, Louise Daniel. *Out of Africa: From West African Kingdoms to Colonization.* Washington, D.C.: Published for the Anacostia Neighborhood Museum of the Smithsonian Institution by the Smithsonian Institution Press [for sale by the Supt. of Docs., U.S. Govt. Print. Off.], 1979.

Inkori, Joseph E. *The Abolition of the Atlantic Slave Trade: Origins and Effects in Europe, Africa, and the Americas.* Madison: University of Wisconsin Press, 1981.

———. *The Chaining of a Continent: Export Demand for Captives and the History of Africa South of the Sahara, 1450–1870.* Mona, Jamaica: Institute of Social and Economic Research, University of the West Indies, 1992.

———. *Forced Migration: The Impact of the Export Slave Trade on African Societies.* Hutchinson university library for Africa. London: Hutchinson, 1982.

Jakobsson, Stiv. *Am I Not a Man and a Brother? British Missions and the Abolition of the Slave Trade and Slavery in West Africa and the West Indies, 1786–1838.* Studia missionalia Upsaliensia, 17. Lund: Gleerup, 1972.

Jennings, Judith. *The Business of Abolishing the British Slave Trade, 1783–1807.* London: Frank Cass, 1997.

Klein, Herbert S. *The Atlantic Slave Trade.* New York: Cambridge University Press, 1999.

———. *The Middle Passage: Comparative Studies in the Atlantic Slave Trade.* Princeton, N.J.: Princeton University Press, 1978.

Law, Robin. *The Oyo Empire, c.1600–c.1836: A West African Imperialism in the Era of the Atlantic Slave Trade.* Oxford studies in African affairs. Oxford [Eng.]: Clarendon Press, 1977.

———. *The Slave Coast of West Africa, 1550–1750: The Impact of the Atlantic Slave Trade on an African Society.* Oxford studies in African affairs. Oxford: Clarendon Press; New York: Oxford University Press, 1991.

LeVeen, E. Phillip. *British Slave Trade Suppression Policies, 1821–1865.* Dissertations in European economic history. New York: Arno Press, 1977.

Manning, Patrick. *Slave Trades, 1500–1800.* Aldershot: Variorum, 1996.

———. *Slavery, Colonialism, and Economic Growth in Dahomey, 1640–1960.* African studies series; 30. Cambridge; New York: Cambridge University Press, 1982.

Mannix, Daniel Pratt. *Black Cargoes: A History of the Atlantic Slave Trade, 1518–1865.* New York: Viking Press [1962].

Miller, Joseph Calder. *Way of Death: Merchant Capitalism and the Angolan Slave Trade, 1730–1830.* Madison: University of Wisconsin Press, 1988.

Northrup, David. *The Atlantic Slave Trade.* Problems in world history. Lexington, Mass.: D.C. Heath, 1994.

Oldfield, J. R. (John R.). *Popular Politics and British Anti-Slavery: The Mobilisation of Public Opinion against the Slave Trade, 1787–1807.* Manchester; New York: Manchester University Press, 1995.

Page, Willie F. *The Dutch Triangle: The Netherlands and the Atlantic Slave Trade, 1621–1664.* New York: Garland Pub., 1997.

Palmer, Colin A. *Human Cargoes: The British Slave Trade to Spanish America, 1700–1739.* Blacks in the New World. Urbana: University of Illinois Press, 1981.

Polanyi, Karl. *Dahomey and the Slave Trade: An Analysis of an Archaic Economy.* American Ethnological Society. Monograph; 42. Seattle: University of Washington Press [1966].

Postma, Johannes. *The Dutch in the Atlantic Slave Trade, 1600–1815.* Cambridge; New York: Cambridge University Press, 1990.

Price, Jacob M. *The Atlantic Frontier of the Thirteen Colonies and States.* Brookfield: Variorum, 1996.

Rawley, James A. *The Transatlantic Slave Trade: A History.* New York: Norton, 1981.

Reynolds, Edward. *Stand the Storm: A History of the Atlantic Slave Trade.* London; New York: Allison & Busby, 1985.

Richardson, David. *The Bristol Slave Traders: A Collective Portrait.* Local history pamphlets; no. 60. Bristol: Bristol Branch of the Historical Association, 1985.

Rodney, Walter. *West Africa and the Atlantic Slave-Trade.* Historical Association of Tanzania. Paper; no. 2. Nairobi: Published for the Historical Association of Tanzania by the East African Pub. House, 1967.

Sanchez, Joseph P. *Explorers, Traders, and Slavers: Forging the Old Spanish Trail, 1678–1850.* Salt Lake City: University of Utah Press, 1997.

Solow, Barbara L. *British Capitalism and Caribbean Slavery: The Legacy of Eric Williams.* Studies in interdisciplinary history. Cambridge [Cambridgeshire]; New York: Cambridge University Press, 1987.

———. *Slavery and the Rise of the Atlantic System.* Cambridge, Mass.: W. E. B. Du Bois Institute for Afro-American Research, Harvard University; Cambridge [England]; New York: Cambridge University Press, 1991.

Stein, Robert Louis. *The French Slave Trade in the Eighteenth Century: An Old Regime Business.* Madison: University of Wisconsin Press, 1979.

Tadman, Michael. *Speculators and Slaves: Masters, Traders, and Slaves in the Old South.* Madison: University of Wisconsin Press, 1989.

Thomas, Hugh. *Slave Trade*. New York: Simon & Schuster, 1997.
University of Edinburgh. Centre of African Studies. *The Transatlantic Slave Trade from West Africa*; [papers and discussion reports contributed to a seminar held June 4th–5th 1965]. Edinburgh, 1965.
Verger, Pierre. *Bahia and the West African Trade, 1549–1851*. Nigeria: Published for the Institute of African Studies by Ibadan University Press, 1964.
———. *Trade Relations between the Bight of Benin and Bahia from the 17th to 19th Century*. Ibadan, Nigeria: Ibadan University Press, 1976.
Walvin, James. *Black Ivory: A History of British Slavery*. London: HarperCollins, 1992.
———. *England, Slaves, and Freedom, 1776–1838*. Jackson: University Press of Mississippi, 1986.
———. *Slaves and Slavery: The British Colonial Experience*. Manchester [England]; New York: Manchester University Press, 1992.

SLAVERY IN THE CONTEMPORARY WORLD

Bales, Kevin. *Disposable People: New Slavery in the Global Economy*. Berkeley: University of California Press, 1999.
Kuklin, Susan. *Iqbal Masih and the Crusaders Against Child Slavery*. New York: Henry Holt, 1998.

UNDERGROUND RAILROAD

Brandt, Nat. *The Town that Started the Civil War*. Syracuse, N.Y.: Syracuse University Press, 1990.
Buckmaster, Henrietta. *Let My People Go: The Story of the Underground Railroad and the Growth of the Abolition Movement*. Columbia: University of South Carolina Press, 1992.
Gara, Larry. *The Liberty Line: The Legend of the Underground Railroad*. Lexington: University of Kentucky Press, 1961.
Hunter, Carol M. *To Set the Captives Free: The Reverend Jermain Loguen and the Struggle for Freedom in Central New York, 1835–1872*. New York: Garland, 1993.

URBAN SLAVERY

Finkelman, Paul. *Economics, Industrialization, Urbanization, and Slavery*. Articles on American Slavery; vol. 10. New York: Garland, 1989.
Goldin, Claudia Dale. *Urban Slavery in the American South, 1820–1860: A Quantitative History*. Chicago: University of Chicago Press, 1976.
Wade, Richard C. *Slavery in the Cities: The South, 1820–1860*. A Galaxy book, GB 209. London; New York: Oxford University Press, 1967.

WOMEN

Finkelman, Paul, ed. *Women and the Family in a Slave Society*. Articles on American Slavery; vol. 9. New York: Garland, 1989.
Fox-Genovese, Elizabeth. *Within the Plantation Household: Black and White Women of the Old South*. Chapel Hill: University of North Carolina Press, 1988.
Gaspar, David Barry and Darlene Clark Hine, eds. *More than Chattel: Black Women and Slavery in the Americas*. Bloomington: Indiana University Press, 1996.
Jones, Jacqueline. *Labor of Love, Labor of Sorrow: Black Women, Work, and the Family from Slavery to the Present*. New York: Basic, 1985.
———. *"My Mother Was Much a Woman": Black Women, Work and the Family under Slavery*. Working paper; no. 45. Wellesley, Mass.: Wellesley College Center for Research on Women, 1980.
Lebsock, Suzanne. *Free Women of Petersburg: Status and Culture in a Southern Town, 1784–1860*. New York: Norton, 1984.
Morton, Patricia, ed. *Discovering the Women in Slavery: Emancipating Perspectives on the American Past*. Athens: University of Georgia Press, 1996.
White, Deborah G. (Deborah Gray). *Ain't I a Woman? Female Slaves in the Antebellum South*. Thesis (Ph.D.)—University of Illinois at Chicago Circle, 1979.
———. *Ar'n't I a Woman? Female Slaves in the Plantation South*. New York: Norton, 1985.
Wood, Betty. *Women's Work, Men's Work: The Informal Slave Economies of Lowcountry Georgia*. Athens: University of Georgia, 1995.

Ziev, Kimberly Anne. *"Chained Witnesses": The Response of Southern Plantation Women to Emancipation*. Thesis (A.B., Honors in Social Studies)—Harvard University, 1993.

PRIMARY SOURCES AND INTERPRETATION

SLAVE NARRATIVES (Criticism and Interpretation)

Andrews, William L. *To Tell a Free Story: The First Century of Afro-American Autobiography, 1760–1865*. Urbana: University of Illinois Press, 1986.

Braxton, Joanne M. *Black Women Writing Autobiography: A Tradition within a Tradition*. Philadelphia: Temple University Press, 1989.

Bromell, Nicholas Knowles. *By the Sweat of the Brow: Literature and Labor in Antebellum America*. Chicago: University of Chicago Press, 1993.

Costanzo, Angelo. *Surprizing Narrative: Olaudah Equiano and the Beginnings of Black Autobiography*. Contributions in Afro-American and African studies, no. 104. New York: Greenwood Press, 1987.

Dean, Ann C. (Ann Coulson). *"There Was a Scene which Angels Witnessed": The Active Function of Narrative Convention in Antebellum Slave Narratives*. Thesis (A.B., Honors)—Harvard University, 1989.

Foster, Frances Smith. *Witnessing Slavery: The Development of Ante-Bellum Slave Narratives*. Wisconsin studies in American autobiography. Madison: University of Wisconsin Press, 1994.

Franklin, H. Bruce (Howard Bruce). *Prison Literature in America: The Victim as Criminal and Artist*. Expanded ed. New York: Oxford University Press, 1989.

Hill, Shannon Elizabeth. *"Free at Last": The Use of the Slave Narrative in Ishmael Reed's* Flight to Canada *and Toni Morrison's* Beloved. Thesis (A.B., Honors in History and Literature)—Harvard University, 1991.

Hopkins, Dwight N. *Cut Loose Your Stammering Tongue: Black Theology in the Slave Narratives*. Maryknoll, N.Y.: Orbis Books, 1991.

Judy, Ronald A. T. *(Dis)forming the American Canon: African-Arabic Slave Narratives and the Vernacular*. Minneapolis: University of Minnesota Press, 1993.

Morgan, Kathryn L. *The Ex-Slave Narrative as a Source for Folk History*. Thesis (Ph.D.)—University of Pennsylvania, 1970.

Richmond, M. A. (Merle A.). *Bid the Vassal Soar: Interpretive Essays on the Life and Poetry of Phillis Wheatley (ca.1753–1784) and George Moses Horton (ca.1797–1883)*. Washington, D.C.: Howard University Press, 1974.

Russell, Sandi. *Render Me My Song: African-American Women Writers from Slavery to the Present*. New York: St. Martin's Press, 1990.

Sanders, Cheryl Jeanne. *Slavery and Conversion: An Analysis of Ex-Slave Testimony*. Thesis (Th.D.)—Harvard University, 1985.

Sekora, John, ed. *The Art of Slave Narrative: Original Essays in Criticism and Theory*. An Essays in Literature book. [Macomb, Ill.]: Western Illinois University, 1982.

Smith, Valerie. *Self-Discovery and Authority in Afro-American Narrative*. Cambridge, Mass.: Harvard University Press, 1987.

Starling, Marion Wilson. *The Slave Narrative: Its Place in American History*. 2nd ed. Washington, D.C.: Howard University Press, 1988.

Williams, Melanie. *Tracing Roots: The Development of the Slave Narrative Tradition in the Works of Three Afro-American Writers*. Thesis (A.B., Honors in English and American Literature and Language)—Harvard University, 1991.

Winter, Kari J. *Subjects of Slavery, Agents of Change: Women and Power in Gothic Novels and Slave Narratives, 1790–1865*. Athens: University of Georgia Press, 1992.

PRIMARY SOURCES

W.P.A. INTERVIEWS

Berlin, Ira, Marc Favreau, and Steven F. Miller. *Remembering Slavery: African Americans Talk About Their Personal Experiences of Slavery and Freedom*. New York: New Press, 1998.

Index to The American Slave. Contributions in Afro-American and African studies, no. 65. Westport, Conn.: Greenwood Press, 1981.

Rawick, George P. *The American Slave: A Composite Autobiography*. Supplement, series 1. Contributions in Afro-American and African studies; no. 35. Westport, Conn.: Greenwood Pub. Co., 1977.
———. *The American Slave: A Composite Autobiography*. Supplement, series 2. Contributions in Afro-American and African studies; no. 49. Westport, Conn.: Greenwood Press, 1979.

ANTHOLOGIES AND RECENT EDITIONS OF SLAVE NARRATIVES

Albert, Octavia V. Rogers (Octavia Victoria Rogers). *The House of Bondage, or, Charlotte Brooks and Other Slaves*. The Schomburg Library of Nineteenth-Century Black Women Writers. New York: Oxford University Press, 1988.
Andrews, William L., ed. *Six Women's Slave Narratives*. The Schomburg Library of Nineteenth-Century Black Women Writers. New York: Oxford University Press, 1988.
Appiah, Anthony, ed. *Early African-American Classics*. New York: Bantam Books, 1990.
Austin, Allan D., ed. *African Muslims in Antebellum America: A Sourcebook*. Critical studies on Black life and culture; v. 5. New York: Garland Pub., 1984.
———. *African Muslims in Antebellum America: Transatlantic Stories and Spiritual Struggles*. New York: Routledge, 1997.
Blackett, R. J. M. *Running a Thousand Miles for Freedom: The Escape of William and Ellen Craft from Slavery*. Baton Rouge: Louisiana State University Press, 1998.
Blassingame, John. *Slave Testimony: Two Centuries of Letters, Speeches, Interviews, and Autobiographies*. Baton Rouge: Louisiana State University Press, 1977.
Bontemps, Arna, ed. *Five Black Lives: The Autobiographies of Venture Smith, James Mars, William Grimes, the Rev. G. W. Offley, [and] James L. Smith*. Documents of Black Connecticut. [1st ed.] Middletown, Conn.: Wesleyan University Press, [1971].
Bruce, Henry Clay. *The New Man: Twenty-Nine Years a Slave*. Lincoln: University of Nebraska Press, 1996.
Coleman, Deirdre. *Maiden Voyages and Infant Colonies: Two Women's Travel Narratives of the 1790s*. Washington: Leicester University Press, 1998.
Cottroll, Robert J. *From African to Yankee: Narratives of Slavery and Freedom in Antebellum New England*. Armonk, N.Y.: M.E. Sharpe, 1998.
Davis, Charles T., ed. *The Slave's Narrative*. Oxford [Oxfordshire]; New York: Oxford University Press, 1985.
Fisk University. Social Science Institute. *Unwritten History of Slavery: Autobiographical Accounts of Negro Ex-Slaves*. Washington. Microcard Editions, 1968.
Gates, Henry Louis, Jr. *The Classic Slave Narratives*. New York: New American Library, 1987.
Gates, Henry Louis, Jr. and William L. Andrews. *Pioneers of the Black Atlantic: Five Slave Narratives from the Enlightenment*. Washington: Civitas, 1998.
Hurmence, Belinda. *We Lived in a Little Cabin in the Yard*. Winston-Salem, N.C.: J.F. Blair, 1994.
Jacobs, Harriet A. (Harriet Ann). *Incidents in the Life of a Slave Girl*. eds. George Hendrick and Willene Hendrick. St. James, N.Y.: Brandywine Press, 1999.
———. *Incidents in the Life of a Slave Girl*. New York: Harcourt Brace Jovanovich [1973].
———. *Incidents in the Life of a Slave Girl*. The Schomburg Library of Nineteenth-Century Black Women Writers. New York: Oxford University Press, 1988.
———. *Incidents in the Life of a Slave Girl: Written by Herself*. Cambridge, Mass.: Harvard University Press, 1987.
Jones, Thomas H. *The Experience of Thomas H. Jones, Who Was a Slave for Forty-three Years*. New York: AMS Press [1975].
Keckley, Elizabeth. *Behind the Scenes, or, Thirty Years a Slave and Four Years in the White House*. The Schomburg Library of Nineteenth-Century Black Women Writers. New York: Oxford University Press, 1988.
Larison, Cornelius Wilson. *Silvia Dubois: A Biografy of the Slav who Whipt her Mistres and Gand her Fredom*. The Schomburg Library of Nineteenth-Century Black Women Writers. New York: Oxford University Press, 1988.
Lester, Julius. *To Be a Slave*. New York, Dial Press [1968].
McCline, John. *Slavery in the Clover Bottoms: John McCline's Narrative of His Life*. Knoxville: University of Tennessee, 1998.

Mellon, James, ed. *Bullwhip Days: The Slaves Remember*. New York: Weidenfeld & Nicolson, 1988.

Mintz, Steven, ed. *African American Voices: The Life Cycle of Slavery*. 2nd ed. St. James, N.Y.: Brandywine Press, 1999.

Nichols, Charles Harold. *Many Thousand Gone; The Ex-Slaves' Account of Their Bondage and Freedom*. Bloomington: Indiana University Press [1969].

———, comp. *Black Men in Chains: Narratives by Escaped Slaves*. New York, L. Hill [1972].

Osofsky, Gilbert, comp. *Puttin' on Ole Massa: The Slave Narratives of Henry Bibb, William Wells Brown, and Solomon Northup*. New York: Harper & Row [1969].

Pennington, James W. C. *The Fugitive Blacksmith; or, Events in the History of James W. C. Pennington*. 3d ed. Westport, Conn.: Negro Universities Press [1971].

Perdue, Charles L., Jr., ed. *Weevils in the Wheat: Interviews with Virginia Ex-Slaves*. Charlottesville: University Press of Virginia, 1976.

Smith, James Lindsay. *Autobiography of James L. Smith: Including also, Reminiscences of Slave Life, Recollections of the War, Education of Freedmen, Causes of the Exodus, etc*. Norwich: Society of the Founders of Norwich, Connecticut, 1976.

Teamoh, George. *God Made Man, Man Made the Slave: The Autobiography of George Teamoh*. Macon, Ga.: Mercer, 1990.

Williams, Isaac D. *Sunshine and Shadow of Slave Life: Reminiscences*. New York: AMS Press, 1975.

Yetman, Norman R., comp. *Life under the "Peculiar Institution": Selections from the Slave Narrative Collection, Library of Congress*. New York: Holt, Rinehart and Winston [1970].

———. *Voices from Slavery*. New York: Holt, Rinehart and Winston [1970].

BIBLIOGRAPHY

Brignano, Russell C. (Russell Carl). *Black Americans in Autobiography: An Annotated Bibliography of Autobiographies and Autobiographical Books Written since the Civil War*. Rev. and expanded ed. Durham, N.C.: Duke University Press, 1984.

SLAVERY AND LITERATURE

Aravamundan, Srinivas. *Tropicopolitans: Colonialism and Agency, 1688–1804*. Durham: Duke University Press, 1999.

Beaulieu, Elizabeth Ann. *Black Women Writers and the America Neo-Slave Narrative: Femininity Unfettered*. Westport, Conn.: Greenwood, 1999.

Bracks, Lean'tin L. *Writings on Black Women of the Diaspora: History, Language, and Identity*. New York: Garland, 1998.

Bromell, Nicholas Knowles. *By the Sweat of the Brow: Literature and Labor in Antebellum America*. Chicago: University of Chicago Press, 1993.

Burnham, Michelle. *Captivity and Sentiment: Cultural Exchange in American Literature, 1682–1861*. Hanover: University Press of New England, 1997.

Cassuto, Leonard. *The Inhuman Race: The Racial Grotesque in American Literature and Culture*. New York: Columbia University Press, 1997.

Clarke, John Henrik, ed. *William Styron's Nat Turner: Ten Black Writers Respond*. Westport, Conn.: Greenwood Press, 1987, c1968.

Davis, Mary Kemp. *Nat Turner Before the Bar of Judgment: Fictional Treatments of the Southampton Slave Insurrection*. Baton Rouge: Louisiana State University Press, 1999.

Diedrich, Maria, Henry Louis Gates, and Carl Petersen. *Black Imagination and the Middle Passage*. New York: Oxford University Press, 1999.

Ellis, Markman. *The Politics of Sensibility: Race, Gender and Commerce in the Sentimental Novel*. Cambridge: Cambridge University Press, 1996.

Ferguson, Moira. *Colonialism and Gender Relations from Mary Wollstonecraft to Jamaica Kincaid: East Caribbean Connections*. New York: Columbia University Press, 1993.

———. *Subject to Others: British Women Writers and Colonial Slavery, 1670–1834*. New York: Routledge, 1992.

Fishburn, Katherine. *The Problem of Embodiment in Early African American Narrative*. Westport, Conn.: Greenwood, 1997.

Gardner, Jared. *Master Plots: Race and the Founding of American Literature, 1787–1845*. Baltimore: Johns Hopkins University Press, 1998.

Gates, Henry Louis. *Figures in Black: Words, Signs, and the "Racial" Self*. New York: Oxford University Press, 1987.

Jackson, Edward Mercia. *American Slavery and the American Novel, 1852–1977*. Bristol, Ind.: Wyndham Hall Press, 1987.

Jones, John Maxwell. *Slavery and Race in Nineteenth-Century Louisiana-French Literature*. [1st ed.] [Camden, N.J.]: Jones, 1978.

Kammer, Martin. *Whitman, Slavery, and the Emergence of* Leaves of Grass. University Park: Pennsylvania State University Press, 1995.

Karcher, Carolyn L. *Shadow over the Promised Land: Slavery, Race, and Violence in Melville's America*. Baton Rouge: Louisiana State University Press, 1980.

Kawash, Samira. *Dislocating the Color Line: Identity, Hybridity, and Singularity in African-American Narrative*. Stanford: Stanford University Press, 1997.

Kinney, James. *Amalgamation! Race, Sex, and Rhetoric in the Nineteenth-Century American Novel*. Contributions in Afro-American and African studies, no. 90. Westport, Conn.: Greenwood Press, 1985.

Kirkham, Edwin Bruce. *The Building of Uncle Tom's Cabin*. Knoxville: University of Tennessee Press, 1977.

Kubitschek, Missy Dehn. *Claiming the Heritage: African-American Women Novelists and History*. Jackson: University Press of Mississippi, 1991.

Lee, A. Robert. *Designs of Blackness: Mappings in the Literature and Culture of Afro-America*. London: Pluto Press, 1998.

Levine, Robert S. *Martin Delany, Frederick Douglass, and the Politics of Representative Identity*. Chapel Hill: University of North Carolina Press, 1997.

Luis, William. *Literary Bondage: Slavery in Cuban Narrative*. The Texas Pan American series. 1st ed. Austin: University of Texas Press, 1990.

McDowell, Deborah E. *Slavery and the Literary Imagination*. Selected papers from the English Institute, 1987; new ser., no. 13. Baltimore: Johns Hopkins University Press, 1989.

Mills, Bruce. *Cultural Reformations: Lydia Maria Child and the Literature of Reform*. Athens: University of Georgia Press, 1994.

Ogude, S. E. *Genius in Bondage: A Study of the Origins of African Literature in English*. Ile-Ife, Nigeria: University of Ife Press, 1983.

Plasa, Carl. *The Discourse of Slavery: Aphra Behn to Toni Morrison*. London; New York: Routledge, 1994.

Rusdy, Ashraf H. A. *Neo-Slave Narratives: Studies in the Social Logic of a Literary Form*. New York: Oxford University Press, 1999.

Sale, Maggie Montesinos. *The Slumbering Volcano: American Slave Ship Revolts and the Production of Rebellious Masculinity*. Durham: Duke University Press, 1997.

Samuels, Shirley. *The Culture of Sentiment: Race, Gender, and Sentimentality in Nineteenth-Century America*. New York: Oxford University Press, 1992.

Sherman, Joan R. *The Black Bard of North Carolina: George Moses Horton and His Poetry*. Chapel Hill: University of North Carolina Press, 1997.

Smith, Valerie. *Self-Discovery and Authority in Afro-American Narrative*. Cambridge, Mass.: Harvard University Press, 1987.

Solomon, Barbara H. *Critical Essays on Toni Morrison's* Beloved. New York: G.K. Hall, 1998.

Thomas, Deborah A. *Thackeray and Slavery*. Athens: Ohio State University Press, 1993.

Van Deburg, William L. *Slavery and Race in American Popular Culture*. Madison: University of Wisconsin Press, 1984.

Vaughan, Alden T. *Shakespeare's Caliban: A Cultural History*. Cambridge [England]; New York: Cambridge University Press, 1991.